ECONOMICS OF WAR AND PEACE: ECONOMIC, LEGAL, AND POLITICAL PERSPECTIVES

Emerald Group Publishing Limited
Howard House, Wagon Lane, Bingley BD16 1WA, UK

First edition 2010

British Library Cataloguing in Publication Data
A catalogue record for this book is available from the British Library

Printed and bound in Great Britain by
CPI Antony Rowe, Chippenham and Eastbourne

ISBN: 978-0-85724-004-0
ISSN: 1572-8323 (Series)

CONTENTS

PART II: INTERNAL CONFLICT: ECONOMIC ASPECTS OF OUTBREAK, ENDURANCE, AND RECOVERY FROM LARGE-SCALE INTRA-STATE VIOLENCE

PART III: TRADE, LAW, INSTITUTIONS AND INTERNATIONAL CONFLICT: NEW PERSPECTIVES ON ENDURING DEBATES

LIST OF CONTRIBUTORS

Aditya Agrawal	School of Business, University of New South Wales at the Australian Defence Force Academy, Sydney, NSW, Australia
Jurgen Brauer	James M. Hull College of Business, Augusta State University, Augusta, GA, USA
Fabrizio Carmignani	School of Economics, The University of Queensland, Brisbane, QLD, Australia
Adrian Gauci	Economic Commission for Africa, United Nations, Addis Ababa, Ethiopia
Benjamin E. Goldsmith	Department of Government and International Relations, University of Sydney, Sydney, NSW, Australia
Peter Hall	School of Business, University of New South Wales Campus at the Australian Defence Force Academy, Canberra, ACT, Australia
Brendan Howe	Graduate School of International Studies, Ewha Womans University, Seoul, South Korea
Jennifer S. Hunt	Centre for International Security Studies, University of Sydney, Sydney, NSW, Australia
Minako Ichikawa Smart	University of Sydney, Sydney, NSW, Australia
Andrew Ladley	School of Government, Victoria University of Wellington, Wellington, New Zealand

ACKNOWLEDGMENTS

This book, and the conference from which most of the papers are drawn, would not have been possible without the support of numerous individuals and organizations. For funding, we thank several organizations within the University of Sydney: the Institute of Social Sciences, the Faculty of Arts, and especially the School of Social and Political Sciences. For important in-kind and operational support, we thank the Departments of Government and International Relations, and Political Economy, within the University, as well as the Peace Science Society (International) and Economists for Peace and Security. We also thank members of the conference organizing committee, Partha Gangopadhyay of the University of Western Sydney, and David Throsby and Tony Bryant of Macquarie University.

We thank all participants in the Third Australasian Conference on the Economics and Politics of War and Peace, held in Sydney in June, 2009. We would especially like to mention Paul Huth and Brian Pollins, both of whom traveled from the United States to give keynote addresses and generously provided advice and feedback to many of the paper presenters, including some in this volume. We also thank Steve Killelea and Camilla Schippa for important participation from the Global Peace Index.

Jane Ford did a tremendous job, in a very short time, copyediting the chapters. Jolyon Spencer and postgrad students from Goldsmith's International Security subject at the University of Sydney provided essential logistical help during the conference.

Finally, we would like to extend special gratitude to Manas Chatterji, who not only found our project of interest for this Emerald series but was also the initiator of the conference series from which the book emerged.

cases do not fit neatly into the emerging general theories of civil war, and perhaps the only clear suggestion of potential escape from the Gordian knot of poverty and violence is that a country, such as Ghana, which is lucky enough to have a period of (relatively) enlightened leadership, can seem to turn the corner and escape the cycle of civil violence and degradation. Their chapter implicitly challenges studies based on statistical analysis of correlations in large-n datasets to more often apply their general findings to specific cases to illustrate their causal plausibility and policy relevance.

Leanne Piggott's chapter, 'Terrorism and violent internal conflict in post-Soeharto Indonesia: Beyond the Jihadi Prism of analysis', on domestic secessionist groups' choices for using terror tactics, or avoiding them, in Indonesia provides a useful perspective on a less-studied aspect of terrorism, domestic rather than international and political rather than ideological or religious. She finds that the Free Aceh Movement (GAM) was more prone to use terror tactics than the Free Papua Movement (OPM); however, GAM also abandoned terror once a basic autonomy agreement was reached with Jakarta, whereas the low-level conflict, including occasional terror attacks, continues in Papua. What is the role of economic factors in the process? Clearly, economic exploitation and grievance in the face of relative deprivation were important motivating factors for both secessionist movements, as was the general feeling of injustice at being incorporated unwillingly into the Indonesian state. However, GAM seemed to adopt terror more actively because it had a more coherent organizational structure and an ideology which more easily justified killing for the cause. OPM's deep internal divisions hindered mustering the resources for terror, it seems, and its origins as a non-violent resistance movement seem to continue to cause moral qualms for some of its members who do not adopt terror as a tactic. Therefore, as with much other research on the topic, Piggott finds limited evidence for economic roots of the choice for the tactic of terror specifically, as distinct from the choice for rebellion in general. It does seem that the diverse preferences of the OPM members prevent them from agreeing on tactics, and then devoting the necessary resources to them, but this diversity of preferences does not seem to be strictly economic in nature

Jennifer Hunt applies prospect theory to an analysis of the relationship between oil price instability and political violence in Iran in her chapter titled 'Great expectations: Prospect theory and oil price volatility in Iran'. She develops an intriguing psychological explanation for the risky behavior of both the conservative ruling elites, and the reform-minded urban publics and their leaders. Hunt's plausible suggestion is that the excessive vote rigging and other actions to guarantee an electoral victory, which seemed likely anyway, shows that the huge economic costs of the fall in oil prices had put the ruling elite in the 'domain of losses', thus predisposing them to such disproportionately risky behavior to retain power they felt might be threatened. The application of prospect theory to mass-level political behavior is rare, but Hunt also makes a plausible case for the resulting 'stolen' election of 2009 putting the opposition collectively into the 'domain of losses', predisposing its members to sustained and risky protest and other anti-regime actions.

Fabrizio Carmignani and Adrian Gauci, in their chapter 'Does fiscal policy differ between successful and unsuccessful post-conflict transitions? Lessons from African Civil Wars', provide strong evidence that answers this question in the affirmative. Their findings add to the policy-relevant knowledge about how to best help states establish a stable peace in the aftermath of internal conflict, showing empirically that increasing the size of government tends to bolster the peace, while economic contraction of the state makes conflict more likely to reemerge. But they provide more specific insights based on their nuanced data on fiscal policy: capital expenditures should increase more than government consumption, and grants to the budget and debt, are positively associated with stability post-conflict given that both revenues and expenditures should grow. Theoretically, the findings point to the equitable distribution of the 'peace dividend' as an important factor in post-conflict transition, strongly suggesting that economic disparities are important causes of cycles of civil war.

Andrew Ladley and Jessie Williams's chapter, 'The Collier challenge: How can reliable transitional financing systems be created in 'Barely Functional' States?' proposes mechanisms for what they term 'buttressing' to support Paul Collier's proposals for international guidance of states' post-conflict transitions. They effectively use the example of the Regional Assistance Mission to Solomon Islands (RAMSI) undertaken with Australian leadership, to demonstrate both the plausibility and the potential effectiveness of the idea. They point to the need to enmesh arrangements for Domestic Internationalised Financial Institutions (DIFIs), as proposed by Collier, into contractual and bureaucratic linkages such that they cannot be easily dislodged or manipulated once local political imperatives exert pressure. This highlights the importance of supporting the efficient and clean financial and distribution functions of DIFIs with strong political defences. The Solomons example is noteworthy because of the role of democratic institutions in preserving RAMSI's role. Their suggestions for Haiti have become even more relevant, given the devastation of the January 2010 earthquake there, which they briefly discuss.

Part III: Trade, Law, Institutions and International Conflict: New Perspectives on Enduring Debates

Brendan Howe's chapter, 'Peace through Trade? Econophoria in Northeast Asia' takes a skeptical view of the supposed pacific effects of international trade and internal capitalist development in Northeast Asia. His wide-ranging essay highlights both the plausible prospects for more pluralistic political development in the People's Republic of China, and the countervailing opportunities for the Chinese Communist Party to manage the political sphere, both having their roots in export-led rapid economic growth. He not only ties democratic peace expectations for the region to economic development, but also considers the possible direct effects of increased intra-regional trade on economic interests and on elite perceptions. Howe's expectation that trade ties have provided a foundation on which peaceful conflict management might now be based is appropriately cautious and reasonable.

Golam Robbani's chapter 'Regional integration and militarised interstate disputes: An empirical analysis', provides a large-n empirical analysis (covering all countries in the world, 1950–2000) of the effect of regional integration, which is predominantly economic, on the likelihood of militarized disputes between states. His analysis, in the spirit of Kantian peace arguments, supports the pacifying effect of such arrangements. But Robbani makes a theoretical contribution in that he thinks extensively about the types of factors which might make regional integration agreements (RIAs) more peaceful. These include the economic benefits of trade and, importantly, the expectation of future economic benefits, the greater certainty that trade barriers will not appear in the future, the increase in foreign investment and functionalist spillover to other areas of cooperation. He also points to the political benefits, such as the interest other RIA parties might have in mediating a dispute among members, and their special knowledge and practices which might facilitate the success of such mediation. Interestingly, and in the vein of security community theories, he also points to the development of mutual trust.

Jedidiah Royal's chapter 'Economic integration, economic signalling and the problem of economic crises' introduces an important note of skepticism regarding the power of economic interdependence to facilitate peaceful conflict resolution during times of economic crisis. He points out that the ability to clearly signal resolve through potentially costly economic moves might be limited in situations of regional or global crisis for a number of reasons. For example, the value of future trade will become uncertain, about the normative and political issues at play. She argues forcefully for the creation of a compensation regime for all civilian victims of such military action, whether the harm results from negligence or not, and whether or not it occurs in the context of a combat situation. The fundamental point that compensating all civilian casualties is required from the perspective of 'fairness' is a compelling one. Her economic analysis points out the actual costs of compensation [illegible] situations are not large. This [illegible] with [illegible] compensation [illegible]. Smart also points out that economic costs of compensation [illegible] in some [illegible] is [illegible]

[illegible]

[illegible]

PART I
MARKETS AND FORCE: FOUNDATIONAL ASPECTS OF THE RELATIONSHIP BETWEEN ECONOMICS AND VIOLENCE WITHIN AND BETWEEN STATES

CHAPTER 2

A METHOD TO COMPUTE A PEACE GROSS WORLD PRODUCT BY COUNTRY AND BY ECONOMIC SECTOR

Jurgen Brauer and John Tepper Marlin

ABSTRACT

Purpose – *The chapter reports on an attempt to compute the size of gross world product (GWP) under the assumption that all violence ceases.*

Methodology/approach – *Spreadsheet-based simulations, given seed values taken from extensive literature review; this is done, for 2007, in nominal foreign exchange–based US dollars (USD) as well as in purchasing power parity (ppp)–based dollars (international dollars).*

Beneficial economic effects from more internal peace (nonviolence within countries) as well from external peace (nonviolence between and among countries) are calculated for each of 140 countries. In addition, we compute sectoral economic effects for the United States.

Findings – *For 2007, the simulations suggest that in a state of nonviolence the world economy could have been larger by 4.8 trillion dollars, or 8.7 per cent of actual GWP, when measured in nominal, foreign exchange–based USD, or by 6.0 trillion international dollars, or 9.2 per cent of GWP, when measured in purchasing power parity values.*

Economics of War and Peace: Economic, Legal, and Political Perspectives
Contributions to Conflict Management, Peace Economics and Development, Volume 14, 13–30

ISSN: 1572-8323/doi:10.1108/S1572-8323(2010)0000014006

Limitations – *The simulations are based on disparate values found in the literature to seed the spreadsheet calculations; various assumptions are made that would need to be confirmed through country- and sector-specific studies.*

Practical implications – *Knowledge of the potential size of forgone economic benefits due to violence can assist to set out global violence reduction goals in order to achieve measurable economic results.*

Originality/value of chapter – *To our knowledge this is the first attempt to calculate the size of the worldwide economic benefits forgone due to violence.*

INTRODUCTION

This chapter reports on the setup of a spreadsheet-based computational method to calculate, for 2007, the size of gross world product (GWP) under the assumption that all violence ceases.[1] Numbers are generated state-by-state and by economic sector (agriculture, industry, services) within each state.[2] In addition, a subsector analysis is provided for the United States to gauge how much money subsectors such as utilities or retail trade or arts, entertainment and recreation 'leave on the table' on account of the GDP-depressing effects of violence. Further, amounts are computed on how much GDP by state might rise when either more internal peace or more external peace (or both) is obtained. The results reported here both abstract from and expand on a lengthy, publicly available commissioned report the authors wrote for the Institute for Economics and Peace (IEP), Sydney, Australia.[3]

THE PROCESS FOR CALCULATING A PEACE GROSS WORLD PRODUCT

So as not to mistake, or be misled about, what we claim, it is important to understand both the conceptual as well as the computational procedure we employed. Fig. 1 represents the conceptual approach. Viewing violent behaviour as an individual and social disease, we agree with the World Health Organization and take a public health view to classify violence into the rubrics of self-harm, interpersonal violence and collective violence (WHO, 2002, 2004). In step 1, we reviewed extensively, but selectively, the disparate and often unconnected literatures on the economic cost these

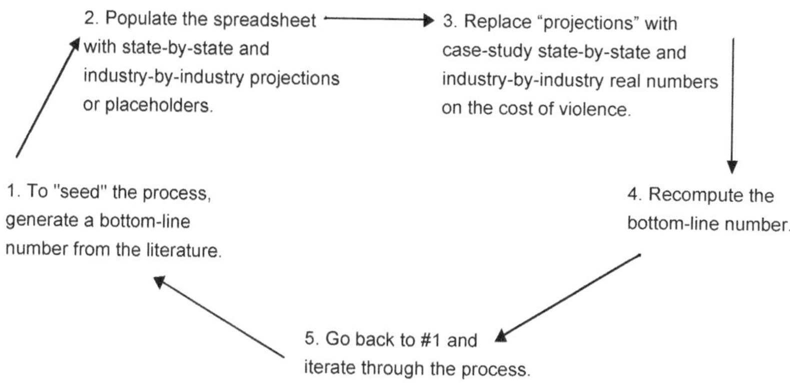

Fig. 1. The Procedure.

forms of violence cause. The objective was not to be comprehensive but to gain sufficient insight from the many case studies on the cost of violence to individuals, to businesses, to economic sectors such as airlines, tourism and the hospitality industries, to the public health system and to entire states. From this, we extracted what we believe is a plausible, indeed conservative, number of the monetary value by which worldwide economic activity is reduced. For 2007, this number, certainly arguable, amounted to USD 4.8 trillion or 8.7 per cent of actual GWP when measured in nominal, foreign exchange–based USD, or purchasing power parity (ppp) 6.0 trillion or 9.2 per cent of GWP when measured in ppp values.[4] This is our bottom-line number. We do not claim that our bottom-line number captures 'the' cost of violence. Rather, it serves as a starting point to seed the computational process. Spreadsheet-based simulations and iterations (discussed in the following text) will continuously revise and refine this number.

Step 2 uses the bottom-line number to populate the spreadsheet which consists of GDP and other data for 140 states, including the sectoral breakdown of GDP into the monetary contributions made by agriculture, industry and services. Actually, there are two spreadsheets. The first makes certain assumptions, easily modified to simulate the effects of changes in the underlying parameters, about the degree to which industry and services in particular are implicated in violence-related economic activity. For example, military expenditure engenders economic activity both in industry (say, production of military hardware) and in services (say, hiring of private military contractors). If all violence, or the threat of violence, were to cease, the economic resources presently devoted to these parts of industry and services necessarily would be reallocated to nonviolence industrial and service activities. As the economic pie per se would not grow, we refer to this effect as the static peace dividend.[5]

We compute the dynamic peace dividend in a second spreadsheet, namely the monetary value of the amount of economic activity set free when violence ceases (this is the aforementioned bottom-line of USD 4.8 trillion or ppp 6.0 trillion). In this second spreadsheet, we take figures produced by the Global Peace Index (GPI) on internal and external measures of peace, and calculate for each state how much of the dynamic peace dividend could be realised if either internal peace occurred, or external peace occurred, or if both came to pass. Further, for the case of the United States, we distribute the dynamic peace dividend, if it were realised, across 20 subsectors of economic activity. In principle, it is possible to compute this distribution across subsectors for other states as well, depending only on the acquisition of detailed sectoral data for each state.

As is true for step 1, at the moment, all numbers in step 2 are placeholders. Step 3 entails either conducting a truly comprehensive literature review so that state and industry cells in the spreadsheet matrix can be filled in with existing empirical evidence. In addition, or alternatively, the work could stimulate research into detailed state-by-state and sector-by-sector case studies that would generate estimates of the cost of violence by (sub)sector and for the statewide economy as a whole. Put differently, the placeholding values in the matrix would be replaced, one by one, by specific estimates gained from specific case studies.

In step 4, cells filled in with evidence from specific case studies can be 'locked' and the bottom-line recalculated. The recalculation would result from combining the original bottom-line seed gained from the general literature review and the specific estimates gained from specific studies. The margin of error would be reduced with each iteration, that is with step 5 of the process.

The remainder of this chapter pertains, very briefly, to step 1, that is how we arrived at the seeding bottom-line number and, extensively, to step 2, generating the placeholder numbers by country, by sector, by subsector and the monetary value of the size of the (internal, external and total) peace dividend that one may expect if violence were to cease.

THE BOTTOM-LINE NUMBER

A companion chapter relates in some detail our review of the literature from which we concluded that it may be no exaggeration to say – staggering as the number is – that GWP could be on the order of 10 per cent higher than it actually is, if all violence were to cease (Brauer & Tepper-Marlin, 2009). Briefly, we reviewed data and literatures on the preparation of war (i.e. primarily military expenditure), on interstate war, on intrastate war, on domestic and transnational terror events, on crime and interpersonal violence and on public health costs associated with self-harm and interpersonal violence.

Although the numbers vary widely across countries and studies, cumulative figures of the annual cost of all violence of up to 10 per cent of GDP are not uncommon. Even in cases of nonwar violence, that is violence other than collective violence, estimates routinely come to 2–5 per cent of GDP. Indeed, a 2006 World Bank working paper put the nonwar cost of crime and violence in Latin American and the Caribbean at 14.2 per cent of GDP for the region (Heinemann & Verner, 2006). Taking our cue from these sorts of results, we calibrated the base scenario coefficients in our spreadsheet to arrive at what we believe is a plausible, indeed conservative, estimate of 4.4 per cent of foreign exchange–based GWP as the current cost of violence (the static peace dividend if all violence stopped) and of 8.7 per cent in addition to current GWP (the dynamic peace dividend). In ppp-terms, the numbers are somewhat larger.

POPULATING THE SPREADSHEET

Foreign Exchange Rate (fx)-Based versus Purchasing Power Parity-Based Values

Because much of the following involves results for particular states, the discussion is couched in ppp terms. The reason for this is that for comparability across states, any one country's currency may be used as the standard of comparison, or numeraire. In practice, this is the US dollar. Nonnumeraire countries' GDPs are converted to the numeraire currency at the average of the prevailing exchange rates for a given time period, usually a calendar year. But annual exchange rate fluctuations greatly affect the resulting US dollar value of non-US economic output. One way economists address this problem is by converting countries' currencies into ppp values. Thus, a haircut that in New York might cost USD 20 and in India USD 1 (at foreign exchange rate conversion) are equally valued under ppp measurement. So, either both are valued at ppp 20 (with the US value being the standard) or both are valued at ppp 1 (with the Indian value being the standard). In practice, the US value is used as the standard, but importantly it is the activity itself that is valued rather than its monetary equivalent as would be the case of foreign exchange rate–based conversions. Although India's ppp 20 haircut, therefore, is an artificial number and cannot be taken at face value, for example as an indicator of the monetary size of its market, the use of ppp permits comparability across currencies and states. Therefore, a dynamic peace dividend for India of ppp 321 billion is only USD 135 billion at the exchange rates of 2007.

Assumption and Calculations

The details are best illustrated by examining an extract from our spreadsheet. The states are alphabetically ordered. The last 9 of the 140 states in our database are displayed in Table 1. The first two numeric columns list the states' GPI rank and numeric score (see www.visionofhumanity.org). This scale stipulates that the lower the score, the more peaceful the country. The score is a combination of 24 factors, 13 pertaining to internal peace and the other 11 to external peace.[6] The relation of GPI to fx-based and ppp-based GPD is displayed in Figs. 2 and 3. The figures show that peacefulness and economic output are associated. The association is stronger for the ppp-based measure. (A linear regression trend line is drawn for convenience.) The causal effects run both ways: peace makes investment safer than otherwise would be the case, and peace thereby stimulates growth and higher

Table 1. Spreadsheet Extract.

State	GPI Rank	GPI Score	log GPI Score	GDP 2007 (ppp, in Billion)	log ppp GDP	Peace Dividend (ppp, in Billion)	PGDP (ppp, in Billion)	ppp GDP Gain (%)
United Kingdom	49	1.801	0.256	2,167.84	3.34	166.06	2,333.90	7.7
United States	97	2.227	0.348	13,807.55	4.14	1,159.56	14,967.11	8.4
Uruguay	21	1.606	0.206	37.36	1.57	4.89	42.24	13.1
Uzbekistan	111	2.377	0.376	64.20	1.81	13.35	77.56	20.8
Venezuela	123	2.505	0.399	334.85	2.52	52.88	387.73	15.8
Vietnam	37	1.720	0.235	221.61	2.35	22.25	243.86	10.0
Yemen	106	2.352	0.372	52.22	1.72	11.29	63.51	21.6
Zambia	53	1.856	0.269	16.09	1.21	3.58	19.67	22.3
Zimbabwe	124	2.513	0.400	2.21	0.34	2.57	4.78	116.2
Sum/average				65,479.67		6,002.47	71,482.14	9.2

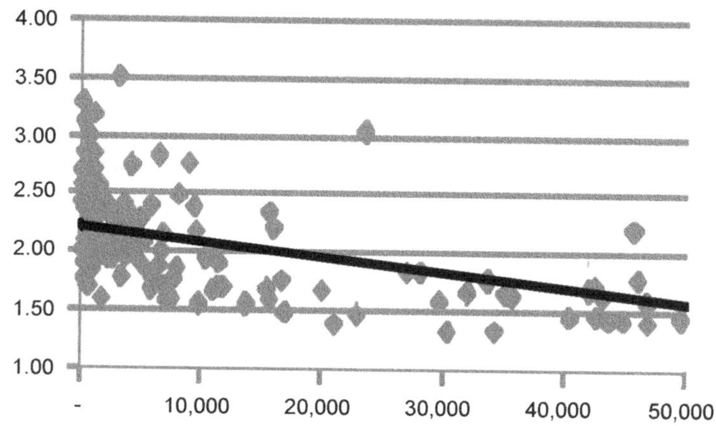

Fig. 2. GPI 2008 (y-Axis) versus 2007 Per Capita fx-Based GDP (x-Axis) for 140 Countries, with Trend Line.

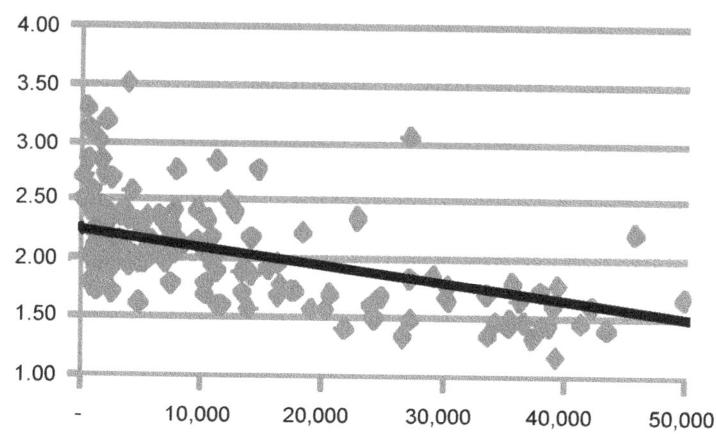

Fig. 3. GPI 2008 (y-Axis) versus 2007 Per Capita ppp-Based GDP (x-Axis) for 140 Countries, with Trend Line.

living standards. In turn, this makes investing in peace more critical as well so as to safeguard the economic achievements. Thus, a virtuous cycle between peace and prosperity can emerge. The World Economic Forum's Business Competitiveness Index and the World Bank's Ease of Doing Business Index correlate with the GPI in a similar way. Basing our dynamic projections of the peace gross domestic product (PGDP) on the GPI itself seems to be a reasonable first approach to take. Calculating the dynamic peace dividend, therefore, links economic gains to the GPI. The following formula is used:

$$\text{Dynamic peace dividend} = \left[\log\ \text{GPI score} \times \frac{\text{ppp GDP}}{\log\ \text{ppp GDP}}\right] \times 1$$

Logarithmic transformations are applied to GPI and GDP to eliminate country-size effects (e.g. larger countries necessarily having a larger actual GDP than smaller countries even if of equal general development status). Thus, the ratio expression in the formula adjusts for the size of a state's economy by using the logarithmic form of the raw data. It then multiplies the result by each state's size-adjusted GPI. The reason for this is that, by construction, a small GPI score means that the country is relatively peaceful to begin with, and stopping violence therefore cannot add much to its already existing GDP. In contrast, a larger GPI score reflects a large upside economic potential to be obtained from peace. Finally, a peace multiplier of size 1 is applied. This multiplier reflects an assumption about how much of an economic boost may be expected from peace.[7] Although we believe it to be plausible, reasonable and conservative, it remains an assumption and is the principal reason why we varied it in scenario analysis from a factor of 0 to a factor of 2 in increments of 0.5. (We discuss this in the following text.)

As may be seen from Table 1, applying the formula yields different effects for different states. Although Uruguay, for example, is a relatively peaceful state, it would receive a larger economic boost (13.1 per cent) than either the United Kingdom or the United States (7.7 per cent and 8.4 per cent, respectively). Note that Venezuela and Zimbabwe, numbers 123 and 124 on the GPI ranks, would receive very differently sized benefits from peace. Venezuela's economy would increase by 15.8 per cent and Zimbabwe's would more than double – a plausible result.

The example of the United States can also be used to show that a peace multiplier of size 1 is a number that is not implausible. From 1991 to 2000, the Clinton-era years following the end of the Cold War, inflation-adjusted GDP in the United States grew at the high rate of an average of 3.7 per cent per year, or roughly USD 300 billion annually (base year 2000). During this time, inflation-adjusted US military expenditure fell from USD 730 billion to USD 607 billion, or about 16 per cent. Projecting this to a military expense of zero dollars, in 2008 terms, generates a nominal USD 1 trillion available to be reallocated between economic sectors right away. It is not unrealistic to believe that a dividend of USD 1.2 trillion could be generated when economy-wide follow-on effects are included, the way the post–Cold War peace dividend appears to have worked in the 1990s.[8]

Scenario Analysis

Table 2 presents results from using different peace multipliers or factors. The line in bold typeface is the base scenario, with a 9.2 per cent boost as extracted from the literature, or about ppp 6 trillion. If a multiplier of 0.5 were used, the gain would be 4.6 per cent. SIPRI (2008) reports that measured world military expenditure alone is 2.5 per cent of GWP. In all likelihood, this is an underestimate, in part because SIPRI counts neither the legacy costs of war such as post-war environmental remediation or health care costs for ex-military service personnel, nor an allocation of interest associated with government budget deficits to finance military expenditure. If these costs were counted as military-related, and therefore, as violence-related, surely, a nonviolent world would at a minimum generate a 4.6 per cent economic boost from the military sector alone. If larger factors are applied, the economic boost can of course be made as large as one desires.

A complementary type of scenario analysis, not pursued here, would involve setting up the spreadsheet in such a way that the economic effects of cuts in GPI (i.e. more peace, less violence) by say 10 per cent could be simulated. (This could be done in a linear or nonlinear way.) Measurable policy goals could be generated by reducing the GPI experimentally and calculating what the dynamic peace dividend effects would be. For example, policymakers could set a goal of reducing their country's GPI score by 10 percentage points over one election cycle and hold themselves accountable in terms of how much measurable progress would have been made.

Table 2. Scenario Analysis.

Factor	Total (ppp-Based)	Gain (ppp-Based)	Percentage Gain (ppp-Based)
× 0.0	65,479.67	0.00	0.0
× 0.5	68,480.75	3,001.08	4.6
× 1.0	**71,481.83**	**6,002.15**	**9.2**
× 1.5	74,482.90	9,003.23	13.7
× 2.0	77,483.98	12,004.31	18.3

Internal versus External Peace

As mentioned, the IEP produces the GPI from a combination of internal and external peace factors. We were given confidential access to the internal and external GPI scores. This enabled us to carry out additional computations. For example, the United Kingdom scores better on internal than on external peace. In contrast, Zimbabwe's internal peace score is worse than its external peace score. Consequently, we would expect that the economic effects of peace for a specific country depend on whether that country is primarily at internal or at external peace (or not), or both, or in what mixture. For example, if state-on-state wars were abolished and the need for military forces disappeared, the United Kingdom would gain relatively much, whereas Zimbabwe would gain relatively little (see Table 3). If, in contrast, civil strife ceased, the United Kingdom would gain relatively little and Zimbabwe would gain relatively much. Specifically, for the United Kingdom about 43 per cent of any gain would come from internal peace, whereas for Zimbabwe about 73 per cent of any gain would stem from internal peace.[9]

As may be seen when comparing the first and last numeric column in Table 3, the weighted economic gain (weighted by internal and external peace) is somewhat smaller than the unweighted gain. This is a result of having more information available with which to run the calculations. (The sum total for the unweighted gain is ppp 6.0 trillion as opposed to ppp 5.9 trillion.)

Drastic differences among countries emerge. For a number of states, internal peace generates 80 per cent or more of the overall peace dividend

Table 3. Gains from Internal versus External Peace.

State	Peace Dividend (ppp Billion)	Internal Peace Dividend	Percentage	External Peace Dividend	Percentage	Weighted Peace Dividend
United Kingdom	166.06	69.06	43.04	91.41	56.96	160.47
United States	1,159.56	578.90	50.65	563.97	49.35	1,142.87
Uruguay	4.89	3.64	76.40	1.12	23.60	4.77
Uzbekistan	13.35	9.76	76.33	3.03	23.67	12.79
Venezuela	52.88	37.47	72.98	13.87	27.02	51.34
Vietnam	22.25	14.33	64.58	7.86	35.42	22.20
Yemen	11.29	8.05	73.44	2.91	26.56	0.96
Zambia	3.58	2.73	79.67	0.70	20.33	3.42
Zimbabwe	2.57	1.83	73.30	0.66	26.70	2.49

(Cambodia, Guatemala, Haiti, Honduras, Jamaica, Kenya, Latvia, Mauritania, and Trinidad and Tobago).[10] This is larger, sometimes much larger, than would have been expected on account of these states' internal GPI alone. For example, for Cambodia, the internal GPI is 65.3 per cent of the combined GPI. But almost 81 per cent of the dynamic peace dividend would be due to internal peace. For other states, less than half of the dynamic peace dividend would come from internal peace (Australia, Canada, Denmark, Iceland, Japan, New Zealand, Norway, Sweden, Switzerland and the United Kingdom). In some cases, this is much smaller than would be expected from their internal GPI. For example, Iceland's internal GPI is 44.7 per cent of its combined GPI. But of the dynamic economic gains of peace, only 27.4 per cent would accrue due to internal peace.

ADDING STATE-SPECIFIC DATA ON THE COST OF VIOLENCE TO FINE-TUNE THE SPREADSHEET

We extracted from our base scenario spreadsheet all South and Central American and Caribbean states to show how steps 3–5 of our procedure would work (i.e. replacing universal placeholders with specific numbers generated from state-by-state or industry-by-industry studies). In ppp terms, the peace multiplier of 1 suggests that these economies could receive an economic boost of about 18 per cent (Table 4, penultimate column). However, a World Bank literature review (for the 1990s) suggests an effect of about 14.3 per cent (Heinemann & Verner, 2006). Assuming this specific review contains 'the' correct number, we would adjust our peace multiplier from 1.0 to 0.8 to get a 14.4 per cent boost in our spreadsheet (Table 4, last column). The spreadsheet cells containing the peace multiplier of 0.8 for 2007 could then be 'locked', and the bottom-line number would be recomputed with the remaining states having a multiplier of 1.

Similarly, a 2006 UNDP study for Guatemala claims a cost of violence of 7.3 per cent for the country (UNDP, 2006, p. 11). One could then 'lock' the spreadsheet cell for Guatemala separately from those of other South/Central American and Caribbean states and recompute again. Thus, every time additional specific information is received, the spreadsheet can be adjusted and recomputed. For example, the UNDP study for Guatemala does not include that state's military expenditure. If one added 0.5 per cent of GDP for military spending, the relevant number would jump from 7.3 per cent to at least 7.8 per cent (since legacy costs and other military-related

Table 4. Fine-Tuning.

Latin America Caribbean	fx-Based PGDP	ppp-Based PGDP × 1.0	ppp-Based PGDP × 0.8
Argentina	0.11	0.10	0.082
Bolivia	0.28	0.19	0.155
Brazil	0.11	0.10	0.082
Chile	0.09	0.08	0.067
Colombia	0.19	0.17	0.137
Costa Rica	0.16	0.14	0.111
Cuba	0.17	0.14	0.111
Dominican Republic	0.20	0.17	0.136
Ecuador	0.21	0.18	0.143
El Salvador	0.26	0.21	0.165
Guatemala	0.24	0.20	0.163
Haiti	0.48	0.36	0.285
Honduras	0.34	0.25	0.198
Jamaica	0.33	0.26	0.211
Mexico	0.11	0.11	0.086
Nicaragua	0.37	0.24	0.188
Panama	0.20	0.17	0.132
Paraguay	0.28	0.21	0.168
Peru	0.15	0.13	0.106
Trinidad/Tobago	0.26	0.25	0.202
Uruguay	0.15	0.13	0.105
Venezuela	0.17	0.16	0.126
Average	0.22	0.18	0.144

costs are not included). If a number of independent studies with different estimates of the cost of violence are available per country, an expert assessment would have to be made of how to combine the various estimates for that country, and the resulting cell could be 'locked' once more – much the same way the peace multiplier of 1 was derived in the first place. Each cell can be hyperlinked to a bibliography of the underlying studies and these, in turn, can be hyperlinked to the studies themselves, possibly on a web server to which the public would have access.

The main message here is that the spreadsheet becomes a handy 'bin' to collect the empirical results of potentially thousands of specific studies on the cost of all aspects of violence. Moreover, the spreadsheet could be updated year-by-year with new GPI and GDP and other relevant data as well.

CALCULATING THE COST SAVINGS OF PEACE FOR ECONOMIC SECTORS

In this section, we spell out how a peace GWP would benefit particular economic sectors. Worldwide, in terms of fx-based 2007 US dollars, agriculture accounts for 3.8 per cent of GWP, industry for 29.8 per cent and services for 66.4 per cent. The GWP figures and the sector percentages are taken from the IMF *World Economic Outlook* and World Bank online data services, and are available by country.[11] It may be argued that although agriculture can engender severe violence, it is not itself a violence industry.[12] Therefore, a shift from violence to peace will reallocate resources within and between industry and services only. Agriculture will benefit from the dynamic peace dividend: as economies grow on account of peace, it becomes safe again to invest in land, livestock, irrigation, farming tools, etc. so that the sector would be expected to benefit and grow. In contrast, the violence portion of industry and services would be converted to peace. Therefore, the current dollar value associated with violence industries and services also is the potential static peace dividend for these sectors, about USD 1.0 trillion for industry and USD 1.4 trillion for services worldwide, both in 2007 nominal USD.

On a country-by-country basis, we look at the ppp-based calculations and, for example find that of the static peace dividend of ppp 6.9 billion available to Venezuela, ppp 3.8 billion (55.1 per cent) would accrue to industry and the remainder of ppp 3.1 billion (44.9 per cent) to the services sector. In terms of the dynamic peace dividend, the gains projected for each country also are allocated across sectors. For example, the expected dynamic peace dividend for Canada is a ppp-based 1.336 trillion. We know that the respective shares of agriculture, industry and services are 2.0 per cent, 28.4 per cent and 69.6 per cent so that Canada could expect dynamic peace dividend effects of ppp 26.7 billion, ppp 379.4 billion and ppp 929.9 billion, respectively, on these sectors. Because the calculations assume that sector shares do not change as a peace economy develops, this is no more than a first approximation. A second approximation would require far more complex modelling.

A subsector, or sectors-within-sectors, analysis requires data on subsector percentage shares in overall GDP. To illustrate, we downloaded GDP information by economic sector and subsector for the United States from the Bureau of Economic Analysis, US Department of Commerce, web site.[13] The sectoral data are coded according to the North American Industrial

Classification coding scheme (NAICS). For 2007, the nominal dollar value of US GDP was USD 13.8 trillion.[14] This breaks down into two-digit sectors and subsectors as shown in Table 5. Sector 11 is the agricultural sector (which consists of farming, forestry, fishing and related activities) and accounted for 1.2 per cent of US GDP in 2007. Sectors 21 through 33 are mining, utilities, construction and manufacturing industries (20.2 per cent), and the remainder are services (78.6 per cent).[15] The corresponding percentages in our spreadsheet for the United States are 1.2 per cent, 22.8 per cent and 76.0 per cent, respectively, but these are actually the CIA data for 2005, not World Bank data for 2007, so it is likely that we are tracking the correct numbers.

If we now believe that the total available dynamic peace dividend to the United States would be USD 1.143 trillion (Table 3, last column), with USD 0.579 trillion stemming from internal peace and USD 0.564 trillion from external peace, this can be allocated to the sector percentages in Table 5. For example, because the wholesale trade sector (NAICS code 42) accounted for

Table 5. United States Economic Sectors (Nominal USD Million, 2007).

Sector	Two-Digit NAICS Codes	USD (in Million)	Percentage
Agriculture	11	167,907.1	1.2
Mining	21	275,012.2	2.0
Utilities	22	281,424.2	2.0
Construction	23	610,841.9	4.4
Manufacturing	31/32/33	1,616,825.8	11.7
Wholesale trade	42	805,319.0	5.8
Retail trade	44RT	892,522.3	6.5
Transportation and warehousing	48/49	407,187.9	2.9
Information	51	586,269.2	4.2
Finance and insurance	52	1,091,415.6	7.9
Real estate, rental and leasing	53	1,719,801.8	12.5
Professional, scientific and technical services	54	1,007,780.5	7.3
Management of companies and enterprises	55	271,251.2	2.0
Administrative and waste management services	56	415,113.0	3.0
Educational services	61	129,531.4	0.9
Health care and social assistance	62	957,440.4	6.9
Arts, entertainment and recreation	71	133,846.7	1.0
Accommodation and food services	72	379,488.5	2.7
Other services, except government	81	315,633.7	2.3
Government	GS	1,742,926.2	12.6
Total final uses (GDP)	T004	13,807,538.6	100.0

5.8 per cent of US GDP, the spreadsheet allocates that percentage to the dynamic peace dividend and says that the wholesale trade sector could stand to gain USD 33.76 billion from internal peace. It could also gain another USD 32.89 billion from external peace, for a total of USD 66.66 billion per year in nominal 2007 US dollars, an 8.3 per cent increase over its 2007 business volume of USD 805 billion.

By design, every sector and subsector would stand to gain the same 8.3 per cent over its current business volume. This is because we do not have information on the violence/peace percentages within each sector or subsector. In time, these may become available as country-by-country analysis reveals actual or estimated percentages. For example, it is a fair guess that the dollar volume devoted to private sector legal services regarding criminal violence is higher in the United States than it is in New Zealand. But whether or not a shift from violence to peace would merely reallocate dollars within private sector legal services, say for more business formation and corporate law, or out of legal services into other sectors is difficult to say at this time. (For New Zealand, however, we estimate an available dynamic peace dividend of only 6 per cent because in terms of the GPI measures it is a more peaceful country than the United States.)

CONCLUSION

The spreadsheet we constructed aims to provide a foundational structure that is logical, coherent and substantive to enable systematic, feasible, replicable, spreadsheet-based computations to be produced by country, sector, subsector and year. The spreadsheet would have these calculations tied-in to the already existing annual production of the GPI. The cost of maintaining the spreadsheet will be comparatively minor. But although the structure now exists, the 'sharing down' of the static and dynamic peace dividend calculations into sectors and subsectors still needs to be completed for states other than the United States.

More important, and more costly, is the need to gradually replace the assumed coefficients underlying our computations with state- and sector-based specific information on the cost of violence. At the moment, we assume a reasonable but uniform peace multiplier of size 1 and applied it across all states. But differences across states imply differences in the multiplier to be used. A comprehensive literature review as well as specifically commissioned studies could, over time, replace the single peace multiplier value with a range of state- and sector-specific values. It might, at first, be easier to apply differentiated multipliers for groups of states, but the ultimate goal should be to aim at state- and sector-specific multipliers, regularly reviewed and updated.

NOTES

1. For convenience, we employ the term violence without indicating each time that we include in this the credible threat of violence or of defending against perceived, implied, threatened or actual violence. For example, most of the time the world military sector is on stand-by status. It represents a threat (or counter-threat) rather than actual perpetration of violence. Similarly, alarm systems and body guards represent, in part, deterrence measures meant to lower the incidence of violence, for example of assault or robbery.

2. Conforming to international law practice, we prefer the use of state over nation-state or country.

3. Available at www.economicsandpeace.org.

4. Unless we quote, we employ standard three-letter codes to denote currencies, e.g. for the US dollar we use USD instead of US$. See http://www.iso.org/ and search for ISO4217 [accessed 1 September 2009].

5. World military expenditure alone amounted to 2.5 per cent of GWP in 2007. When one allows for the under-measurement of military expenditure and adds in other violence-related spending, for example on private security services, private and public health care costs, the entire criminal justice system and so on, it is probably an understatement to assume, as we did, that the total amount of GWP presently devoted to violence-related economic activity is 4.4 per cent. Our intention was to err on the side of understatement. See Brauer (2007, 2009) on estimates for U.S. military expenditure.

6. *Internal*: level of distrust in other citizens; number of internal security officers and police per 100,000 people; number of homicides per 100,000 people; number of jailed population per 100,000 people; ease of access to weapons of minor destruction; level of organised conflict (internal); likelihood of violent demonstrations; level of violent crime; political instability; respect for human rights; volume of transfers of major conventional weapons, as recipient (imports) per 100,000 people; potential for terrorist acts; number of deaths from organised conflict (internal). *External*: military expenditure as a percentage of GDP; number of armed services personnel per 100,000 people; UN deployments 2007–2008 (percentage of total forces); non-U.N. deployments 2007–2008 (percentage of total forces); aggregate number of heavy weapons per 100,000 people; volume of transfers of major conventional weapons as supplier (exports) per 100,000 people; military capability/sophistication; number of displaced people as a percentage of the population; relations with neighbouring countries; number of external and internal conflicts fought during 2000–2005; estimated number of deaths from organised conflict (external).

7. This assumption is based on the bottom-line number extracted from the literature. Initially, we intended to put in 10 per cent, and a peace multiplier of 1.1 would have accomplished that. Instead, we went with the round number of 1, which implied a bottom-line number of 9.2 per cent of ppp–GWP.

8. Note in passing that because of both the military and the economic size of the United States, 24.3 per cent of the worldwide dynamic peace dividend effect, in fx-based terms, comes from the United States. In ppp-terms, this would be 19.3 per cent.

9. For example, for the United Kingdom, its 2007 ppp-measured actual GDP is multiplied by the logarithm of its overall GPI score. The more peaceful a country is to begin with, the smaller its GPI score and hence, the smaller the additional potential benefit it can receive from peace. To account for economic size differences among states, the result for each country is divided by the logarithm of the country's ppp-measured actual GDP. Finally, the resulting number is adjusted by a peace multiplier derived from the literature such that the sum of the peace dividends across all countries comes to about 9 per cent of GWP. For the United Kingdom, this comes to about I$166 billion.

To compute a weighted peace dividend, the logarithms of the internal and external GPIs are weighted according to a preset ratio determined by the producers of the Global Peace Index (60 per cent for internal peace; 40 per cent for external peace), and the procedure explained in the prior paragraph is applied to the logarithm of the weighted GPI. For the U.K., the weighted peace dividend comes to about I$160 billion, of which the internal peace dividend then accounts for 43 per cent (I$69 billion) and the external peace dividend for the remaining 57 per cent (I$91 billion). [I$ = international dollars, i.e., purchasing power parity adjusted numbers.]

10. As mentioned as a rule, fx-based calculations may be appropriate for certain global statements, but country-by-country analysis is better done on a ppp basis.

11. Certain data gaps have been filled by recourse to the CIA World Factbook.

12. Actually, this is an assumption. Just as a truck driver working for a private security firm would be part of the service industry serving violence or violence prevention, food raised to feed armed forces would become part of the agricultural sector serving violence or violence prevention.

13. http://www.bea.gov/industry/gdpbyind_data.htm [accessed 11 April 2009].

14. Recall that for the United States, the ppp-values equal the USD values.

15. As an example, the mining subsector (NAICS code 21) within industry is itself subdivided into oil and gas extraction (code 211), mining, except oil and gas (code 212), and support activities for mining (code 213). These amounted to USD164.6 billion, USD45.3 billion and USD65.0 billion, respectively. Similar subdivisions are made in the other industry and service top-level categories, so that the overall detail available is considerable.

ACKNOWLEDGMENTS

We acknowledge research assistance by Ms. Deanna Liderman and Mr. Ian Scheffer. Dr. Brauer also acknowledges the hospitality of Professor J. Paul Dunne at whose home in Bristol, United Kingdom, much of the underlying work for the research reported in this chapter was conducted. The research was commissioned and funded by the Institute for Economics and Peace (www.economicsandpeace.org) in conjunction with its work on the 3rd annual Global Peace Index (www.visionofhumanity.org) released in June 2009. The project was facilitated by Economists for Peace and Security, Annandale-upon-Hudson, New York, USA (www.epsusa.org).

REFERENCES

Brauer, J. (2007). Data, models, coefficients: The case of United States military expenditure. *Conflict Management and Peace Science*, *24*(1), 55–64.

Brauer, J. (2009). The trillion dollar military. Available at http://www.aug.edu/~sbajmb/abc156.pdf. Accessed 10 April 2009.

Brauer, J., & Tepper-Marlin, J. (2009). Nonkilling economics: Calculating the size of a peace gross world product. In: J. E. Pim (Ed.), *Toward a nonkilling paradigm* (pp. 125–148). Honolulu, HI: Center for Global Nonkilling.

Heinemann, A., & Verner, D. (2006). *Crime and violence in development: A literature review of Latin America and the Caribbean*. World Bank Policy Research Working Paper 4041 (October), The World Bank, Washington, DC.

Stockholm International Peace Research Institute [SIPRI]. (2008). *SIPRI yearbook 2008: Armaments, disarmament and international security*. New York: Oxford University Press.

United Nations Development Programme [UNDP]. (2006). *El costo econòmico de la violencia en Guatemala*. Tegucigalpa: Programa de las Naciones Unidas para el Desarrollo.

World Health Organization [WHO]. (2002). World report on violence and health. In: E. G. Krug, L. L. Dahlberg, J. A. Mercy, A. B. Zwi, & R. Lozano (Eds), Geneva: WHO. Available at http://whqlibdoc.who.int/publications/2002/9241545615_eng.pdf. Accessed on 15 April 2009.

World Health Organization [WHO]. (2004). In: H. Waters, A. Hyder, Y. Rajkotia, S. Basu, J. A. Rehwinkel & A. Butchart (Eds), *The economic dimensions of interpersonal violence*. Geneva: WHO. Available at http://whqlibdoc.who.int/publications/2004/9241591609.pdf. Accessed 15 April 2009.

CHAPTER 3

PRIVATISING MILITARY PRISONS: THE CASE OF THE UNITED STATES

Aditya Agrawal and Keiran Sharpe

ABSTRACT

Purpose – *This chapter aims to contribute to the policy debate on private sector involvement in traditionally core defence activities through rigorous economic analysis. Punishment and correction in the US military prisons have traditionally been considered as a core activity that has been governed, regulated and managed by the military service personnel. It has been shown however, that military facilities such as stockades and brigs have often failed to meet their correctional objectives – a quality issue.*

Methodology – *The chapter constructs a case study to illustrate the method of analysis. Well-trained and motivated military custodial personnel play an important correctional role but are not available in sufficient numbers in military prisons. It is therefore proposed to source these services through the private sector. Specifically, the chapter proposes that private sector providers should provide custodial personnel for stockades and brigs. Traditionally the private sector has been employed to reduce costs, rather than improve quality. This chapter adapts and applies the framework developed by Hart, Shleifer and Vishny (1997) to study the governance model and incentive regime that could enable the use of the*

Economics of War and Peace: Economic, Legal, and Political Perspectives
Contributions to Conflict Management, Peace Economics and Development, Volume 14, 31–51

ISSN: 1572-8323/doi:10.1108/S1572-8323(2010)0000014007

private sector, reduce the risk of excessive cost cutting and enable quality outcomes to be achieved.

Findings – *This chapter argues that private sector involvement could effectively increase the contestability of supply.*

Implications – *The chapter demonstrates the scope for private sector involvement to increase quality, rather than just decrease costs. It follows that the private sector can contribute to core national security outcomes. However, this implication needs significantly more exploration for specific contexts.*

Value – *The adopted mode of analysis provides a template for rigorous analysis of similar proposals in the future.*

INTRODUCTION

Contracting out civilian prisons to private service providers was a hot topic during the privatisation debate in the 1990s (Hart, Shleifer, & Vishny, 1997). In the 2000s, the debate has focussed on using private military contractors (PMCs)[1] in providing military services (Singer, 2008, p. 9, 53). This chapter considers the scope for private sector providers to fill the shortfall of custodial personnel in military prisons and improve the quality of detention outcomes. Specifically, this chapter focuses on the detention of military prisoners (as opposed to prisoners of war) and considers the detention of military personnel in the US military correctional facilities: stockades and brigs. This is because a considerable amount of non-economic literature discusses various aspects of military imprisonment by the US military. Furthermore, the US military detention system has quality issues and the United States has led the way in contracting out non-core activities to private military companies.

Traditionally, defence procurement has involved the private sector to cut costs and increase efficiency. Sectoral allocation of defence activities focuses on cost-quality tradeoffs (Markowski & Wylie, 2009). Hart et al. (1997) have developed a formal information economic theoretic approach to studying the incentive structure in sectoral allocation decisions around the cost-quality focus. *This chapter adapts their fixed price-based model to a fixed quality incentive contract situation and formally investigates the feasibility of the proposed involvement. To our knowledge, PMC use in the contemporary security environment has not been subjected to this form of economic incentive analysis.* The analysis concludes that a feasible incentive regime can be constructed for quality incentive contractual situations involving the private sector in traditionally core military services.

This chapter is structured as follows. The correctional challenges posed by stockades and brigs are discussed in the next section. The following section considers the case for using the private sector to provide confinement officers for stockades and brigs. Then the proposed private sector governance and incentive regime is analysed through the lens of the cost–benefit framework developed by Hart et al. (1997). The discussion section reports the results on the modelling of cost-quality tradeoffs incentives. It considers the management issues, compares the results of this chapter's analysis with the results of the traditional Hart et al. model, and the implications for private military contracting. The chapter concludes with suggestions for possible extensions and directions for further work.

THE PROBLEM: INSUFFICIENT SUPPLY OF CUSTODIAL PERSONNEL TO REHABILITATE PRISONERS

Military detention in the United States is not achieving its correctional objectives (Brodsky & Eggleston, 1970, pp. 28, 29). Hasenritter observes

> [The] correctional 'program' has developed as a result more of pushes and pulls from external pressures than as an internally generated product of rational planning to meet certain objectives. As a result, it has often produced a 'hodge-podge' of policy, just as do all 'systems' created largely by compromises between conflicting external pressures. Of course no program in any organization the size of the Army (in fact no program anywhere) exists without the unpleasant necessity of compromising with other competing goals and objectives. Still, some aspects of the Army have been relatively more powerful than others, and it is in this relative sense that the writers refer to the *long term powerlessness of corrections* vis-à-vis other systems which impinge or interface with it.
>
> [Another] problem is that the area is relatively peripheral to the Army's central missions and ... *the number of persons involved is few*. Corrections seem to have become a function often preempted in practice by demands of objectivity in less important areas. (Haasenritter, December 2003) (emphasis added)[2]

A recent study commissioned by the American Correctional Association affirms the shortages in correctional staff[3]

> Results from a 2004 study indicate that 44 per cent of the 44 US correctional systems and four Canadian systems that responded to a work force survey face serious difficulties in recruiting and retaining an adequate staff of qualified correctional officers ... the field of corrections finds itself facing unprecedented work force challenges as it enters the 21st

> century. Correctional agencies are competing with other criminal justice, governmental and private agencies for potential applicants. Although the number of correctional employees expanded from 300,000 to more than 750,000 (150 per cent) between 1982 and 1999, the growth has not kept up with the increased demand for correctional officers, according to the study. Current nationwide projections estimate that in the next decade, the US will need an additional 490,000 correctional officers to fill new positions required by the growth in the prison population and to replace correctional officers who terminate employment ... Based on these trends, Carroll and Moss predict that corrections will be second to the health care profession on the list of fields that are most likely to be affected by an upcoming shortage of workers ... As a result of the aforementioned factors, recruitment and selection are among the critical issues facing corrections, regardless of an agency's size. (Sumter, 2008)

The basic objective of military imprisonment is to protect military order (Henshel, 1970, p. 33).[4] Military facilities exist for the restraint, punishment and correction of prisoners (Hankoff, 1970, p. 46). The US military's equivalent to the civilian jail, in the sense of a 'holding area' or a 'place of brief incarceration for petty crimes' is known as the guardhouse or stockade in the Army and the Air Forces, and the brig in the Navy.[5] These facilities have from 2 up to 500 men,[6] serve holding, treatment and correctional purposes, and are often controlled at the local level[7] (Brodsky & Eggleston, 1970, p. 16). Persons who are confined and no longer participate in basic training are transferred out of their basic units into a replacement company. This company also includes apprehended individuals from other military areas, deserters and anyone else who does not participate in training (Bushard & Dahlgren, 1970, p. 60, 61). The aim is to rehabilitate short-term prisoners, whereas long-term prisoners (sentences of two years or more) are often dishonourably discharged. Such prisoners are also often transferred to civilian facilities after two years to serve the remainder of their sentence.[8] Essentially, a military prisoner can move from the replacement company back to the basic unit (military rehabilitation), civil society (normal discharge after serving sentence) or civil prison/civil society (dishonourable discharge).

The US process of military justice includes:

- court martialling of a prisoner;
- assessment by a national military court (henceforth referred as the Court)[9] of his/her suitability for rehabilitation;
- detention and rehabilitation tenure with a replacement company at a specific detention facility and
- monitoring by the local 'mental hygiene' facility which then makes a recommendation to the Court.

The Court then decides whether the prisoner should be dishonourably discharged, receive a normal discharge, be transferred to a civil prison or returned to service. Rehabilitative procedures include training in useful military trades[10] or trade employment and mature use of military discipline. A rehabilitative company provides an intermediate step between the replacement company and basic training. In addition, a Clemency Board can monitor a prisoner and can suspend the sentence of a deserving prisoner. There is also a parole system for employable prisoners, and a mental hygiene consultation service acts as the central initiating agency to examine and monitor prisoners, provide psychotherapy as required, and recommend individual rehabilitation programmes or transfer to the rehabilitation company, clemency, parole, discharge, etc. (Bushard & Dahlgren, 1970, pp. 64–67).

The custodial personnel must work together with the mental hygiene team to develop and implement an appropriate treatment plan. They must recognise that it is essential to champion non-delinquent patterns of behaviour to rehabilitate prisoners (Bushard & Dahlgren, 1970, p. 67). Rehabilitation requires *custodial personnel who can serve as appropriate models*, whom prisoners can emulate in successfully interacting with their environment (Brodsky & Eggleston, 1970, p. 22).

However there are several problems with the quality of custodial personnel at stockades and brigs. As Brodsky and Eggleston (1970, p. 16) observe

> A major problem in stockade operations is that stockades are controlled at the local post levels. The commanding officer of the post is responsible for making basic decisions about stockades. One important result of this local control is that the stockade has low priority on the post, *since military posts do not exist for the purpose of running good stockades*. Indeed, some commanders see bad images of stockades as a useful deterrent to soldiers. Thus the seeking of the deterrent image plus disinterest in military corrections – except for the use of prisoners in sweeping streets and packing groceries – contributes to inefficient and problem-producing stockades.
>
> A second by-product of this local control is *staffing*. In many posts, stockades receive personnel drawn involuntarily from various other units. The least desirable men in the donating units are relinquished permanently and some stockades become staffed in part by misfits and unmotivated custodial personnel, rather than by individuals who can make positive contributions [italics added for emphasis].

Custodial personnel do not generally serve as positive and effective role models (Brodsky & Eggleston, 1970, p. 16). Personnel are more interested in enforcing a dependable routine focused on custody and control rather than correction. The problem of rehabilitating prisoners is not a core issue and does not warrant much attention from the local post military hierarchy.

Custodial personnel concerned with handling prisoners are the lowest ranking, least experienced and youngest of the brig personnel, and they are often prone to personal expressions of hostility. Misbehaviour and hostility chain reactions, such as acting out anger towards superiors on prisoners, are common in the highly authoritarian environment of these detention facilities (Hankoff, 1970, p. 54). Interviews report frequent use of the expression, 'the brig [is] there to break these men' and they use an entire arsenal of provocation, humiliation and abuse to achieve their ends (Hankoff, 1970, p. 51). Many sentries feel that stern physical measures are proper and they see themselves as dispensing personalised true justice, leading to sadistic practices (Hankoff, 1970, pp. 52, 55, 56). Although a strict and disciplined routine and procedural code has a stabilising influence on prisoners, it can also be anti-rehabilitative and tyrannical (Miller, 1958). The brig manual is intended to prevent the worst case behaviour of custodial personnel and does not set standards or establish rewards for better performance (Hankoff, 1970, p. 50). Since career military personnel command and run the facility, there are no measures for personnel accountability, correctional performance measurement or assessment which leads to inertia (Hankoff, 1970, p. 54).

Professional intervention in penal systems has often had disappointing results. The crucial area of attack is the attitudes, particularly of custodial personnel. Attention should be given in the first instance to change the attitudes of custodial personnel as this would appear to be most rewarding in its overall rehabilitative effect on prisoners (Hankoff, 1970, p. 59).

WHERE THE PRIVATE SECTOR COULD BE INVOLVED

At this stage, the US military can have alternative solutions to this problem including:

- choosing and transferring good-quality custodial personnel to problem stockades and brigs;
- re-specifying the incentive regime making prisoner rehabilitation higher priority for the local commander;
- using civilian custodial personnel from other areas of the public sector;
- allowing the private sector to provide suitable personnel; etc.

Haasenritter observed in his survey article on the US military correctional system

> The skills developed in operating military prisons have become critical in operating detention camps throughout the world during military conflicts (enemy prisoners of war) and the global war on terrorism (detention camps in Guantanamo Bay, Cuba and Bagram, Afghanistan). Despite all this, as are state and federal systems, the military correctional system are under scrutiny for divestiture and privatisation, and its future is uncertain. This is not the first time the military has looked at getting out of the prison business. (Haasenritter, December 2003)

This chapter investigates the costs and benefits of private sector provision, specifically it considers the possibility of a national military body hiring a PMC to recruit and provide private custodial personnel within the overall military framework of a stockade or brig.[11] The ownership, governance and management of the facility is still provided by the military but the provision of custodial personnel is contracted out to the private sector. The PMC personnel would have stronger incentives for correction and rehabilitation with assessment taking place as before. These correctional goals can be communicated to PMC personnel using metrics such as *Correction Pass Rate* (*CPR*).[12]

The government objective is to improve quality (quality contract), and a CPR-based measure can be set as the baseline performance measure with rewards for additional performance (incentive contract) and penalties for less than baseline performance. This type of contract is in contrast to (1) a fixed price contract which is relevant if the performance of the activity rather than the outcome is being reimbursed or (2) a cost reimbursement (cost plus) contract which would leave room for contractor manipulation without sufficient government safeguards. Fig. 1 summarises sector choice and contract-type choice. To improve quality the PMC can hire non-commissioned officers (NCO) who have retired from the Services. These returned NCOs can serve as positive and realistic role models. Regulation and oversight can be provided by a company officer managing these personnel, thus serving as a link between the company and the rest of the military structure.

THE CLASSIC HSV MODEL

Considerable economic literature deals with the relative advantages and disadvantages of using private suppliers for delivery of public goods. Government contracting advocates note that private suppliers deliver public goods at a lower cost than public agencies (Logan, 1990). Critics of

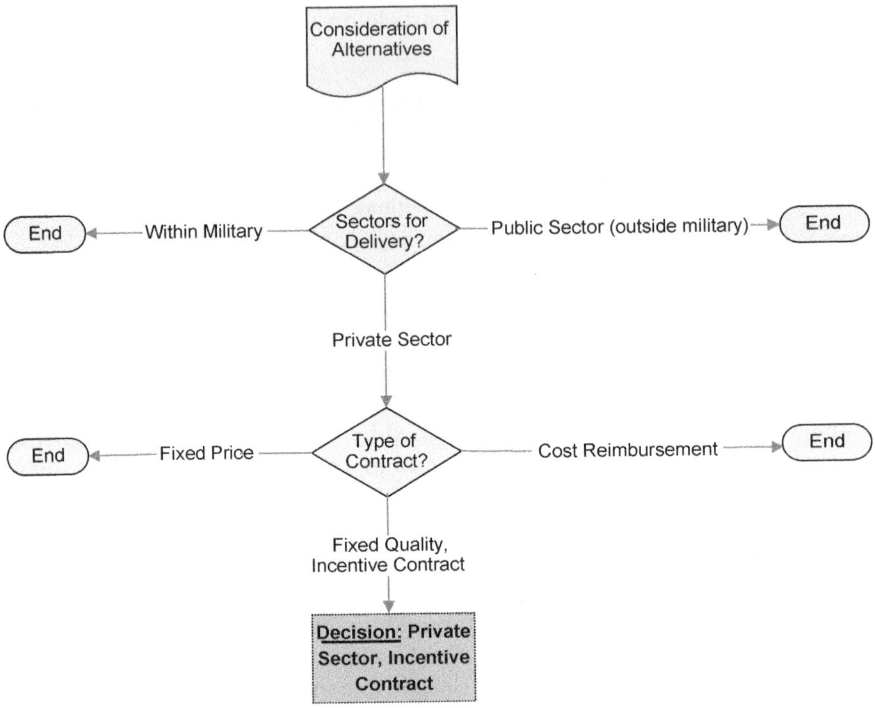

Fig. 1. Decision Flowchart – Proposal Considered (With Indication of Alternatives).

government contracting emphasise that the quality of public services is likely to decline (Shichor, 1995).

Hart et al. (1997) (henceforth referred to as the HSV model) have developed a formal model for examining cost-quality tradeoffs between private and public provision. The model introduces concepts such as:

- incomplete contracts (contracts where important unforeseen contingencies are excluded);
- residual rights of control (power and control issues that are implicit in a negotiation) and
- interaction between incomplete contracts and residual rights of control in terms of contingencies arising in incomplete contracts that place greater power in the hands of the owner of residual rights.

The model allows for two types of innovation: cost innovation (which may impact adversely on quality) and quality innovation (which normally results in higher cost of service provision). The HSV model examines contractual incentives under different scenarios of public and private ownership and service delivery. It also includes considerations of ex post competition, corruption and patronage.

INNOVATION: ADAPTATION OF THE HSV MODEL

The HSV paper studied a *fixed price contract*, assuming a profit maximising private supplier. In the proposal outlined, the private sector is being introduced to *improve quality* rather than reduce costs. This represents a departure from both the HSV analysis and the traditional way PMC is used. However, cost-quality tradeoff issues must be studied to determine whether the governance regime and incentive structure allows the PMC to meet the required quality outcomes intended. Therefore, this chapter adapts the basic methodology of the HSV model to analyse a fixed quality incentive contract situation where the government is attempting to equate profit (the incentive for the private supplier) with the quality of detention outcomes (the incentive for the government).[13] The following analysis formally examines a possible governance and incentive regime that could achieve this objective.

ANALYSIS: CAN THE GOVERNANCE REGIME ACHIEVE INTENDED QUALITY OUTCOMES?

The facility for military detention is denoted by F. F is maintained for the holding, restraint and correction of military prisoners. Activities by the custodial personnel are a subset of the entire activities of the detention centre. F is owned, managed and regulated by the military G, and a private sector employer P is chosen through an auction to hire and manage custodial personnel. P hires M, a private manager, to manage custodial personnel and liaise with office staff at F. Residual rights of control in case of uncontracted for contingencies, all information pertaining to the activity and facility remain with G.

P_0 is the price of the basic good defined as the provision of holding services and basic correctional output (CPR) for a specified length of time (the length of the contract). It is assumed that the contract timeline includes ex ante negotiations for defining the basic good, metrics for periodic verification and regulation of contractual activities, and finally ex post renegotiation or termination of the contract. It is also assumed that G will insert clauses in the contract for short notification termination in case of extraordinary circumstances. B represents the benefit to society of the role of custodial personnel in the restraint and correction of military prisoners and C is the cost to produce the detention outcomes including hiring, maintaining, managing and replacing custodial personnel. B_0 is the baseline number of corrections that would be needed for G to pay P the baseline salary P_0. If P fails to reach B_0 then P would be penalised, and if P surpasses B_0 then he would be rewarded with bonuses. The specification of the reward/punishment is done as per a scale designed according to the measure of the CPR.[14]

Cost and quality innovations can be made and implemented, with the permission of G,[15] and are represented by the effort variables e and i, respectively (measured in utility terms). $b(e)$ represents the reduction in social benefit due to effort e exerted towards cost innovations. $c(e)$ represents the corresponding decrease in costs due to cost innovation effort e. $\beta(i)$ represents the increase in social benefit due to effort i exerted into quality innovations (and is assumed to cause a rise in costs[16]). Both innovations are incentivised compared to a regular military service contract in that satisfactory holding and correctional performance is rewarded with another contract for the private employer at the end of the contractual period, in a competitive marketplace.[17] This reward constrains excessive tendency to cut costs while making it beneficial for M to invest in low-quality impact cost reductions. Quality innovations are defined as some manner of achieving better holding performance measured by the CPR. It is assumed that in order to incentivise quality innovations, on passing verification, G will absorb the entire costs of quality innovations and reward P in the ex post renegotiation stages through contractual renewal in a competitive marketplace.

Assumptions in the HSV model have physical meaning in this proposal. $b(0) = 0$ means that if the effort e expended on cost innovation is 0 then the quality degradation as a result is also 0 follows naturally. $b' \geq 0$ and $b'' \geq 0$[18] means that major reductions in quality of personnel, or management of personnel would result in more rapidly decreasing quality. This has physical meaning in that private provision is already partly a cost-based decision (due to the competitive auction) and the residuum of possible cost innovations before the quality meter goes into the danger zone is small.[19] If the private provider makes major cost reductions (e.g. a dramatic decrease in quality of custodial personnel), then the detrimental impact on quality increases more significantly than the cost reduction. $c(0) = 0$: this assumption suggests that if P puts no effort into cost innovation then no cost reduction can result follows naturally. $c'(0) = \infty$, $c'(\infty) = 0, c' > 0$ and

$c'' < 0$: these parameters indicate that physically the rate of the cost reduction function increases more quickly at lower levels of e as cost innovations may exist due to reasons such as cost efficiencies through customisation to the particular stockade or brig, etc. However as the auction for awarding P the contract is competitive, larger e levels produce diminishing rates of cost innovations. Again the residuum of permissible cost reductions before intolerable quality reductions start to occur is small. Furthermore this margin of difference between cost reduction and quality reduction keeps increasing, with quality reduction outweighing corresponding cost reductions earned through them. This is because the loss of holding and correctional performance removes the reason for the presence of the private provider. $\beta(0) = \infty, \beta' > 0, \beta'' < 0, \beta'(\infty) = 0$: this shows that physically as more effort i is put into quality innovations, the corresponding quality improvement is greater. However, since there is a limited extent to possible improvement of correctional performance due to better performance by custodial personnel, the rate of quality improvement decreases. This has intuitive appeal as custodial personnel are an important but small part of F, and have a limited impact on correctional outputs. $c' - b' \geq 0$: proposals for cost reductions that are implemented in F have the feature that the cost reduction net of quality reduction is positive. Intuitively P in consultation with M submits proposals which accrue some benefit to itself in cost reduction, and G assesses whether the quality reduction is *tolerable* before allowing implementation. Hence this condition must hold for the innovation to be allowed to be implemented.

The total costs for private sector employer P to provide social benefit B might be represented as

$$C + e + i = C_0 - \left(\frac{1}{2}c(e)\right) + e + i - \alpha\beta(i) \quad (1)$$

All terms are expressed in utility units convertible to financial estimations. C_0 denotes the initial estimation of costs by P. The benefits of cost reduction are shared between G and P (50:50 as per Nash bargaining). This relationship can be read to mean that the total cost is equal to

- the baseline cost minus any cost reduction benefits due to cost innovations
- plus the cost of any efforts expended to develop and implement cost and quality innovations
- minus cost decreases due to quality innovation benefits (cost of implemented quality innovations are absorbed by G).

It is also assumed that e, i and C are observable but not to a third party and therefore not verifiable or enforceable, hence need to be regulated through local negotiations. This ensures that P cannot be sued by G through legal enforcement controlled by G. The system of checks and balances is still maintained because P is regulated by G through termination clauses. α represents the financial estimation (in utility terms) of reputational capital, monetary remuneration (as per the incentive clauses in the original contract) and renegotiation leverage gained by P through implementing quality innovations, where $0 \leq \alpha \leq 1$.[20]

The general payoff to P is

$$P_0((\text{CPR}_{\text{achieved}} - \text{CPR}_{\text{baseline}}) * \text{Scale}) - C_0 + \frac{1}{2}c(e) - e - i + \alpha\beta(i) \quad (2)$$

which is essentially the baseline salary adjusted by actual performance, minus costs plus weighted benefits of quality innovations.

The payoff to G is

$$\begin{aligned} &B_0((\text{CPR}_{\text{achieved}} - \text{CPR}_{\text{baseline}}) * \text{Scale}) \\ &\quad - (P_0(\text{CPR}_{\text{achieved}} - \text{CPR}_{\text{baseline}}) * \text{Scale}) - b(e) + \frac{1}{2}c(e) + \beta(i) \end{aligned} \quad (3)$$

P_0 represents the basic, contracted salary paid by G to P. B_0 represents the initial contracted social benefit measured by CPR. The relationship reads as

- the baseline output adjusted according to actual performance
- minus baseline salary adjusted according to actual output
- minus output decreases due to cost innovations
- plus half of the benefits of cost innovations
- plus the benefits of quality innovations.

Any innovation introduced by P becomes organisational knowledge in the facility and therefore the full $\beta(i)$ belongs to G for future use in the same or a different facility.

Eq. (2) represents P's payoff. P and G are assumed to have a standard, formal principal-agent relationship bound by a contract, preventing effective collusion. Optimal effort levels e and i for P can be computed from first order conditions for Eq. (2) as

$$\frac{1}{2}c'(e) = 1 \quad (4)$$

$$\alpha\beta'(i) = 1 \quad (5)$$

Eq. (4) explains that at the social optimum, the marginal financial benefit[21] of spending extra effort (for *P*) to reduce costs must equal the marginal cost of the extra effort, which equals one. Eq. (5) explains how the marginal financial estimate of benefit (to *P*) of spending extra effort to improve quality must equal the marginal cost of the extra efforts, which again equals one. *P* has an incentive to cost innovate as it benefits with half the rewards and possible renegotiation benefits. Furthermore cost reduction-related quality impacts are checked (and taken responsibility for) by *G*. *P*'s incentive for quality corrections (above and beyond the basic goals in the initial contracted price P_0) depend on the estimate factor α. However *P* has to share the innovation with *G*.

Discussion – Related Management Issues

This section briefly considers some issues and qualifications relevant to the proposal. Accountability is a serious concern in most private sector allocation decisions.[22] *G* owns, regulates and manages most functions within *F*, and owns residual rights of control is uncontracted for contingencies. The actions of *P* are visible and partly verifiable (between *G* and *P*, though not always to a third party such as a court). Therefore *P* is *accountable* to *G*. *Adverse selection* and *moral hazard* possibilities are reduced because *P* recruits through performance-based selection from a pool of ex-military custodial personnel[23] who understand military pedagogy[24] (therefore reducing chances of adverse selection) and have the incentives to perform and a desire to remain employed in future contracts (therefore reducing the chances of moral hazard). Information rent issues do not occur because as owner, *G* retains all *information*, and provides *P* with the required information, which can be withdrawn as required. *G* can attempt to recover auction costs, and costs of managing *P*, through the cost–benefits gained by selection through competitive auction. The central intention however is to involve *P* to improve the *CPR*. *G* must assess whether P_0 is a viable and sustainable transfer payment from the public to the private sector, though it can be easily justified in cases where *G* cannot find enough high-quality custodial personnel or where base correctional standards in the contract are equal to the transfer payment. Part of the transfer payment may also be recovered through taxes levied on *P* that may not apply in case of the service being provided by *G*. Benefits of *competition* can be earned by a planned selection of *P* among several vendors, and renegotiation and renewal of contract based on *P*'s performance. Since *G* is the sole buyer, *G* retains market power as a monopsony and can extract all rents if its privatisation mechanism design is efficient.

Issues of *corruption* and *corporate patronage* of vendors may dilute some of the benefits. A possible solution would be to rotate vendors within fixed time intervals, and ensure that choice of *P* is done through a public auction regulated by a national commission rather than at the local level. Military officer trade unions may cause issues. However a mixed model of using junior non-commissioned officers and private high-quality custodial personnel might prove satisfactory to the unions, beneficial to correctional performance, and the training of junior military custodial personnel. *G* underwrites all contingencies and insurance costs, therefore making the proposal comparatively low risk for *P*. Since the Court independently examines the detention cases before and after correction tenure, this reduces the risk of collusion between *P* and relevant staff at *F*, or between *G* and the Court.

RESULTS COMPARED WITH CLASSICAL HSV

The general HSV model concludes that *e* is inefficiently high and incentive for *i* is inefficiently low *under private ownership*. Verification and visibility are more difficult to achieve because *M* has the residual rights of control. An example is armed security, where the private owner over-emphasises cost reductions rather than responsible security provision for profit maximisation. The result is less than ideal security provision, and in some cases it even causes collateral damage to national security outcomes. An example is the use of Blackwater private security guards during the Iraq war to reduce costs. Although cost efficient, these guards did not have legal checks and balances imposed on them (the quality constraints) that are required of standard US military personnel. This resulted in them firing on Iraqi civilians in 2007 causing significant damage to the US war image as a responsible power.

The general HSV model concludes that under *public ownership*, since *M* has no residual rights of control and cannot extract the benefit of the innovation for future use (except through a possible reputational and promotional benefit), incentive to exert either *e* or *i* is inefficiently low. The alternative example is the public sector owner produces the standard product without emphasising innovation in weapons production. An adversary who can achieve innovation in the stated weapon will be at an advantage in the area of operation. A historical example is when the British first built and deployed an air force in WWI and then in post–WWI for imperial policing. It was the Germans who successfully developed the use of the Luftwaffe as support for their Blitzkrieg operations leading to successful operations in the Battle for France. Public sector failure to innovate can have significant negative impacts on national security outcomes.

In the stated analysis, since P may derive $\frac{1}{2}c(e)$ and $\alpha\beta(i)$, therefore the incentive for both cost and quality innovations may be higher. Since P needs to negotiate with G for *every* significant innovation (due to high visibility and verification), innovations are better regulated preventing systemic risk. P can introduce quality innovations to keep itself employed in future contracts, and it has incentive to implement cost innovations for its own benefit without causing damage to the correctional or holding objectives for which it is employed. Hence this mixed model proposal yields (in theory) superior results.

Extending the Model – Implications for Private Military Contracting and Conflict

This model which has incentives for private sector contractors to provide cost and quality incentives in defence service provision could have wider application in the military. Historically, combat-focused activities, including logistic support in areas of operations, have been the domain of the military. However, US combat operations in Iraq have seen a major increase in the use of PMC services with the ability to use force in direct combat zones and in quasi-combat roles. For example, in Iraq, PMCs are deployed as armed guards protecting transport convoys and buildings in areas of direct operations such as Baghdad. Several reasons have emerged for the increasing significance of PMCs in the security arena, in particular, post-colonial conflicts and the rise of non-state aggressors and terrorists. Conflicts long suppressed or manipulated by the superpowers re-emerged at the end of the Cold War. Once superpower support was withdrawn, several post-colonial states collapsed and private players entered the market of achieving and maintaining order. The rise of non-state actors and terror groups such as Al-Qaeda has led to *asymmetric warfare* intensifying and new requirements for warfare which standard militaries are not prepared for.

A vacuum in the security market has been caused by a range of factors, including the:

- failure of the world community (United Nations Security Council, North Atlantic Treaty Organization, etc.) to regulate these new actors;

- global downsising of militaries especially in support areas, the increase in force *op-tempo*;
- availability of resources and tools for warfare into the reach of private actors;
- weakness of government forces to prevent coups and
- decline of larger powers such as United States and international bodies such as the United Nations to be involved in conflict or to prosecute them (Colonel Tim Spicer, November 22, 1998; Singer, 2008, Chapter 4).

Private players are filling this vacuum and becoming increasingly critical security players. For example, only 30 countries ratified the 1989 treaty against the practice of using contractors in combat zones. The United States is taking a lead in private sector involvement in historically core defence activities. In 2001, the then US Secretary of Defense Donald Rumsfield spelled out the 'Rumsfield Doctrine' which stated that 'governments cannot die and so we need other incentives for the bureaucracy to adapt and improve' (Scahill, 2004, p. xiv), that the 'Pentagon is jeopardising the lives of men and women in uniform' and the need for a 'small footprint' approach (Scahill, 2004, pp. xiv, xv) involving the private sector into the defence of the country. Furthermore in 2006, the Pentagon Quadrennial Defense Review included PMCs as part of the US Total Force in the War against Terror (Scahill, 2004, p. xvii). In this context, the private sector is seen to have an advantage over the public sector in the provision of services.

The competitive advantage of private enterprise derives from lower cost overheads as these entities normally do not have to maintain legacy structures (such as obsolete Service units or government departments). They also have

- greater agility and geographic mobility of supply;
- scope for provision of tailored services using technically competent and requirements-oriented ex-soldiers (often from non-combatant countries) and
- surge capability (Avant, 2004, 2005).

Within this context, this chapters' analytical contribution is a method to study the incentives for PMC personnel compared to a public personnel, when performing a traditionally core activity.

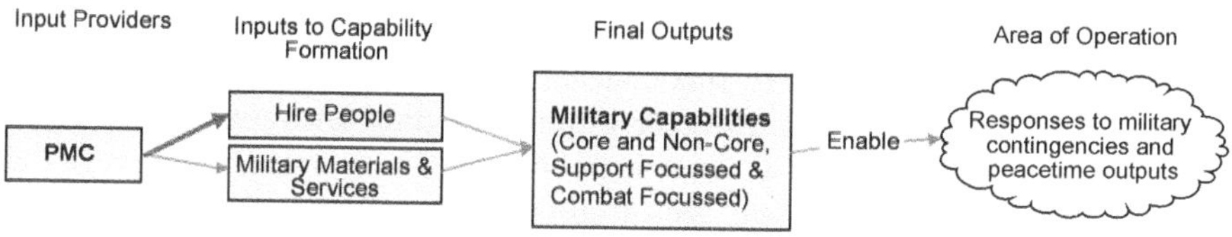

Fig. 2. Investigating the Expanded Use of PMCs.

IMPLICATIONS: THE ROLE OF PRIVATE SECTOR CONTRACTORS

Private contracting has traditionally been used to support cost cutting measures (Hart et al., 1997) and as gap fillers (Scahill, 2007, p. 57). This chapter's formal analysis demonstrates that a feasible incentive structure can be constructed to enable private contracting to expand into improving the quality of defence activities. In the context of the classical Defence value chain the role of the Private Military Company (PMC) input provider can be expanded to providing people (Fig. 2). Providing people in the defence value chain means to provide uniformed personnel who serve in or manage Defence activities, particularly in core activities. This would include providing armed security in operations, actual combat operations on land, sea or air and management of core command and control systems.

By providing people for defence activities, PMCs can contribute as inputs to core national security outcomes. This is significant because as the United States-led War on Terror intensifies, the need for PMC involvement as gap fillers in actual combat operations will increase. Nonetheless, the expanded use of private military contractors by defence must not decrease the quality of intended national security outcomes. This implication needs to be explored further, beyond an incentive analysis, for specific contexts and specific defence activities, to be robust and scalable enough for actual decision making.

CONCLUSION

This chapter has attempted to rigorously analyse a preliminary proposal to incorporate the private sector in providing military detention services to improve correctional performance and incentivise innovations. Stockades and brigs are considered as a general case study. Several avenues of further work exist. More detailed study of Single Service (such as Army) stockades and brigs, as well as maximum security and prisoner of war interrogation facilities could be considered. Analysing real applications could supplement the theoretical examination in this chapter. The current proposal considers private custodial personnel, however other personnel and governance roles could also be privatised. As a larger segment of military detention is brought under the purview of private sector allocation, more complex issues of governance, power and control, information structures and information rent, allocation of taxes and subsidies, etc. would also become relevant. Such a broadening of scope would allow the study to contribute to the more general question of sectoral allocation of defence activities, and more widely, public goods.

NOTES

1. In capitalist countries, where the means of production are largely privately owned, military supply chains have always involved a mixture of public and private activities. PMC can be defined broadly, to include all specialised suppliers of military-specific goods and services (a global business worth hundreds of billions of dollars each year), or narrowly, to focus on specialised logistic support services such as maintenance of military equipment, the provision of armed security, garrison support, etc. (Institute, 2005). In this proposal, the broader definition is adopted as the term PMC represents all private input into the defence production chain.

2. This last line maybe interpreted to mean that correctional objectives are often de-emphasised using the excuse of need for objectivity. Furthermore, higher priority is often accorded to other military base functions at the cost of quality degradation to the correctional programme.

3. The report referred to is A 21st century Workforce for America's Correctional Profession, available at the American Correctional Association Inc. website, http://www.aca.org/Workforce/workforce_r1.asp.

4. Crime in the military services means insubordination against military authority, either in peace or war. Military justice has its own code of laws and correctional branches within the Services are responsible for implementing the military justice system. Attorneys, prosecution, defence, the judge and the jury are all military personnel (Brodsky & Eggleston, 1970, p. 5). Military detention facilities are separated from civilian prisons to avoid what the military see as the 'detrimental environment of civilian state penitentiaries' (Brodsky & Eggleston, 1970, p. 16).

5. Facilities for war time detention of enemy soldiers are considered outside the purview of this study.

6. To provide some reference of scale, the US military correctional system was established in 1873. The US Marine Corps are also responsible for running prisoner of war, terrorist and detainee camps. Currently, the system has 59 facilities designed to confine inmates on the basis of sentence length, geographical location and treatment programs. The total operational capacity of the facilities is 3,249 and the

military, on average, confines 701 inmates for every 100,000 service personnel. There are three levels of confinement, level 1 for pre-trial and post-trail inmates of up to one year, level 2 for sentences up to seven years (our focus in this paper) and level 3 maximum-security confinement facilities of which there is only one, US Disciplinary Barracks (USDB) at Fort Leavenworth. Today the return to duty program is small and only the Air Force maintains an active, structured facility and programme. Other services maintain their goal as proper return to civilian life (Haasenritter, December 2003).

7. In this study, the terms stockade and brig are used interchangeably.

8. See http://en.wikipedia.org/wiki/Military_prison. Retrieved on 25 July 2009.

9. It is assumed that judgements by the Court are relatively independent from local post-collusions. Such an independent means of decision making is central to the success of this proposal, and correction in general.

10. The work is meant to be useful and menial, however not degrading. Pointless menial labour is avoided (Bushard & Dahlgren, 1970, p. 65).

11. Stockades and brigs are managed in such a way that corrections come low on the list of priorities for the local commanding officer. This officer is often not interested in improving correctional performance so change needs to be recognised and implemented at the national level.

12. Defined as number of corrections per hundred prisoners in a year. Correction is defined as the movement of military prisoner from replacement company to basic military unit (a full correction counted as 1), civil society with completion of sentence and normal discharge (counted as 1/2) and civil society/civil prison with dishonourable discharge (counted as 0).

13. By which it is meant a contract based on achievement of quality outcomes measured by a quality metric index, calibrated to a basic quality provision that is contracted for, rewards for additional performance, and penalties for lack of performance as per basic provision expectations.

14. To put it more formally, P would receive $P_0 + ((\text{CPR}_{\text{achieved}} - \text{CPR}_{\text{baseline}}) * \text{Scale}) + \alpha\beta(i)$. Scale represents the bonus payments based on the scale of achievement (designed to become a penalty if the difference is negative). $\alpha\beta(i)$ is the (current and anticipated) benefits from cost-incurring quality innovations. Quality innovations are discussed further in Eq. (1).

15. An alternative would be for a 'more black box' approach involving G to simply measure the correction pass rate, and allow P to implement innovations without permission. A greater amount of regulation than strictly necessary has been specified to mitigate risk, allows G to derive full knowledge of innovations, and prevent serious changes due to mis-applied innovations that could jeopardise G's position.

16. If a quality innovation does not cause a rise in costs, it can be subsumed as a cost innovation with positive $b(e)$ and $c(e) = 0$.

17. Is there a competitive marketplace available? This is a determinant of the sourcing strategy and would be determined before this analysis would be undertaken. However, it is anticipated that this would not be a comparable problem to traditional military outsourcing. Most PMCs today act as global resource allocators maintaining large databases of employment contacts. They draw from an international employee pool of ex-military personnel readily available due to global downsising of militaries due to the end of the Cold War and the gaps in the security market. Hence they have

low barriers to entry (Singer, 2008, pp. 74–78). Furthermore the short expected lifespan of contract, seen as a gap-filler, ensures lower dependency and therefore a more easily formed competitive marketplace. Arms production and maintenance, however, have much higher outlays and higher barriers to entry (traditionally controlled by the government sector indirectly) due to a longer expected specialised dependence. Hence the availability of a competitive marketplace in theory would be possible in case of this proposal.

18. b' refers to the first derivative of b and b'' to the second derivative.

19. The threshold value would depend on the characteristics of a specific implementation.

20. It is possible for P to value benefit α as 0 meaning P sees no benefit in implementing quality innovations. Similarly P may set α as 1 as P is able, through various means, to acquire the entire benefit of implementing quality innovations. G must endeavour to create a situation where α is as close to 1 as possible, whereas maintaining appropriate checks and ensuring social benefits are not adversely affected.

A possible mathematical expression of α might be, $\int_t^{\infty} \pi(\text{payoff})\mathrm{d}t$ representing a summation over an (in theory) infinite time series of the relationship between G and P, of some fraction π (maybe greater than 1) of the payoff to P (see Eq. (2)) received through renegotiation success, reputational benefits, etc.

21. Half the financial benefit goes to G, after G has checked and is satisfied that the cost innovation is tolerable.

22. This discussion is stated from G's perspective. However P would have several common and some different concerns from G. Specific concerns would include the reliability and credibility of G, ensuring the lack of collusion and incorrect manipulation of the Court's correctional judgements by G or the local post (manipulation of independent means) feasibility of achieving B_0 given P_0 (a hard budget constraint) for a given F, etc. The feasibility is especially important because G controls all inputs except the custodial personnel, and P would need to assess whether CPR requirements can be achieved with this limited influence (assessment of calibration). This is representative of the generally closed nature of the military and the traditional difficulty in private sector involvement in the military.

23. This is indicated as a preference by G however P is not bound to limit itself to this pool. G can evaluate tender proposals during source selection to test feasibility of recruitment strategies proposed by different possible private suppliers.

24. It can be a condition of employment that all custodial officers undergo military pedagogy training. Ex-military custodial officers will have the added benefit of experience applying the pedagogy. The detention facility manual can also be studied as part of this orientation.

REFERENCES

Avant, D. (2004). The privatization of security and change in the control of force. *International Studies*, *5*, 153–157.

Avant, D. (2005). Private security companies. *New Political Economy*, *10*(1), 121–131.

Brodsky, S. L., & Eggleston, N. E. (Eds). (1970). *The military prison. Theory, research, and practice*. Carbondale, IL: Southern Illinois University press.
Bushard, B., & Dahlgren, A. W. (1970). A technic for military delinquency management. In: *The military prison: Theory, research and practice* (pp. 60–75). Carbondale, IL: Southern Illinois University Press.
Colonel Tim Spicer, Q. I. A. G. (1998). Inside Lt. Col. Spicer's new model army. *Sunday Telegraph*, 22 November.
Haasenritter, D. K. (2003). The military correctional system: An overview. *Corrections Today*, pp. 58–61. Lt. Col. David K. Haasenritter is senior correctional adviser to the deputy assistant secretary of the Army for Manpower and Reserve Affairs, December.
Hankoff, L. D. (1970). Interaction patterns among military prison personnel. In: S. L. Brodsky & N. E. Eggleston (Eds), *The military prison: Theory, research and practice* (pp. 46–59). Carbondale, IL: Southern Illinois University Press.
Hart, O., Shleifer, A., & Vishny, R. W. (1997). The proper scope of government: Theory and applications to prisons. *Quarterly Journal of Economics*, *112*(4), 1127–1161.
Henshel, R. L. (1970). Military correctional objectives: Social theory, official policy and practice. In: S. L. Brodsky & N. E. Eggleston (Eds), *The military prison: Theory, research and practice* (pp. 46–60). Carbondale, IL: Southern Illinois University Press.
Institute, A. S. P. (2005). *War and profit: Doing business on the battlefield*. Technical Report, ASPI.
Logan, C. H. (1990). *Private prisons pros and cons*. New York: Oxford University Press.
Markowski, S., & Wylie, R. (2009). Using commercial discipline to improve Australian defence procurement: Misplaced enthusiasm? *2009 Pacific Rim Conference of the Western Economic Association International, Session 52: Issues in Defence and Security Economics*, Ryukoku University, Kyoto, Japan.
Miller, P. (1958). The prison code. *American Journal of Psychiatry*, *114*, 583–585.
Scahill, J. (2007). *Blackwater: The rise of the world's most powerful mercenary army*. New York: Nation Books.
Shichor, D. (1995). *Punishment for Profit*. Thousand Oaks, CA: Sage Publications.
Singer, P. W. (2008). *Corporate warriors: The rise of the privatized military industry*. Ithaca, NY: Cornell University Press.
Sumter, M. (2008). The correctional work force faces challenges in the 21st century: A study by the American correctional association inc. Available online at http://www.thefreelibrary.com/The+correctional+work+force+faces+challenges+in+the+21st+century.-a0183302026. Retrieved 26 November 2009.

CHAPTER 4

ARMS EXPORT CONTROLS AND THE PROLIFERATION OF MILITARY TECHNOLOGY

Peter Hall and Robert Wylie

ABSTRACT

Purpose – *To examine the implications of arms export controls on the international spread of weapons production and innovation.*

Methodology/approach – *The chapter analyses predicted responses to arms export controls, drawing on existing literature. It considers incentives to potential buyer countries to develop their own substitutes and a case study of Australia's response to US denial of access to electronic warfare self-protection (EWSP) technology for fighter aircraft.*

Findings – *Spurred by the US denial of access to relevant EWSP, Australia devoted many years to developing a homegrown substitute. Although Australia achieved some success, the United States ultimately granted Australia access to the technology. Australia then abandoned research, design and development (RD&D) on EWSP for fast jets in 2009. Cause and effect remain a matter of debate.*

Research limitations/implications – *Insight into the real-world value of the theory is limited by the use of a single case study. Such cases supported by publicly available information are, however, scarce. Countries seeking*

Economics of War and Peace: Economic, Legal, and Political Perspectives
Contributions to Conflict Management, Peace Economics and Development, Volume 14, 53–68

ISSN: 1572-8323/doi:10.1108/S1572-8323(2010)0000014008

to circumvent export controls must expect to incur high costs and uncertain outcomes.

Practical implications – *Policy-makers should be wary about committing large budgets in developing substitutes for new technologies denied them through export controls. Such efforts may, however, offer the possibility of putting suppliers under pressure unavailable from other actions.*

Social implications – *Arms export controls designed to limit proliferation of weapons create incentives for states to develop their capabilities for new arms production and to develop new weapons-related knowledge.*

Originality/value of the chapter – *This chapter provides a new case study which illustrates an innovative approach to arms export control analysis.*

INTRODUCTION

Arms control continues to be a key focus in the study of defence and peace economics (see, e.g. Smith, 2009). Export controls designed to stifle the international proliferation of arms can, nonetheless, create pressures that lead to an even more undesirable outcome – the more widespread development, internationally, of military production and innovation capabilities. Denied direct access to the military assets they seek, countries have an incentive to invest in the capabilities required to make the weapons for themselves. Formal economic analysis has pointed to conditions under which countries will invest to undertake domestic production in the presence of arms export controls (Levine & Smith, 2000; Levine, Mouzakis, & Smith, 2000), but that work offers only limited analysis of the range of possible responses to arms export controls. And in taking research, design and development (RD&D) expenditure as a proxy for innovation, it disguises the arduous and uncertain nature of the process that countries must often pursue if they wish to develop 'home-made' substitutes for technologies they have been denied. This prevents existing analysis from acknowledging that such uncertainty can lead to faulty perceptions about the potential effectiveness of arms export controls.

In this chapter, we begin by outlining the range of choices open to a potential recipient of new military technology to identify the range of possible actions for a nation in this position. We then consider the implications of these potential actions for suppliers and how the relationship between recipients and suppliers might, under uncertainty, shape innovation in military technology. We are, thus, able to analyse factors that determine whether and how the capability to produce new military technology will diffuse and, with it, how use of the system will proliferate. As an illustration of the general analysis, we then present a case study that examines Australia's response to US denial of access to advanced electronic warfare self-protection (EWSP) systems for use in FA-18 aircraft. This history ran from the 1980s until domestic efforts to develop an Australian substitute were called to a halt in mid-2009.

FRAMING THE CHOICES COUNTRIES FACE WHEN OBTAINING WEAPONS

Any country can obtain military capability in world markets *at a price* (Levine & Smith, 1997). Sometimes price is infinitely high: the seller (or its government) forbids sale of arms at any finite, positive price to another country. This is the case of *export control.*

Whether the price of an imported system lies below or at infinity, potential buyers have a range of options to consider, each including substitutions in production or use. Suppose first that a weapons system is priced below infinity and could be obtained from one or more alternative suppliers. Then potential buyers will observe or make judgments about current and expected future weapons prices and could

- wait, that is obtain the system (or a close technical substitute) in future rather than now (*intertemporal substitution*);
- make rather than buy, that is make the system (or a close technical substitute) domestically rather than import it (*import substitution*);
- switch, that is import the system (or a close technical substitute) from one supplier rather than an existing one (*supplier substitution*);
- stand pat, that is neither make nor import the system (nor a close technical substitute). In this case, countries may be more or less ambitious in or capable of adapting their existing military capabilities, using existing capability inputs.

Under full arms export control, the current price to potential buyers is infinitely high. 'Waiting' means considering whether the system will ever become available at a finite price – and, if so, at what price. 'Making now' means considering whether to produce domestically a system that would not otherwise be available at all. 'Switching now' implies seeking a supplier who might offer the system at a finite price. 'Standing pat' means accepting the infinite price as a complete bar on importing and deciding whether or not to adapt national military capability in the light of that.

MAKING THE CHOICE ABOUT HOW OR WHETHER TO OBTAIN WEAPONS

In this section, we outline the factors influencing potential buyers in making their choice. It has been common to focus more on import substitution than the other substitution possibilities and we leave that option until last.

In relation to *intertemporal substitution*, buyers are more likely to postpone purchases if they judge that the import price will fall relatively quickly and substantially over time or that new versions of a system, at the same or even a higher price, will become available in future. In responding to export controls, nations must judge how long it might be until the seller is prepared to trade at some subinfinite price – and whether it is worth the wait. Potential buyers may seek to *encourage relaxation* of the controls by embarking on a programme of import substitution.

In the general case of *supplier substitution*, countries will seek to reveal which supplier offers best value for money, and if a current supplier is judged inferior in terms of price and/or quality and/or delivery performance, an alternative may be used. If export controls are imposed by one or a subset of foreign producers (but not all of them), supplier substitution becomes a particularly important option for buyers if a current supplier now denies access to its exports. Faced with a bar on obtaining weapons from one source (or a subset), buyers will weigh up the relative benefits of supplier substitution among foreign producers and import substitution.

The 'stand pat' option occurs when a country chooses not to import weapons that it could obtain if it were prepared to pay for them. Making such a choice is equivalent in its effects to having such a choice imposed upon it by export controls. But neither route implies that *domestic technological and organisational substitutions* will not occur. For example, a country denied access to signature-minimising technology for submarines may redesign its war-fighting doctrine and organisational arrangements to dispense with submarines altogether.

In relation to *import substitution*, results from the existing literature provide at least partial guidance on how buyers decide what to do. Levine et al. (2000) stylise the international market for arms to comprise a small number of hi-tech weapons supplier countries and a large number of buyer countries, some of which also produce low-tech weapons. At the core of the model lies the determination of a switch point at which it becomes worthwhile for a non-producer country to establish a domestic industry producing low-tech arms – which will, to an extent, substitute for hi-tech imports. If there are large fixed costs, the average cost of achieving a given level of military capability with domestic production can be below its marginal cost with only imported arms, thus covering the initial investment (Levine et al., 2000, p. 56).

Levine et al. find that at any *given* hi-tech arms import price (which could, in principle, include infinity), local production of low-tech weapons will occur more widely: (i) the lower are the set-up costs of potential new producers (ii) the more import-competitive locally produced substitutes are or appear to be. Starting from any finite price for the hi-tech import, a *rising* price leads to an increasing number of countries becoming low-tech arms producers (Levine et al., 2000, p. 65). Expectations about future hi-tech weapons prices are also potentially important. Here, Levine and Smith (2000) discover that the greater is future uncertainty about the price of arms imports, the greater is the disincentive for importers to produce substitutes. Greater uncertainty makes it harder for a country to judge whether it is worthwhile to incur large, non-recoverable (i.e. sunk) production setup costs (p. 893).

Although the Levine et al., and Levine and Smith analyses are set up in terms of hi-tech exports and low-tech substitutes, it is a relatively short step to argue that the same conclusions will apply if we ask about import substitution in general. No country setting out to replace imported weapons systems with its own product will be able to generate a perfect substitute; there will always be differences. Whether the difference is described as hi-tech versus low-tech is merely a matter of nomenclature. What this implies is that raising the price of arms exports may *encourage proliferation* by inducing investments in other countries to produce substitutes. Since arms export control is equivalent to raising the price to an infinitely high level, the encouragement to proliferation is *maximised.* That is not to say, however, that arms export control is either necessary or sufficient for proliferation. It is not necessary because, even at finite prices, import substitution may appear attractive. It is not sufficient because a complete ban on exporting arms will not, of itself, induce a country to set up an arms industry. It depends on the setup costs and the willingness with which the country (or its government) will sacrifice consumption to meet those costs.

IMPLICATIONS FOR SUPPLIERS

Suppliers considering imposing arms export controls are likely to take responses of potential customers into account when making their initial decision and subsequently implementing it. In controlling arms exports, suppliers incur the following threats:

1. The controls deny firms in supplier nations the potential return on export sales that would have been earned in the absence of the controls.
2. Successful import substitution enables an erstwhile customer potentially to become an alternative source of supply to third countries.
3. Countries that make their own systems may pose a new military threat to suppliers.

These dangers only become pressing, however, if another country is successful in developing an alternative system to the point of successful operational deployment.

Suppose that suppliers initially think that most non-producers believe reinventing a weapons system is too costly or unpredictable even to contemplate. Suppliers will then perceive only limited incentives to adjust any export control policy. But the incentive structure changes if it starts to become apparent that countries denied access to the controlled system could develop a substitute for themselves. Now the cost of the arms export control to suppliers becomes the sum of lost export sales and the costs associated with new production occurring elsewhere, counted both in terms of increased threats to security and new competition in export markets. Suppliers face increased incentives to head off the possibility of other countries proceeding further towards production by exporting the technology to them.

Suppliers as technological leaders, however, always enjoy an asymmetric advantage which they may exploit in determining whether and when to change their position. Leaders know better than followers what lies ahead in terms of the unsolved problems and ongoing RD&D costs associated with a 'catch-up' programme. Even as incentives for withholding the technology decline, the initial supplier still retains the upper hand. It knows from the development stage followers have reached, both how much their own interests are truly threatened and when the burden of rising costs and continuing uncertainty will render followers most susceptible to abandoning local production.

IMPLICATIONS FOR INNOVATION

Attempts to develop a substitute weapons system imply greater challenges than are apparent by viewing them as isolated expenditures on RD&D. But the prospect of failure may be a poor disincentive to undertaking the work. This is partly because genuine uncertainty infuses the innovation process and also because the prospect of failure is often not recognised by innovators who may be more influenced by the raw value of anticipated success rather than the low probability they should attach to achieving it.

This leads to the conclusion that those who seek to control arms exports may systematically underestimate the probability that countries denied access will seek to develop substitutes – and encourage other countries more than they had anticipated to develop strategically valuable new technological knowledge, even if that knowledge is not likely to be converted into operational systems. Levine et al. (2000) argue that import substitution might be discouraged by imposing controls on the equipment required to produce the substitute weapons – or by measures which have implications for innovation. One suggestion is to strengthen the intellectual property regime protecting relevant technological knowledge; the other is to enhance the technological specifications of the weapons export, thus making substitution by a (lower-quality) imitation less effective (Levine et al., 2000, p. 65). A natural extension of the latter argument is that supplier countries might see it as being in their interests to complement arms export control by an accompanying strategy of ongoing RD&D designed deliberately to render existing knowledge obsolete. In that case, far from discouraging investment in new arms technology, arms export controls would only contribute to an ongoing process of military innovation. That said, the offsets literature finds that even when offsets suppliers willingly transfer technology to offsets-demanding states, the capabilities they develop often lie behind the leading edge (Brauer & Dunne, 2004).

ELECTRONIC WARFARE SELF-PROTECTION: US EXPORT CONTROL AND AUSTRALIAN INDIGENOUS INNOVATION

To this point in the chapter, we have been concerned with general principles. We now apply this framework to a particular case: the use of EWSP systems in Australia's combat aircraft.

Technical Background

Electronic warfare (EW) is about ensuring use of the electromagnetic spectrum by one's own forces (and those of friends and allies) while denying it to adversaries.

EW technologies can be divided into receivers, emitters and decoys. Modern EW suites often combine all these elements (Puttre, 2004). Receivers are the focus of the case study in this chapter, and within that technology, innovation in *threat warning systems* that warn flight crew that they are being tracked by the targeting radar of a surface-to-air missile (SAM) battery or an air-to-air missile radar operated by hostile aircraft. *Passive* threat warning systems typically comprise sensors that either 'stare' at a fixed sector of the electromagnetic spectrum or scan a wider portion of that spectrum surrounding the host platform. (Unlike active warning systems, they make no emissions that signal their presence to radar detection devices.) Our case study concentrates on innovation in the passive *radar* warning receiver (RWR) – the simplest and most essential element of any EW suite, and also the most commonly found. The pursuit of tactical advantage has fostered intense innovation in RWR technology for decades.

PERFORMANCE, INNOVATION AND CONTROL IN ELECTRONIC WARFARE

The efficacy of RWR systems depends on

- accurate, timely information about hostile radars stored in the warning system's threat library;
- signal processing capability sufficiently advanced to identify/categorise, locate and prioritise the threat posed by hostile radars and to discriminate between hostile and friendly radars illuminating the host platform.

Gathering and processing information about the electronic signatures of hostile radars is a matter for national intelligence services. But technological innovation is the key to improving the sensitivity, speed and precision with which the RWR can process signals from hostile and friendly radars.

Focusing specifically on RWR innovation, we can illuminate the impact on an innovation follower (in the present chapter, Australia) of an innovation leader (in our chapter, the United States) denying access to weapons technology. We concentrate on RWR developed by the US military for three reasons:

1. The US military is one of the innovation leaders in this field.
2. To maximise the gain from investment in such innovation, the US government controls the international diffusion of US-developed RWR technology closely.
3. Australia, like others seeking to emulate the US military, seeks to maximise its military capability at minimum cost by accessing US innovation in military technology.

As US friends and allies became aware of the tactical advantage US forces gained by effectively exploiting EW technology, they sought to emulate it. Where US friends and allies procured US aircraft, policy attention in both customer and supplier communities shifted away from, say, release of airframe and engine technologies and focused increasingly on access to the most up-to-date EW technology. For customer countries like Australia, effectively exploiting US aircraft capability increasingly depended on having the ability to manage the EW technology embedded in the aircraft. This included the ability to program threat libraries embedded in RWR. Conversely, the US Government took as much care to protect this technology as it did to protect its intelligence about electronic signatures used to populate RWR threat libraries. Selective release to US friends and allies of EW technology and of intelligence about electronic signatures became an increasingly important tool of US statecraft. It managed the release of EW technology and related equipment via the export licensing process pursuant to the International Traffic in Arms Regulations (ITAR), whereas intelligence exchange about electronic signatures was managed under government-to-government arrangements.

Historically, although the United States shared information about hostile radar signatures (e.g., those operated by Warsaw Pact forces) with its friends and allies relatively readily, it was much less forthcoming with information about the electronic signatures of Western, particularly US aircraft operated by US forces. Hence, the RWRs used by non-US operators of US-origin aircraft could 'see' radar emissions by US adversaries but were 'blind' to radar emissions by US-origin aircraft whoever operated them.

THE UNITED STATES CONTROLS RADAR WARNING TECHNOLOGY

The mainstay of Australia's current air defence capability is the McDonnell Douglas F/A-18A Hornet aircraft, almost all 75 of which were assembled in Australia between 1984 and 1990. Fitted to the aircraft were AN-ALR-45 RWRs which had their origins in the Vietnam War era. (In US military terminology, the 'AN' prefix denotes joint service, whereas the designation ALR can be decoded as follows: 'A' signifies 'airborne', 'L' signifies countermeasures and 'R' signifies passive countermeasures.)

Australian procurement of the F/A-18 provided for extensive Australian industry involvement intended to, among other things, ensure local industry could support the aircraft by repairing, maintaining and adapting the aircraft and its systems during the service life of the aircraft. The F/A-18 industry programme also provided for 'designated work'. This was defined as work of strategic significance – that is, industry activity underpinning Australia's self-reliant operation of the aircraft – which would not otherwise have been undertaken in Australia, and for which the government was prepared to pay a cost premium. A key element of the F/A-18 designated work involved supplying and supporting aircraft systems. According to a review of the F/A-18 industry programme (Department of Defence, 1994), this included

- final assembly and test of the inertial navigation system;
- partial manufacture, assembly and test of Head-Up Displays and of the multipurpose display group;
- assembly, burn-in and acceptance testing of flight control computers;
- design, development and production of avionics fault tree analyser hardware and software and
- assembly and test of radars, including manufacture of radar processors.

The key point, for the purposes of this chapter, however, is that this otherwise comprehensive list makes no mention of local industry involvement in supply, repair, maintenance and adaptation of electronic countermeasures fitted to the aircraft. This is even more significant given that local industry involvement was seen at the time as critical for defence self-reliance and figured prominently in the strategic guidance of the day.

In the event, according to the review, 21 of the passive electronic countermeasures were repaired by the Royal Australian Air Force (RAAF) in-house, whereas 25 were repaired in the continental United States.

The report does not indicate where the all-important AN/ALR-45 RWR was supported. Over 20 years later, however, it is now clear that, despite vigorous attempts by Australia to obtain the information required for local support of these systems in the interests of self-reliant operation of the F/A-18A, the aircraft's RWRs were returned to the United States for repair, maintenance and upgrade as a matter of US policy (Wylie, 2006).

IMPLICATIONS OF DENYING AUSTRALIAN ACCESS TO THE TECHNOLOGY

The AN-ALR-45 RWRs in Australia's F/A-18A aircraft were configured for operations against Warsaw pact forces. They were not programmed to detect radar emissions of US and other Western origin aircraft operating in South East Asia. Worse, Australia could not repeat earlier success it had had in reconfiguring the threat libraries of its fleet of F111 tactical bomber aircraft. In the case of the F/A-18A, the threat library of AN-ALR-45 RWRs was embedded in the system's hard-wired programmable signal processor and the US government denied Australian government requests for access to the algorithms that determined the operations of the processors and, hence, which radar frequencies it could 'see'.

The then Minister for Defence, the Honourable Kim Beazley, explained the significance of this denial in his valedictory speech to Parliament in 2007:

> The radar of our Hornet could not identify most of the aircraft in this region as hostile – in other words, our front line fighter could not shoot down people who might be the enemies in this region .... (Beazley, 2007)

Denying access to the algorithms that would permit local reprogramming and upgrade of the F/A-18 RWR and upgrade of the F111 EW capability diminished Australia's tactical advantage in regional air combat capability. This prompted Australian governments, first, to press for release of the algorithms at senior US political levels and, second, to initiate an indigenous RWR development programme.

AUSTRALIA'S RESPONSE: THE ALR-2002 RADAR WARNING RECEIVER

Australia responded to this US denial of the RWR technology by escalating its efforts to develop electronic countermeasures for the F111, F/A-18A and other combat aircraft operated by the Australian Defence Force. This response focused on locally developing the ALR-2002 RWR. Looking back, Beazley described the climate of the times in the following memorable terms:

> I went to the United States and, for five years, it was up hill, down dale and one knock-down drag-out after another with Cap Weinberger, Dick Cheney and Paul Wolfowitz. I tried to get the codes of that blasted radar out of them. In the end, we spied on them and we extracted the codes ourselves – and we got another radar that can actually identify them, otherwise I would not be talking about it now. We got a radar that was capable of doing the shoot-down and the rest of what we wanted. (Beazley, 2007)

Given that the United States would not provide access to the technology, Australia sought to develop its own. Although Beazley does not say so explicitly, it seems apparent that, in the late 1980s–early 1990s, the Australian defence policy community turned to the Defence Science and Technology Organisation (DSTO) to ascertain whether it would be feasible to develop locally a tactically satisfactory RWR for selected ADF aircraft. By 1992, reportedly after some 15 months work, DSTO had developed a RWR Concept Technology Demonstrator, designated ALR-2002. It then licensed this to AWA Defence Industries (AWADI) for full-scale engineering development (FSED) as a precursor to undergoing the RAAF's acceptance test and evaluation process. FSED proceeded on the basis that ALR-2002 would be adapted in various versions for the F/RF111 strike aircraft, the ADF's fixed wing C130 transport aircraft, ADF Blackhawk and Chinook helicopters – and for the F/A-18 fighter aircraft.

The ALR-2002 RWR was developed as a modular system, capable of being fitted to several types of fixed and rotary wing aircraft in the Australian Defence Force inventory. It detects and determines the direction of emission of incident radar, analyses and classifies the signals, and provides an aural and visual warning to its host platform crew as to which signals pose a threat. AWADI was responsible for developing the ALR-2002 software, including the key signal processing algorithms.

In 1998, the Defence Department consolidated into a single project the previously disparate upgrades of EWSP in the various strike, transport and rotary wing aircraft operated by the Australian Defence Force. Based on the ALR-2002, the consolidated project was designated AIR 5416 – 'Echidna'. The programme to upgrade the F/A-18 Hornet was more complex and proceeded separately, but initially aimed to include the ALR-2002 RWR.

Stewardship of the project changed throughout its life as AWADI was bought by BAE Systems in 1996. Along with Tenix Defence, BAE Systems now became involved in an initial design activity for Project Echidna.

This activity involved BAE Systems and Tenix analysing systems requirements, architectural and detailed designs down to the subsystem level with the aim of adapting the modular ALR-2002 to the requirements of fixed and rotary wing aircraft. The initial design activity was completed in December 2002. In December 2004 and February 2005, Defence awarded contracts worth a total of AUD 160.5 million to BAE Systems and Tenix Defence to develop, integrate and install ALR-2002-based EWSP capability in fleets of C-130 Hercules transport, Black Hawk and Chinook aircraft.

Subject to satisfactory contract negotiations, this EWSP capability was to extend to an RWR designed and manufactured by Australia for the Hornet aircraft, again based on the ALR-2002 (Hill, 2005). But it was not to be. In November 2006, a new Minister for Defence, Dr. Brendan Nelson, announced that the government had decided not to upgrade the F/A-18A with the Australian-sourced BAE Systems ALR-2002. It decided instead to use the US-sourced Raytheon ALR-67 (V3) which was, by this, stage standard equipment on US Navy's F/A-18C/D aircraft deployed on 2003 operations in Iraq. The ALR-67 (V3) system was also fitted to US Navy's F/A-18E/F (Super Hornet) aircraft. The Australian government announced in March 2007 it would be purchasing 24 of these Super Hornet aircraft to provide an interim strike capability pending procurement of the Joint Strike Fighter being developed by Lockheed Martin (Nelson, 2007). Australia now had access, via the US supplier with US government approval, to an EWSP system for its F/A-18s for which it spent well over a decade working to create an independent substitute.

We have been able to explain why Australia set out on the road to import substitution. According to its then Defence Minister, 'the radar of our Hornet could not identify most of the aircraft in this region as hostile ... (so) our front line fighter could not shoot down people who might be the enemies in this region' (Beazley, 2007). The United States denying access to the entire EWSP technology package, including algorithms that would permit local reprogramming and upgrade of the F/A-18 RWR, thus undermined Australia's tactical advantage in regional air combat capability. But the circumstances around Australia abandoning the project require further discussion.

Dr Nelson's 2006 announcement contained the following passage:

> BAE Systems Australia has been developing a RWR – the ALR 2002B. This is an Australian developed technology that shows great promise. The Government is not and will not be risk averse in encouraging innovation and in obtaining the best capability. However, we have concluded that this technology cannot be delivered within the necessary timeframe. Ensuring the success of the extensive Hornet upgrade and Australia's regional superiority is the most important priority and requires us to progress

> with another, proven option. Accordingly, the Government has now decided to fit the Raytheon ALR 67-(V3) RWR to the entire F/A-18 fleet, so there is low integration risk. The ALR-67 (V3) will be progressively fitted to the F/A-18 from 2008 with Full Operational Capability achieved in 2011.

This suggests two things. First, Australian work on its indigenous RWR for the FA-18 was still in progress and incomplete towards the end of 2006, 15 years after efforts to develop a substitute for US systems had begun. Second, the ALR-2002B was being rejected in favour of a Raytheon system viewed as a 'proven option' with 'low integration risk'. This apparently implied that the indigenous capability remained to prove itself serviceable in the F/A-18 and entailed a higher risk of failing either technical or interoperability criteria.

The decision to equip the F/A-18 with the imported ALR-67 (V3) rather than the indigenous ALR-2002 reflected an internal Defence debate about the acceptability to Defence of the cost, schedule and technical risk inherent in integrating the domestic solution to various ADF aircraft. The government's decision to equip the less electronically demanding C130 fixed wing transport aircraft and Army helicopters with the ALR-2002 suggests that the associated cost, schedule and technical risk were acceptable to the Defence stakeholders involved. Conversely, the additional cost, schedule and technical risk involved in equipping the much more electronically complex F/A-18 aircraft with the ALR-2002 became less acceptable to the RAAF, especially as it became clear that Australia could obtain the proven ALR-67 (V3) on acceptable terms. In addition, by fitting it to the RAAF's F/A-18A aircraft, Australia could take advantage of US experience and minimise the risk involved.

According to the 2009–2010 Defence Portfolio Budget Statements, BAE Systems had fitted an ALR-2002 RWR and other elements of an EWSP system to a Blackhawk for testing. Subsequently, however, a new Minister for Defence, Senator John Faulkner (2009), announced what is probably the final chapter of the ALR-2002 saga. He noted that, although the trials of ALR-2002 on the Blackhawk were continuing, the system had not been fitted to any operational aircraft. He added that the Blackhawks were to be phased out after 2012, further undermining the case for persevering with the ALR-2002 project.

CONCLUSION

The ALR-2002 saga shows how the decision of a military technology leader to deny a technology follower access to an innovation may prompt the follower to emulate the innovation independently. The leader here is the United States, the follower Australia and the innovation is EWSP for combat aircraft.

We have argued that countries in Australia's position can respond to technology denial in a number of ways. Australia pursued its domestic substitute with great promptness and determination, suggesting it attached a high level of importance to having a system to protect its assets in areas in which it expected its combat aircraft to operate. The record suggests that DSTO was able to master the relevant RWR technology within 15 months. In contrast, and despite over 15 years of effort, the Australian defence innovation system was unable to satisfactorily integrate that technology into all the ADF platforms where it was required, in particular the F/A-18. There is little hint of this sort of painful and lengthy process in analysis where innovation and new capability development are proxied by a simple RD&D variable.

We do not know whether US decision-makers had expected Australia to labour so persistently, and at considerable cost, to develop a domestic substitute. We can only speculate (on the basis of the Beazley's remarks noted earlier) that perhaps they had not. But 15 years later, by making available the Raytheon ALR-67 (V3) system for Australia's F/A-18s, the United States effectively reduced the incentives for Australia to persist with its efforts to develop EWSP for this aircraft. Ultimately, it was in the interests of the US government to do this, both to ensure that the capabilities of a key ally remained interoperable with related US forces and to fend off the threat of competition from a new source. In fact, Australia had gained – and continues to exploit – potentially valuable additional independent capability in EW innovation.

REFERENCES

Beazley, K. [Member for Brand]. (2007). Hansard, House of Representatives, Canberra, Thursday, 20 September 2007 (pp. 37–44). Available at http://www.aph.gov.au/Hansard/reps/dailys/dr200907.pdf. Accessed on 19 May 2009.

Brauer, J., & Dunne, J. P. (Eds). (2004). *Arms trade and economic development: Theory, policy and cases in arms trade offsets*. London: Routledge.

Department of Defence (Industry Involvement and Contracting Division). (1994). *Review of the F/A-18 industry program*. Department of Defence, Canberra.

Faulkner, J. [The Honourable]. (2009). Governance and defence: Some early impressions. Available at http://www.minister.defence.gov.au/FaulknerSpeechtpl.cfm?CurrentId = 9361

Hill, R. [Senator]. (2005). Adelaide based company awarded major defence contract. February 16, 2005. (Press release). Available at http://www.minister.defence.gov.au/2005/160205.doc. Accessed on 19 May 2009.

Levine, P., Mouzakis, F., & Smith, R. (2000). Arms export controls and emerging domestic producers. In: P. Levine & R. Smith (Eds), *Arms trade, security and conflict* (pp. 55–77). London and New York: Routledge.

Levine, P., & Smith, R. (1997). The arms trade. *Economic Policy*, *25*(October), 336–370.

Levine, P., & Smith, R. (2000). Arms export controls and proliferation. *Journal of Conflict Resolution*, *44*(6), 885–895.

Nelson, B. (2006). Minister for defence press release 149/2006: Ensuring Australia's Air Combat Capability Edge. Monday, 13 November 2006. Available at http://www.minister.defence.gov.au/Nelson. Accessed on 30 March 2009.

Nelson, B. (2007). Announcement of the Australian government's decision to acquire 24 F/A-18F Block II Super Hornet Multi-role aircraft, Fairbairn, Australian Capital Territory, Australia, 6 March 2007. Available at http://www.minister.defence.gov.au/Nelson. Accessed on 28 May 2009.

Puttre, M. (Ed.) (2004). *The international electronic countermeasures handbook*. Norwood, MA: Horizon House Publications.

Smith, R. (2009). *Military economics: The interaction of power and money*. London: Palgrave Macmillan.

Wylie, R. (2006). Unpublished speech to Canberra Chapter of the Committee for Economic Development of Australia, 28 September 2006.

PART II
INTERNAL CONFLICT: ECONOMIC ASPECTS OF OUTBREAK, ENDURANCE, AND RECOVERY FROM LARGE-SCALE INTRA-STATE VIOLENCE

CHAPTER 5

PROBING THE ROLES OF GOVERNANCE AND GREED IN CIVIL STRIFE IN WEST AFRICA

Helen Ware and Dele Ogunmola

ABSTRACT

Purpose – *This chapter aims to explore the causes of civil war in West Africa, including the perspectives of those directly involved, both those involved voluntarily and those involved against their will. To this end, we examine the three contiguous war – afflicted coastal countries of Sierra Leone, Liberia and Ivory Coast and as a counterweight, Ghana which has escaped civil war.*

Methodology – *Brief country case studies are used to explore the motivations of leaders and followers which often diverge. This chapter examines four West African countries:*

- *Sierra Leone and Liberia, which have suffered classic brutal, 'third war' civil wars (Holsti, K. (Ed.). (1996). Wars of the third kind. In:* The state, war and the state of war. *Cambridge: Cambridge University Press).*
- *Ivory Coast, once seen as the West African 'beacon of stability' (Royce, E. (2003).* Testimony. *US House of Representatives Subcommittee on Africa, 2nd February, p. 12) but now suffering a seventh year of civil conflict.*

Economics of War and Peace: Economic, Legal, and Political Perspectives
Contributions to Conflict Management, Peace Economics and Development, Volume 14, 71–87

ISSN: 1572-8323/doi:10.1108/S1572-8323(2010)0000014009

- *Ghana, the counter case, which has so far survived multiple military coups without descending into national conflagration.*

To demonstrate the basic features these countries share in common and to suggest some areas where they diverge, we present core socio-economic data in Table 1.

The respondent data on which much of the analysis is based was collected by Dele Ogunmola from individual interviews, and focus group discussions. In the case of Ivory Coast, there was also an e-interview with a medical missionary who experienced the early stages of the war. Given the tense nature of the situation, for both the individual interviews and the focus groups the selection of participants was purposive. People were selected who were willing to talk about their involvement and could represent a range of different roles and experiences. Thus, for example, the Makeni focus group quoted was recruited at Sumbaya village, which was virtually razed by the rebels. Minor warlords were interviewed but not, regrettably, randomly selected. We also refer to the interviews of ex-rebels conducted in 2009 by John-Idriss Lahai, a former member of the Sierra Leonian Civil Defence Forces and current PhD Student at the University of New England.

Findings – *Interviewing in these countries still requires courage on both sides, and while we accept that respondents (especially those at risk of prosecution) may well prevaricate, the overall impression is one of the striking frankness. Most argued that the war was messy and the participants had mixed motivations. The findings confirm that, while grievances play a significant role in providing the fuel for West African civil wars, the greed of both national and international players serves to prolong them. Though Sierra Leone and Liberia experienced opportunistic wars, the Ivory Coast is torn apart over the definition of citizenship. Ghana has survived due to leadership which facilitated economic growth, curbed corruption and prioritised provision of basic services.*

Limitations – *This is not the place to detail the multitude of coups, wars and treaty negotiations that make up the troubled history of the region (see Adebajo, A. (2002).* Building peace in West Africa: Liberia, Sierra Leone and Guinea-Bissau. *Boulder, CO: Lynne Rienner. Parallel timelines for each country would demonstrate many interactions across the region, such as the spread of subaltern coups, but at the cost of presenting a long and confusing history. It is enough to stress that these colonially defined countries are linked across borders that are porous to ideas, rebels, refugees and diamonds alike.*

INTRODUCTION

Civil war in West Africa is in many ways more a local or cross-regional, rather than a national phenomenon. Often it has as many international as national elements. It is relatively easy to understand secessionist civil wars, where ethnic groups fight to carve out their own new states. It is more difficult to understand West Africa's rebels without a cause, who want to take over the national government without a defined ideological platform, as in a nation-wide coup. The rebels claim that their aim is to introduce cleaner, fairer government and because their own leaders are so often demonstrably corrupt, such claims appear implausible. But our interviews with the followers suggest that they are making a rational bet: either everyone will get to benefit from a fairer sharing of the spoils or at least they themselves will get to benefit because their side will have gained power and will be directing the spoils their way. Many join the rebels simply to protect their own home villages. Rebels have a very local perspective. They aim to take over national governments in the capital because this is still the way to control the distribution of the spoils. Good governance as an ideology may mean national equity or just a new set of winners (Bodea & Elbadawi, 2007).

> Creating and arming organizations is costly and wars are destructive and risky. Thus a fundamental question is why wars ever occur at all. If the competing groups are rational, both should prefer a bargained solution to a destructive conflict. (Blattman & Miguel, 2009, p. 10)

The realities of West Africa are in stark contrast to this rational view of war and its costs. In Liberia for example, the rebel leader Charles Taylor, educated in economics in the United States in the 1970s, was apparently motivated, at least partly by greed, to lead a rebellion (Kich, 2008, 2009). For Taylor, creating and arming rebels was not costly, it was quite cheap and in any case financed by the Libyans and the diamond dealers. The destructive nature of war was no concern of his. Rebel leaders usually put their lives on the line – but if only motivated by greed, why become a rebel instead of a robber or corrupt official (Brett & Specht, 2004)? Our interviews with youths from the slums of Sierra Leone and Liberia, many of whom faced the choice between thievery and rebellion, show one overwhelming emotion: frustration with the powers that be that failed to make a better world in which youth has a chance of a job with prospects for the future.

An unemployed urban youth tosses a coin to decide whether to join the army or the rebels – or, in the case of Sierra Leone's 'sobels' (soldiers by day and rebels by night), both. Is he/she driven solely by greed or is lack of access to any other means of feeding oneself a genuine grievance (Arnson & Zartman, 2005)? Once the war has broken out, even the marginal option of returning to the village to grow subsistence food crops where land is available, is no longer viable because the fighters strip the harvest like locusts.

In weak states, groups have to form, cohere and persuade their members to risk their lives with the incentives of infrequently paid wages, loot, promises of future reward and protection from harm. War in this region is so dirty because governments and rebels alike can mainly offer looting plus negative sanctions. Fighting by untrained troops is often associated with a short and confused belligerent 'haze' in which overwhelming tension and fear can only be resolved by immediate violence (Richards, 1996). Motivation to join a rebellion can also arise from the rebel leader's charisma, group ideology or the pursuit of justice or vengeance (Lahai interviews).

Young men are a vital element in civil wars (Collier, Hoeffler, & Rohner, 2009). One reason is simply that they are unemployed and looking for something to do and a source of income. The other, much less discussed, factor is the highly subordinate role of young men within traditional society. Writing about the potential role of traditional authorities in re-establishing peace can be more romantic than realistic (Ferme, 2001; Assefa, 2004). This may work where there is still considerable respect for the traditional authorities but Western-influenced education has often destroyed this respect for tradition. Also many of these authorities are, by modern standards, very corrupt and as much part of the problem as part of its solution. Corruption has long been associated with land allocation and alluvial diamond mining at the local level (Gberie, 2005). Also in pre-colonial days making war was often a significant part of youths' raison d'etre. Appealing to tradition, therefore, often means accepting the equation of manliness with military valour (Richards, 1996).

In war-time Sierra Leone relative stability was achieved when armed youth remained close to home and tied to local customs, or became integrated to new communities on the basis of the customary institutions of their chief. The community protection units, the Kamajors, engaged in looting and unrestrained violence when away from their base areas but their elders kept them under control when nearer to home (Reno, 2003). Local chiefs in downstream mining regions used initiation rights to engage Civil Defence Force (CDF) soldiers with local hunting customs, ensuring reciprocal protection. This was unlike the chaos of the Kono region where new chiefs had been imposed by the Sankoh government (Reno, 2003). But sometimes the CDF also went bad (Keen, 2005, p. 268). The RUF deliberately killed chiefs to generate political and institutional instability and/or because chiefs had been corrupt. Large-scale diamond smuggling was only possible as long as the war went on, which meant that neither government leaders nor the rebels had much incentive to bring the war to a close (Keen, 2005, p. 50; Snyder & Bhavnani, 2005).

At first sight, the claim that civil wars are caused by the collapse of the national government might appear a statement of the obvious. Yet, there clearly are examples such as Sri Lanka, where a strong centralised national state was forced to fight a secessionist group that wished to carve out its own nation. But, as noted, in West Africa the object is usually not secession but to topple the national government, with the result being an exceptionally bloody and widespread coup (Ali, 2000). Existing governments cling, however ineffectively, to power because the participants are engaged in an all-or-nothing struggle and because the sources of wealth within the country are very limited (Arnson & Zartman, 2005). This pattern also applies to states with very limited resources, lootable or otherwise, such as Mali.

LIBERIA: FIRST CIVIL WAR 1989–1996 AND SECOND CIVIL WAR 1999–2003

By the late 1980s Liberia had effectively ceased to exist as a state. The government was criminalised, exclusionary, exploitative, negligent and predatory. It collected taxes but failed to provide even the most basic social services. In the 1980s, 65 per cent of the population still had no access to modern healthcare. In 1989, the ruling class, descendants of returned American slaves and comprising 6 per cent of the population, owned and controlled 70 per cent of the wealth of this bitterly poor country (Kich, 2008, p. 27). In 1988, in the absence of any social safety net, the recorded urban unemployment rate was 36 per cent (UNDP, 1990).

Young people in Liberia who acquire an AK 47 can be seen as the equivalent of youths getting credit cards in the West (Utas, 2008). Young Liberians enlisting in rebel armies follow earlier labour and educational migration inside as well as outside the country.

> Once rural young men could spend a few years working on the plantations and return home able to afford a farm, a wife and a few modern items. Urban youths with education could formerly get jobs.

But by the 1990s, they could 'only increase their stakes in the social chess board by taking up arms' (Utas, 2008, pp. 112, 120).

Charles Taylor was elected President of Liberia in 1997, in a free and fair election, because he threatened that if he was not elected he would re-start the civil war, and people apparently believed him. The Friends of Liberia (1987) group which included former U.S. President Carter and several American Congressmen, had set out eight conditions for free and fair elections and found that in general they had been met. Ironically, a vote for Taylor became a vote for peace (Kich, 2008). The people, despite massive grievances and continuing scope for greed, were unwilling to fight any more. For warlords, war is usually a winning game (although, as Taylor may have finally discovered, the trick is in knowing when to leave with one's winnings) (Wantchekon, 2004; Sexsmith, 2009).

The Collier–Hoeffler (2004) analysis of civil war clearly reveals that one of the best predictors of a civil war is a previous civil war. As elsewhere, the causes of the second civil war in Liberia were the same as for the first:

> As soon as the [first] war was over, and a new government was installed, things quickly reverted to the way they were before the war. Abuse of power, corruption, manipulation of ethnic division, abject poverty, alienation, oppression of a large sector of the population, and hopelessness of the youth were still rampant (Assefa, 2004, pp. 1–2).

Security sector reform had not worked and national reconciliation had not been achieved. Warlord militias remained. Bureaucracies remained as corrupt and incompetent as they were before the war. This was a country which had never known good governance (Ellis, 2007, p. xxvii). There were still no effective checks on the power of the executive available to curb corruption.

Charles Taylor explained his regime's dismal performance by ethnic scape-goating his opponents. From 1997 to 1999 his government committed 367 political murders (US State Department 1999, p. 97). Taylor looted the Treasury, diverted the budget to his personal security and failed to pay government salaries.

When both civil wars had ended, 1 in 17 Liberians had died, and 1 in 3 had been displaced. Today, 40 per cent of children under five years old suffer from malnutrition-induced stunting. War and HIV/AIDS have orphaned 230,000 children. Half a million children, mostly girls, do not attend school and two-thirds of students are taught by untrained teachers. Armed groups along the borders with Guinea and Ivory Coast still recruit children as soldiers (UNICEF, 2009). Any government clearly continues to face immense challenges.

SIERRA LEONE: CIVIL WAR 1991–2002

> The tragedy of Sierra Leone is that her people are among the poorest in the world while the country is among the richest. The reasons for this are entirely man-made ... God blessed this land with an abundance of resources. Just a relatively few people are responsible for the misery and hardship suffered by so many (Peter Penfold, former British High Commissioner to Sierra Leone quoted by Davies, 2000, p. 349).

The war in Sierra Leone was initially organised by radical university students and launched from neighbouring Liberia (Davies, 2000, p. 351). Libyan finance and training can be blamed for starting the rebellion (Davies, 2000). At its core were economic decline and poverty, high youth unemployment, violations of the rule of law, government dysfunction, rural isolation and regional and ethnic grievances. Diamonds have prolonged the war, but so too has external support of the government which has bolstered or re-instated a collapsing state and also induced a tendency not to negotiate or to rebuild state security (Smilie, Gberie, & Hazleton, 2000). The current model of state sovereignty privileges the government in power as the recipient of support from the international community but this is not necessarily a good recipe for peace.

Before the war, one child in four died before reaching age five, per capita income was USD300 whereas GDP growth through the 1980s averaged 0.5 per cent per annum (Table 1). The elitist educational system provided no technical or vocational education and consequently numerous school drop outs on the streets in the cities joined those who arrived through rural–urban migration. So what did anyone who contemplated joining the rebels have to lose other than their life? Many believed it possible to buy 'medicine' to make one invincible. Conditions were exacerbated over Siaka Stevens' 17 years of despotic rule during which he co-opted ghetto youths, fed with drugs and false promises of employment, to brutalise opponents. Civil society, the judiciary and traditional rulers were co-opted or suppressed (Keen, 2005). In 1960s, 70 per cent of foreign exchange earnings came from diamonds. When Stevens allowed free-for-all mining, official diamond exports fell from two million carats in 1970 to less than 200,000 in 1984.

Young men, talking about how they came to join the rebels presented a mixed picture of sharing common grievances and weighing up the opportunities offered. Some had been offered as much as USD500 per month (more than a year's income) 'plus loot' to fight in Liberia. Some joined to protect their families or under peer pressure from their friends (Lahai interviews). The only disincentive mentioned was the high risk of death.

Table 1. Basic Socio-Economic Data.

Indicator	Ghana	Ivory Coast	Liberia	Sierra Leone
Population in millions 1988[a] 2007[b]	14.0 22.9	12.0 20.0	2.4 3.3	4.0 6.3
HDI rank from bottom 1986[a] 2009[b]	30th 30th	32nd 16th	26th 13th	4th 3rd
Percentage of population under 15[b]	40	41	44	44
Under 5 mortality per 1,000[a]	146	142	147	266
Gross enrolment ratio[b]	57	38	58	45
Percentage of adults literate 1985[a] 2007[b]	54 65	42 49	35 56	30 38
GNP per capita 1987 USD[a]	390	1,120	450	300
GNI per capita USD ppp method[c]	1,430	1,690	362	679
Land area (km^2)[b]	230,000	318,000	98,000	71,000
Export Concentration Index 1995/2006[d]	0.44/0.44	0.27/0.32	NA	0.55/0.54
1986: Armed forces as percentage of teachers[a]	14	13	55	20
1986: Military expenditure as percentage of GDP[a]	0.9	1.2	2.2	1.2
Gem diamond exports estimate 1,000 carats 1995/1998[e]	126/640	53/204	60/60	113/50

[a]UNDP Human Development Report 1990.
[b]UNDP Human Development Report 2009.
[c]World Development Indicators Database, World Bank 2009.
[d]UNCTAD 2008 Economic Development in Africa: Export Performance 2000–2006.
[e]1998 Annual Report US Geological Survey 'Gemstones'.

Most analyses of reasons for fighting reference young men, yet women fighters are quite common. The proportion of female fighters among the Sierra Leone factions comprised between 10 per cent and 30 per cent (Sierra Leone TRC, 2004, Ellis, 2007). Half of these female fighters had received military training. The skewed Liberian disarmament process registered 2–4 per cent of women (Utas, 2005). Forced female participation in war should be understood in the traditional context of forced marriages. Moving from sexual slavery to fighting, the girls were given formal lectures on the necessity of overthrowing the corrupt and inefficient government. They were promised cash and status. They were told: 'As long as you are holding a gun, you have power over those who don't'. Some interviewed said it gave them more status and power and it was exciting. One said: 'I was eager to become a soldier so that I would be able to resist threats and harassment from other soldiers' (Denov & Maclure, 2006, p. 78). Wives, especially those in polygamous marriages, sometimes joined to get loot to provide for their families (Sierra Leone TRC, 2004; Lahai interviews).

Any examination of the motivations of followers has to take into account the overall confusion and the extent of forced recruitment. One of our interviewees was a woman who had joined the RUF because her husband had been arrested by the army which falsely accused him of being a rebel. She was in the bush, three months pregnant, after the rebels killed her parents, when the rebels forced her to join them to replace her absent husband. An elderly woman was forced to join up with her. When asked what caused the civil war, in which she had fought, the woman simply replied that she did not know. She said that the rebels were fighting to end the war. 'Some people said that the rebels were fighting because they wanted our leader Foday Sankoh to be released from jail in Nigeria, others denied it saying they are fighting for the common cause, for patriotism', she said (Makeni Interview 1). Asked specifically about whether the war was caused by a struggle over diamonds she said:

> No I don't see it ... that way. Diamonds were not the reason that triggered the war. The war has ended and they still mining diamonds. They were mining diamonds during the war .... It is because I am suffering I will harm other people? The reason was not poverty. It was their wish. The leaders of the rebellion were urban dwellers. They had not lived in the bush. Rebellion is not something you do spontaneously. They could not just form a group and decide to live in the bush ... They had planned something that took us one hundred years backward ... It is clear that there were Liberians among the rebels who invaded Sierra Leone. (Makeni Interview 1)

But her strongest feelings were reserved for the horrible likelihood that there might be another war. 'When we were in Kono, there was a problem between ethnic groups. Some people would say the discord between the Temne and the Mende would lead to another war. We did advise them not to think of it or even try it. Those who say that did not and do not know the bitterness of war. Some of us have tasted it. I know the bitterness of war' (Makeni Interview 1).

Another interviewee had been forced to join the RUF, because the group had killed 'my dad, my mom, my uncle ... and [the rebels] said that they were fighting for the poor so I had to be on their side' (Makeni Interview 2). In her view the war had come about because a lot of people were suffering with no employment, no hope and no opportunity.

> A lot of people say that Sierra Leone is rich. But why are we poor? It is only the people in the government who can explain that to you. A lot of people were not happy with what they were doing with our money. I think poverty, selfishness of our leaders

> led to the war. And when the RUF came to recruit a lot of people followed them. Because they promised to change things for the better if they won the war. (Makeni Interview 2)

One interesting question relating to the causes of war in Sierra Leone is whether the state was unusually guilty of spending too little on the military. The level of military expenditure rose from a mere 1 per cent of GDP in 1990 to 6 per cent since the mid-1990s (Davies, 2000, p. 350). Thus, when the civil war broke out, the army numbered no more than 2,000 persons. This meant that money was not spent on using the army to soak up some of the young unemployed and deter rebels before war broke out in 1991.

In Sierra Leone, unlike Liberia or Ivory Coast, the rebels were not marginalised members of the power elite. Rather, 'a marginalised social group, in this case youths, appropriate[ed] the language of revolution from radical college students to contest political power' (Abdullah, 2004, p. 2). Davies, a local academic, points to the 'ideological barrenness and the low social standing of the rebels (including the leadership)' but he recognises their grievances. Jusu (2005) and Abdullah (2004) argue that war in Sierra Leone was originally the result of a political project involving legitimate struggles to right the wrongs resulting from the extreme inequity of Sierra Leonean life. The RUF did have a manifesto: Footpaths to Democracy, published in London in 1995. The women interviewees said this manifesto was used to indoctrinate rebel recruits in the field. Conflict diamonds 'produced a war-prolonging congruence of interests among the war protagonists – the rebels and allied neighbouring countries, the army and other pro-government forces, and sometimes the government itself' (Davies, 2000, p. 359).

In 1997, Liberia exported 5.8 million carats of diamonds to Belgium while Ivory Coast exported 885,000 and Guinea exported 533,000. This stands in contrast to official production records which put the Liberian production at around 150,000 carats, Guinea's 205,000 and Ivory Coast virtually nil (Smilie et al., 2000). Many in the Sierra Leone government and army favoured prolonging the war because of the gains they were making from diamonds and the looting of consumer goods and agricultural produce. Members of the army sold arms to the rebels, defected en masse and attacked defenceless civilians rather than the rebels. An ultimate example of the economic rationality of the participants saw the creation of 'sobels', who were government-paid soldiers by day but looting rebels by night. Similarly combatants organised cease fires in which soldiers and rebels peacefully mined alluvial diamonds side-by-side in Kono and Tongo Fields. By the end of the war, following the profits, 95 per cent of the Sierra Leone military had joined the rebels.

IVORY COAST: CIVIL WAR 2002–PRESENT

In the Ivory Coast, rebellion began in mid-September in the Northern quarter of the country with approximately 750 military personnel who were to be mustered out but did not agree to do so peacefully. They occupied the second largest city, Bouake, with a population of perhaps 600,000 people plus three lesser towns (Gberie, 2004; Galy, 2007; Timeline Ivory Coast, 2009). An American medical missionary on the ground described to us how just 19 men with guns could take over an upcountry town of 8,500 in the Ivory Coast as there were no defenders and the rebels had superior weapons (e-interview 2). The situation was totally fluid as locals decided to stay or to go via bush paths into neighbouring Liberia or Guinea. Daily life continued, with medicines supplied by market women from Guinea, who still crossed unmolested into this war zone to ply their trade.

Partly because the country is francophone, we hear little about the civil war in Ivory Coast, which was sparked off by the bloody mutiny noted earlier. For most of the long (1960–1993) Presidency of Houphouet-Boigny, Ivory Coast was seen as a prosperous and growing paragon of economic and political stability. Indeed N'Diaye (2001) set out to write about why the country had avoided coups, only to be over-taken by events. Equally, the World Bank commissioned, but left unpublished, a study of how the Ivory Coast had avoided civil war. Conflict in the Ivory Coast was based on the shortage of new land for cocoa growing (Woods, 2003). Given complex ethnically linked land-exploitation patterns described by Leach and Fairhead (2000) 'changes in the forest rent lay the basis for increasing conflicts between different ethnic communities only when available tropical forest land has nearly disappeared. At this point, the cost of reclaiming land with violence is less than trying to mobilise the increased labour and capital costs to maintain the forest rent' (Woods, 2003, p. 643).

Until the early 1990s, Ivory Coast was remarkable because foreigners had similar rights to citizens: they could vote, buy land and participate in government. A quarter to a third of the population was immigrants, mostly

Mossi Muslims from Burkina-Fasso to the North. Then, as foreigners increasingly lost their rights, Northern Muslims, who were undoubtedly locally born also felt excluded from the state and came under physical attack. In a country where so many residents were born abroad but most people have no identity papers, many immigrants and nationals alike, felt very insecure. The combination of falling cocoa prices and the lack of further virgin forest to exploit resulted in growing conflict and then war (Leonard & Oswald, 1995).

The war split the country between the rebel-held North and the government held-South. For some time UN peacekeepers patrolled a buffer zone between North and South maintaining a tenuous situation described as 'No Peace, No War'. The Medical missionary quoted above kept track of the rebels he encountered, most were young men aged 18–23 with squad leaders up to age 30. Many were Liberians who explained: 'I had no job in Liberia and was told we would be paid'. Some who had participated in the Liberian Civil war some 5–10 years earlier admitted that they simply enjoyed fighting and had another war in which to do it (e-interview 2). Thus it is now possible to have an international career as a rebel in West Africa. These interviews suggest that rebel bands of foreigners driven by greed, fight along side local residents who are fighting to define national identity and the scope of democratic rights.

The Ivory Coast is due to hold its national elections in early 2010 but conflict continues. The crucial disagreement is over the definition of a citizen for electoral purposes. Repeatedly stalled negotiations have at least clarified what the points at contention are

- resignation of the President
- new elections
- re-instatement of the rebels into the national army
- re-definition of citizenship and eligibility for election to include those with only one Ivorian parent.

None of these objectives is directly economic, although political changes might indirectly allow access to economic goals. Land, which is not a lootable resource, is a much more important source of contention than diamonds. However, just as Sierra Leonean diamonds had been exported via Ivory Coast, the latter exported diamonds via Ghana and Mali. In 2006, the United Nations reported that USD23 million of diamonds from the Ivory Coast had been exported through Ghana and Mali (Global Witness, 2006).

GHANA: COUPS BUT NO CIVIL WAR

Ghana gained its independence in 1957 and Kwame Nkrumah was Prime Minister and then President until he was deposed by the country's first coup in 1966. Since then, Ghana has experienced three more successful coups and six failed attempts to seize power by force. It has also experienced five relatively free and fair national elections. Ghana has had one small, localised war: the Guinea Fowl War of 1994, but this was quashed before spreading beyond the North (Adjepawn, 2008). Looking at the factors for civil war feasibility beyond greed and grievance (Collier et al., 2009) there are no obvious reasons why Ghana should have escaped the fate of its neighbours (Table 1). Ghana contributes 19 per cent of the world's cocoa production whereas the Ivory Coast provides 35 per cent (International Cocoa Organization, 2009), so both countries are heavily reliant on cocoa prices.

Two of Ghana's successful coups were led by Flight-Lieutenant Jerry Rawlings, who was subsequently elected President in 1992. Rawlings, in power for 19 years in total, was very different from the leaders who took Sierra Leone and Liberia to war. Although capable of publicly executing three of his surviving predecessors, he had a genuine interest in the welfare of his fellow citizens and remained relatively untainted by corruption (Nugent, 1995). As does the current President of Liberia, Ellen Johnson Sirleaf, Rawlings has mixed, part-European parentage, which gives him the advantage of not being identified as part of a single ethnic group or beholden to it. Most importantly, Rawlings transmuted from being a socialist, whose economic policies failed, to a successful follower of the IMF, delivering some USD5 billion in support and economic growth. Even when he was effectively a dictator, he promoted some democracy at the grass roots level through the People's Defence Committees.

Amos Sawyer, interim President of Liberia (1990–1994), wrote a blueprint *Beyond Plunder: Toward Democratic Government in Liberia*. He argued for shared sovereignty:

> What African countries need is a fundamental shift away from a system of unitary government so that there can be several centres of authority underpinned by a system of shared sovereignty in which ordinary people acting as empowered citizens can meaningfully participate in an array of governance institutions at local, provincial, national, and even regional scales where necessary. (Sawyer, 2005, p. 107)

Rawlings shared this vision (Rawlings, 2007). We cannot know how effective leaders with a similar code might have been in Sierra Leone or

Liberia. Rawlings seized power from within the military (not as the leader of a rebel force entering from abroad) and once in power, he gained mass support with the slogan 'Let there be light [electricity] for rural people, for they are Ghanaians too' (Adedeji, 2001). Strong economic management helped to calm troubled waters and to assuage conflicts that might have otherwise overtaken the country.

CONCLUSION

We have presented four case studies of neighbouring states. Sierra Leone and Liberia are countries where, long before the wars, the social contract was already broken. The state in those countries failed to provide basic justice, services and equity to the point where this failure in itself became the grounds for war. In contrast, in Ivory Coast, the governing faction of a functioning state made a deliberate decision to attempt to hold onto political power by breaking the social contract through denying citizenship to the third of the population who had a parent born outside the country. As Ghana has demonstrated, West African countries can survive multiple violent political changes, provided the government continues to provide basic services to everyone.

For those countries endeavouring to recover from civil war, the goal must be to deliver basic services across the country as rapidly as possible. Restoring the unfair discrimination which obtained before the war is not a formula for peace (Keen, 2000). Youths who have learnt to live by demanding goods at gun-point are unlikely to accept a life of hazardous penury. Fundamentally, the cases are not strongly consistent with mono-causal arguments, nor do they seem to follow very similar patterns that lead to compelling generalizations. The interview evidence and general complexity of events in each country suggest a daunting mix of causes and circumstances that have contributed to the terrible conflicts these societies have endured. It does seem that the case which avoids devastating conflict, Ghana, might have just been fortunate to have a relatively enlightened and skilled leader, or at least one who prioritised economic development.

This study has found that leadership, governance, growth and equity surely do matter in maintaining peace in West Africa. In addition, there is an urgent need to develop mechanisms to constrain absolute government and corruption and thus reduce the rewards for those who seize power. Nonetheless, the ground-level evidence from participant interviews suggests daunting complexity in the West African wars. The four cases suggest that strong, relatively enlightened leadership may be a crucial factor which provides a plausible escape from cycles of violence and despair in the region.

REFERENCES

Abdullah, I. (2004). *Between democracy and terror: The Sierra Leone civil war*. Dakar: Codesria.

Adedeji, J. (2001). The legacy of J.J. Rawlings in Ghanaian politics, 1979–2000. *African Studies Quarterly*. Available at http://www.africa.ufl.edu/asq/v5/v5i2a1.htm

Adjepawn, Q. (2008). Conflict and Poverty in Ghana, Ph.D. thesis, University of New England, Armidale NSW.

Ali, A. A. G. (2000). The economics of conflict in Africa: An overview. *Journal of African Economics*, *9*(2), 235–243.

Arnson, C., & Zartman, W. (Eds). (2005). *Rethinking the economics of war: The intersection of need, creed, and greed*. Baltimore, MA: Johns Hopkins University Press.

Assefa, H. (2004). Peacebuilding in a globalizing Africa: The role of religious institutions and leaders. *Peace Colloquy* (6), 1–12.

Blattman, C., & Miguel, E. (2009). *Civil war: A review of 50 years of research*. Working Paper No. 166. Center for Global Development, Washington.

Bodea, C., & Elbadawi, I. A. (2007). *Riots, coups and civil war: Revisiting the greed and grievance debate*. World Bank Policy Research Working Paper 4397. Washington.

Brett, R., & Specht, I. (2004). *Young soldiers: Why they choose to fight*. Boulder, CO: Lynne Rienner.

Collier, P., & Hoeffler, A. (2004). Greed and grievance in civil war. *Oxford Economic Papers*, *56*(4), 563–595.

Collier, P., Hoeffler, A., & Rohner, D. (2009). Beyond greed and grievance: Feasibility and civil war. *Oxford Economic Papers*, *61*(1), 1–27.

Davies, V. A. B. (2000). Sierra Leone: Ironic tragedy. *Journal of African Economies*, *9*(3), 349–369.

Denov, M., & Maclure, R. (2006). Engaging the voices of girls in the aftermath of Sierra Leone's conflict: Experiences and perspectives in a culture of violence. *Anthropologica*, *48*(1), 73–85.

Ellis, S. (2007). *The mask of anarchy: The destruction of Liberia and the religious dimensions of an African civil war*. New York: New York University Press.

Ferme, M. (2001). *The underneath of things: Violence, history and the everyday in Sierra Leone*. Berkeley, CA: University of California Press.

Galy, M. (2007). Politologie d'une Rebellion.Une 'Gouvernace par la violence' au Nord de La Cote d'Ivoire? *Cultures et Conflits*, *65*, 137–155.

Gberie, L. (2004). *The crisis in Ivory Coast*. June 24, Znet.

Gberie, L. (2005). *A dirty war in West Africa: The RUF and the destruction of Sierra Leone*. London: Hurst & Co.

Global Witness. (2006). *The truth about diamonds: Conflict and development*. London: Global Witness.

International Cocoa Organization. (2009). Available at http://www.icco.org/statistics/production.aspx. Retrieved on 10 February 2010. The full reference is http://www.icco.org/statistics/production.aspx

Jusu, A. (2005). *Problems in Sub-Saharan African economic development: An analysis of the economic causes of civil wars*. Ph.D. thesis, New School University, New York.

Keen, D. (2000). War and peace: What's the difference? *International Peacekeeping*, *7*(4), 1–22.

Keen, D. (2005). *Conflict and collusion in Sierra Leone*. Oxford: James Currey.

Kich, G. K. (2008). *Liberia's first civil war: The crisis of underdevelopment*. New York: Peter Lang.

Kich, G. K. (2009). The roots of the second Liberian civil war. *International Journal on World Peace*, *26*(1), 7–30.

Leach, M., & Fairhead, J. (2000). Neo-Malthusian deforestation analyses in West Africa's dynamic forest landscapes. *Population and Development Review*, *26*(1), 17–43.

Leonard, E., & Oswald, M. (1995). Cocoa smallholders facing a double structural adjustment in Cote d'Ivoire: Responses to a predicted crisis. In: F. Ruf & P. S. Siswoputranto (Eds), *Cocoa cycles: The economics of cocoa supply*. London: Woodhead.

N'Diaye, B. (2001). *The challenge of institutionalizing civilian control: Botswana, Ivory Coast and Kenya in comparative perspective*. Lanham, MD: Lexington Books.

Nugent, P. (1995). *Big men, small boys and politics in Ghana: Power ideology and the burden of history 1982–1994*. London: Pinter.

Rawlings, J. J. (2007). Interview with Jessie Jackson. Available at http://www.jjrawlingsinfo/about.html

Reno, W. (2003). Political networks in a failing state: The roots and future of violent conflict in Sierra Leone. *Internationale Politik und Gesellschaft*, *2*(1), 44–66.

Richards, P. (1996). *Fighting for the Rainforest: War, youth and resources in Sierra Leone*. London: James Currey.

Sawyer, A. (2005). *Beyond plunder: Towards democratic governance in Liberia*. Boulder: Lynne Rienner.

Sexsmith, K. (2009). Violent conflict and social transformation: An institutionalist approach to the role of informal economic networks. *European Journal of Development Research*, *21*(1), 81–94.

Sierra Leone TRC. (2004). Feminisation of poverty. Sierra Leone Truth and Reconciliation Commission Report, Vol 3b, Chapter 3. Available at http://www.sc-sl.org/

Smilie, I., Gberie, L., & Hazleton, R. (2000). *The heart of the matter: Sierra Leone, diamonds and human security*. Ottowa: Partnership Africa.

Snyder, R., & Bhavnani, R. (2005). Diamonds, blood and taxes: A revenue-centred framework for explaining political order. *Journal of Conflict Resolution*, *49*(4), 563–597.

Timeline Ivory Coast. (2009). Available at http://timelines.ws/countries/IVORYCOAST.HTML. Retrieved on 18 November.

UNDP. (1990). *Human development report*. New York: Oxford University Press.

UNICEF. (2009). UNICEF Humanitarian Action Report 2009. UNICEF, New York.

US State Department. (1999). *Liberia human rights reports, 1997–1999*. Washington: US State Department.

Utas, M. (2005). West African warscapes: Victimcy, girlfriending, soldiering: Tactic agency in a young woman's social navigation of the Liberian war zone. *Anthropological Quarterly*, *78*(2), 403–430.

Utas, M. (2008). Abject heroes: Marginalised youth, modernity and violent pathways of the Liberian civil war. In: J. Hart (Ed.), *Years of conflict: Political violence and displacement.* Oxford: Berghahn Books.
Wantchekon, L. (2004). 'Warlord' democracy: A theoretical investigation. *American Political Science Review*, *98*(1), 17–33.
Woods, D. (2003). The tragedy of the cocoa pod: Rent-seeking, land and ethnic conflict in Ivory Coast. *Journal of Modern African Studies*, *41*(4), 641–655.

CHAPTER 6

TERRORISM AND VIOLENT INTERNAL CONFLICT IN POST-SOEHARTO INDONESIA: BEYOND THE JIHADI PRISM OF ANALYSIS

Leanne Piggott

ABSTRACT

Purpose – *Since September 2001, most studies of terrorism have focused on the motives and operations of transnational terrorist groups, especially Islamist jihadi groups. Yet statistics from the past decade indicate that most terrorist attacks occurred within violent internal conflicts. Indonesia is a case in point. Following the fall of the Soeharto regime in 1998, terrorism became a hallmark of separatist and inter-communal violence that cost the lives of thousands of Indonesians. The aim of this chapter is to look beyond the jihadi-focused prism of terrorism studies and to examine the secessionist conflicts in Aceh and Papua to determine why and to what extent terrorism was used by the Free Aceh Movement (GAM) and the Free Papua Movement (OPM) respectively, and the role that economic factors played in the process.*

Economics of War and Peace: Economic, Legal, and Political Perspectives
Contributions to Conflict Management, Peace Economics and Development, Volume 14, 89–105

ISSN: 1572-8323/doi:10.1108/S1572-8323(2010)0000014010

Methodology – *By synthesising the causes of violent internal conflicts and of terrorism, a framework of societal and organisational factors is constructed to explain why terrorism was used by GAM and OPM, and why, in the case of GAM it stopped, while in the case of OPM, it continues.*

Findings – *In general, socio-economic and political factors rather than religious ideology explain why terrorism was used by GAM and continues to be used by OPM in their respective secessionist conflicts. Economic grievances fuelled by resource exploitation and inequitable sharing of resource rents have been contributing factors.*

Originality/value of chapter – *The analysis departs from previous approaches, which have focused primarily on the causes and course of the conflicts themselves and not on when and why such conflicts have included terrorist attacks.*

INTRODUCTION

The vast literature on terrorism that followed al-Qaeda's attacks on New York and Washington on 11 September 2001 provides numerous explanations of what terrorism is, why terrorists choose such a violent *modus operandi*, and what they seek. Most works, which are written by Western scholars, focus on the motives and operations of transnational groups[1] which are responsible for attacks on democratic states, especially Islamist jihadi groups,[2] and in particular al-Qaeda. Others have examined asymmetrical conflicts in which transnational jihadi terrorist groups are pitted against local and/or international military forces, as in Iraq and Afghanistan. Accordingly, the role of religious ideology within transnational groups is highlighted as a 'root cause' of contemporary terrorism. Yet statistics on terrorist attacks over the past decade indicate that most occurred in the context of violent internal conflicts in which domestic actors were prevalent, operating outside the framework of transnational groups. Indeed, the available data indicates that domestic incidents of terrorism are substantially higher in number than international incidents, with correspondingly higher figures for injuries and deaths (Stepanova, 2008; Derin-Güre, 2009). Further, in cases that involve secessionist groups, socio-economic and political factors rather than religious ideology provide a more comprehensive understanding of why terrorism occurs.

Indonesia is a case in point. In the wake of the economic crisis that preceded the fall of the Soeharto regime in 1998 and the political instability that followed, long-standing separatist conflicts in Aceh, East Timor and

Papua intensified, whereas pre-existing inter-communal grievances ignited a wave of violence in Kalimantan, Maluku and Sulawesi, claiming the lives of more than 10,000 Indonesians. Terrorism became a hallmark of the violence that spread across the archipelago, although for most perpetrators it served as an additional tactic within a wider arsenal of violent acts driven first and foremost by local socio-economic and/or political factors. One exception was the transnational Islamist jihadi group, *Jemaah Islamiya* (JI), infamous for its bombings of tourist sites and international hotels in Bali and Jakarta, which views terrorism as a key instrument in its strategy to overthrow the secular Indonesian state and replace it with an Islamic state or Caliphate (Chalk, Rabasa, Rosenau, & Piggott, 2009). Yet despite the predominance of terrorist attacks carried out by domestic groups motivated by locally related factors, religious and ideological factors remain the prism through which terrorism in Indonesia is analysed. Although not ignored, other drivers of terrorism in the post-Soeharto era, including economic factors, have received less scholarly attention.

Accordingly, the purpose of this chapter is two-fold: first, to provide a framework for analysing why terrorism is used by domestic groups as a tactic within violent internal conflicts. This is done by synthesising common factors that are present in the literature on the causes of violent internal conflict and literature on the causes of terrorism. The framework identifies three broad societal factors and three broad organisational factors. The second aim is to apply the model to the separatist conflicts in Aceh and Papua to determine why terrorism was used by the Free Aceh Movement (GAM) and the Free Papua Movement (OPM) respectively. The extent to which economic factors played a role in the process will be considered. The priority given to a causal analysis of terrorism as a tactic in these conflicts is a unique undertaking, as scholarly attention has focused on the causes and aspects of the conflicts themselves and not on when and why such conflicts have included terrorist attacks. Both case studies will show that economic factors, among other material causes, have contributed decisively to these conflicts and the link to terrorist actions, although not to the exclusion of religious and other ideological factors.

THE RELATIONSHIP BETWEEN VIOLENT INTERNAL CONFLICT AND TERRORISM: A SYNTHESISED MODEL

Although there is no universally agreed definition of terrorism in international law or among scholars, a non-exhaustive review of the academic literature provides the following list of key determinants. Terrorism is

- a form of political violence, with political aims and motives;
- a means, not an end;
- the use or threat of violence against civilian and other non-combatant targets as distinct from military targets;
- intended to generate fear in the wider civilian population to further a political (including ideological) purpose;
- conducted by non-state actors, who constitute either a cell or organization and
- aimed ultimately at an audience that is not the immediate victim/s but a government against which the terrorists hold a grievance and/or from which they seek some action.

Combining these components, terrorism may be understood as an act or threat of violence carried out by a group against civilians (or non-combatants) for the purpose of coercing or intimidating a government into acting or acquiescing in a manner that the terrorists believe will produce a desired political outcome (however interpreted). A range of techniques is employed by terrorists, the most common of which are bombings, kidnappings (also a source of finance), assassinations, hijackings of aircraft and the taking over of ships and buildings with hostages.

As for the goals of terrorists, these are as diverse as terrorist organisations themselves. However, when attempting to provide a causal analysis of why a group involved in an internal violent conflict might choose to use terrorism as a means to achieve its political end, terrorism is often noted as a 'weapon of the weak', a tactic used by 'those on the outside without the power or access to military command, but with grievances against the strong in an asymmetric warfare situation' (Intriligator & Coissard, 2008, p. 163). Crenshaw (1981) summarises the argument as follows:

> [terrorism is] an attractive strategy to groups of different ideological persuasions who challenge the state's authority. Groups who want to dramatize a cause, to demoralize the government, to gain popular support, to provoke regime violence, to inspire followers, or to dominate a wider resistance movement, who are weak vis-à-vis the regime, and who are impatient to act, often find terrorism a reasonable choice. (p. 398)

Clearly, not all violent political conflict involves terrorism and not all terrorism occurs within the context of violent internal conflict. What circumstances, then, would motivate a group involved in such a conflict to view terrorism as a legitimate means to their political end? The following factors emerge from a review of the literature concerning the causes of violent conflict on the one hand, and of the so-called root causes of terrorism on the other. They can be categorised into three broad *societal factors* and three broad *organisational factors*.

Societal factors:

- *Political, economic and/or social grievances*, including political repression and discrimination. Also economic deprivation, including exploitative economic systems and inequitable profit distribution from the sale of natural resources and discrimination based on ethnicity, religion, etc.
- *Political, economic and/or social upheaval*, the causes of which include democratic transition, economic mismanagement and recession. Also rapid modernisation, demographic changes including urbanisation, social marginalisation and rootlessness, and a sense of humiliation and hopelessness.
- *Weak or failed social contract*, including lack of good governance, the rule of law and institutional breakdown. In addition, economic stagnation and the breakdown of revenue and/or power-sharing agreements between the state and various stakeholders.

Organisational factors:

- *Group affiliation and differentiation*, based on ethnicity (race, language, religion), tribal affiliation and/or geography. Group identity is crucial for effective mobilisation around collective grievance, achieved by calling on cultural markers, which might include a group's common values, myths and rituals.
- *Charismatic leadership*, most often drawn from social elites. The group's leader is critical for 'identifying the external enemy as the cause, and drawing together into a collective identity otherwise dissimilar individuals who may be discontented and aggrieved, but who, without the powerful presence of the leader, would remain isolated and individually aggrieved' (Post, 2006, p. 21).
- *Legitimising ideology*, the drivers of which include ethnic or nationalist aspirations, secular (leftist or rightist) or religious beliefs.

In relation to economic factors in particular, Stewart (2002) identifies the importance of 'horizontal inequalities', namely, the existence of severe inequalities between groups as distinct from vertical inequality within groups. The former lead to conflict when 'there are such inequalities in resource access and outcomes, coinciding with cultural [including ideological] differences' (Stewart, 2002, p. 2). Gurr (1970, 2006) sheds further light on the way in which economic grievances might fuel conflict, which he refers to as 'relative deprivation'. This occurs when a group perceives a discrepancy between its value expectations (goods and conditions of life to which people believe they are rightfully entitled) and its value capabilities (goods and conditions people think they are capable of attaining or maintaining, given the social means available to them) (Gurr, 1970, p. 13). Conflict becomes probable when the rise in a group's expectations is not matched by a rise in its capability to realise those expectations. Conflict becomes inevitable when discontent is politicised and there is no political recourse to address a group's frustration. At this point, leadership takes on a central role in organising and directing the aggrieved group. The leadership works with an ideology that draws on a set of beliefs derived from the group's own cultural and historical experience. In this way the grievance is legitimated in the minds of group members and these beliefs also provide the rationale for violence. As Gurr (2006) explains: 'Militant and exclusionary ideologies – extremist nationalism, jihadist doctrines, militant Hinduism – all frame disaffected people's ideas about what is possible, permissible, and required' (p. 91).

A particular source of grievance that predisposes a society to violence including terrorism is the inequitable distribution of resource rents. Frustration is heightened, explains Murshed (2009), when there is a concomitant lack of investment by the political centre in regions from which the resources are extracted, and when, in instances of colonialism, institutionalised mechanisms favour settlers over indigenous populations. Internal conflicts where resource grievances are at play, together with environmental damage, loss of land rights and forced migration are also well documented (Humphreys, 2005). In order to resolve such conflicts peacefully, Murshed (2009) argues, a viable social contract is required, constituting a framework of widely agreed rules, both formal and informal, that govern the allocation of resources and development funds.

In what follows, the case studies of Indonesia's separatist conflicts in Aceh and Papua are profiled, using the foregoing framework of causal societal and organisational factors. As will be evident, perceptions of socio-economic deprivation were a primary cause of grievance, articulated through nationalist separatist ideology. Significantly, the conflict in Papua has more recently taken on an inter-communal dimension as tensions have grown between the indigenous Christian and Muslim-settler populations. Although economic factors have played a role in these groups' decision to carry out terrorist attacks, to-date religious motivation has not.

CASE STUDIES

Indonesia's economic crisis of 1997–1998,[3] and increasing popular demand for democratic reforms, led to the fall from power of Soeharto and his military-backed regime after 32 years of authoritarian rule. Soeharto's two immediate successors, B. J. Habibie and Abdurrahman Wahid, began the process of lifting repressive political controls and opened the country to democratic and economic reform, initiating the so-called *Era Reformasi*. Although providing the foundations for Indonesia's successful but fragile transition to democracy, the economic and political upheaval triggered a wave of violence across the archipelago, reigniting the long-standing secessionist conflicts in Aceh and Papua.

TERRORISM IN ACEH[4]

From 1976 to 2005, the *Gerakan Aceh Merdeka* (GAM – Free Aceh Movement) conducted a separatist campaign in Aceh. This consisted primarily of guerrilla warfare against military and police targets but they also attacked Javanese and Batak immigrants. The former were seen as symbolising colonialism in the land of Aceh, and the latter as representing Christianity among Muslim Acehnese (Tadjoeddin, 2002). Terrorism was used as a tactic against communities and leaders whom GAM believed did not support Acehnese independence. For example, GAM burned down state-run orphanages and schools, and murdered teachers, some 50 in 2002 alone, in protest against the state curriculum that promoted Aceh as an integral part of the Republic of Indonesia (Schulze, 2003).

Terrorism was also used against corporations which GAM saw as working with the central government in Jakarta to exploit Aceh's natural resources without benefiting the Acehnese people. It targeted oil and gas facilities, and the Lhokseumawe industrial complex. Between 1999 and 2001 alone, GAM is believed to have been responsible for more than 50 attacks on ExxonMobil's company cars and threatening employees with violence. In April 2001, ExxonMobil was forced to shut down its operations at Lhokseumawe for four months. Bombs were also set off at PT Newmont Nusa Tenggara in 2000 and 2001, whereas five oil wells belonging to PT Caltex Pacific Indonesia were set alight in Simpangbatang, and an oil pipeline was severed in Bangko (Tempo, 2001). Beyond the province, GAM was also linked to the 2001 terrorist bombing of the basement car-park in the Stock Exchange Building in Jakarta. Since the peace agreement and

Memorandum of Understanding were signed in 2005, a small number of terrorist attacks have occurred, largely as a result of economic disputes related to the sharing of receipts from the sale of resources and the allocation of development and reintegration aid (World Bank, 2009).

CAUSAL FACTORS OF TERRORISM IN ACEH: SOCIETAL FACTORS

Grievances against the Jakarta Government

The secessionist conflict in Aceh was driven by a long history of grievances by the local population against the central government in Jakarta. These included

- The long-maintained contention that the 1949 inclusion of the province within the Republic of Indonesia was illegitimate and an act of Indonesian (or more specifically, Javanese) colonisation.
- The military's human rights abuses and the inequitable distribution of natural resource wealth back to the province (large oil and gas deposits were discovered in the early 1970s) (ICG, 2001b).
- High levels of poverty, unemployment and the general lack of economic opportunities (World Bank, 2008).
- The fact that Javanese immigrants outnumbered local Acehnese people in top government and professional positions (Tadjoeddin & Chowdhury, 2009).

Upheaval with Political Change in Indonesia

GAM's efforts at secessionist violence intensified following the economic crisis in 1997 and the democratic reforms that occurred in the wake of Soeharto's fall in 1998. These efforts particularly intensified after President Habibie rejected the call by Acehnese civil society groups in 1999 for a referendum on independence similar to that granted to East Timor.[5] The transition from authoritarian rule to partial democracy in Indonesia increased the conflict, explains Ross (2003), because while it now became possible for the Acehnese to express more freely their grievances towards Jakarta, 'the electoral system was too weak to facilitate a peaceful solution' (p. 19).

Social Contract: Central Government's Lack of Credibility

Until the 2005 MoU, the Indonesian government failed in its efforts to resolve the conflict in Aceh by agreement with the Acehnese. The central government lacked credibility and elected officials were unable to control the military and the relentless human rights abuses it inflicted on the local population.

CAUSAL FACTORS OF TERRORISM IN ACEH: ORGANISATIONAL FACTORS

Group Affiliation: Growing Popular Support

From its inception in 1976 until its formal dissolution following the 2005 MoU, GAM grew from 'a small, armed organization with an intellectual vanguard into a popular resistance movement' (Schulze, 2004, p. viii). Its initial members were local Acehnese as well as those living in neighbouring Malaysia. In the wake of the 1998 resurgence, it is reported that the size of the organisation grew to some 3,000 regular fighters, and as many as 24,000 militia members, with support from 75 per cent of villages throughout the province (ICG, 2001a). Many of the recruits were children of people who had been killed or tortured by the military 'offering them the opportunity to avenge their parents' (Ross, 2003, p. 24).

Charismatic Leadership

GAM's founder, Hasan di Tiro, was a member of a prominent Acehnese family and grandson of Teungku Chik di Tiro, a renowned hero of Aceh's war against Dutch colonial rule. After studying and working for some years in the United States, he returned to Aceh in early 1976 to fight for Acehnese independence to free its people from 'all political control of the foreign regime of Jakarta' (Schulze, 2004, p. 6). Three years later, he fled to Sweden, where he and those who followed him set up an Acehnese government-in-exile. Even from afar, di Tiro's personality was able to unite the community and provide a focal point for the separatist movement.

Ideology: The Power of Nationalism

Although the Acehnese are known for their particular religiosity, GAM's ideology was first and foremost nationalist, the central pillars of which were to free Aceh from Javanese colonialism and human rights abuses, and end the theft of its natural resource rents by the Indonesian government and international companies (Aspinall, 2002). Its leaders focused on the Arun gas complex at Lhokseumawe, claiming that Acehnese would accrue all of its riches if the province became independent. Terrorism was legitimised for these purposes. In an effort to justify terrorist attacks on ExxonMobil personnel and property in Lhokseumawe, for example, one GAM representative was reported as saying that such attacks would cease when the company agreed to two conditions: 'First, the payment of income taxes to the "nation" of Aceh. Second … to get[ting] rid of its TNI [Indonesian military] and police guards. If these two conditions are met in full, 'Then we would be fully prepared to let them continue exploration in Aceh' (Tempo, 2001).

GAM ENDS ITS TERRORIST CAMPAIGN

In the wake of the devastating tsunami of 26 December 2004, which took the lives of more than 170,000 Acehnese and left 500,000 homeless, both the Indonesian armed forces and GAM announced unilateral ceasefires. Negotiations to bring a final end to the conflict began in Helsinki in January 2005 and ended with the signing of a Memorandum of Understanding (MoU) between GAM and the government of President Susilo Bambang Yudhoyono on 15 August 2005. In accordance with the MoU, a new social contract was established between the central government and the Acehnese. GAM abandoned its demand for independence, demobilised its troops (numbering some 3,000), surrendered its arms and ended its terrorist campaign. In exchange, significant numbers of Indonesian troops were withdrawn from Aceh. The province was granted 70 per cent of revenues earned from all of Aceh's present and future hydrocarbon resources, and autonomy in civil and judicial administration excluding foreign affairs, external defence, national security, monetary and fiscal matters, justice and freedom of religion (Aspinall, 2005). In July 2006, the Indonesian parliament passed the 'Law on the Governance of Aceh', which gave formal legal effect to the MoU. Local elections were held in December 2006, in which former GAM members won control of a majority of provincial and district offices along with the position of governor and deputy. In May 2008, it officially changed its party name to *Partai Aceh* (The Aceh Party).

Although the success of the 2005 MoU in addressing local economic and other grievances has enabled a reduced Indonesian security force presence and a significant, overall reduction in violence, including acts of terrorism, current circumstances suggest that it is too soon to relegate the separatist conflict in Aceh to history. Growing disquiet is evident among many Acehnese regarding the new local government's failure to allocate oil and gas revenues equitably within the province and to devise and implement effective development programs. There has been minimal economic and social reintegration of former GAM members. Allegations of corruption and poor governance abound. As one villager put it, 'in place of the struggle for independence, unemployment and poverty are now the greatest threats to peace' (Padden, 2009). Thus after four years of reconstruction in Aceh, economic grievance continues to fuel conflict and dissent. The prevailing peace thus remains fragile while the new social contract rests on shaky ground.

TERRORISM IN PAPUA[6]

Since 1965, *Tentara Pembebasan Nasional* (National Liberation Army – TPN), the armed wing of the *Organisasi Papua Merdeka* (Free Papua Movement – OPM) has conducted a separatist campaign in Papua against the central government of Indonesia, comprising attacks against military and police targets, and on occasion, acts of terrorism. The latter have included the kidnapping of Indonesian and foreign hostages, and sabotaging gold and copper mining operations. In 2002, for example, at least 10 people were injured when a convoy heading the US-owned Grasberg gold mine near Timika was ambushed. The mine's operator, PT Freeport Indonesia, is believed to cooperate actively with the government's security forces in suppressing Papuans' pro-independence activities.

CAUSAL FACTORS OF TERRORISM IN PAPUA: SOCIETAL FACTORS

Grievances – Indonesia's Post-Colonial Invasion of Papua

The origins of the secessionist campaign date back to the highly controversial circumstances in which Papua came to be included in the

Indonesian Republic.[7] The majority of indigenous Papuans believe that their first step towards independence was taken while they were still under Dutch rule, and that Papua was only incorporated into Indonesia as a result of the latter's illegal invasion and occupation of Papuan land. During Soeharto's rule, the government pursued a policy of settling Papua with Muslims from more populated islands, providing them land and facilitating their employment in government positions.

In response to Papuan secessionist activities, the Indonesian military has conducted a brutal campaign of repression featuring unchecked human rights abuses by the security forces which have resulted in the deaths of tens of thousands of Papuan civilians and the internal displacement of many more (Chauvel, 2005). Fuelling further the Papuans' grievances against the central government is the vast disparity between the province's natural resource wealth and its pronounced lack of development. Papua possesses vast tracts of timber and mineral deposits and one of the world's largest gold and copper mines (the Grasberg site in Mimika district), operated by the US mining company, Freeport McMoRan. Yet in spite of the province's GDP being 50 per cent higher than the national average (due mainly to mining), most Papuans are impoverished, and those districts that have the highest proportion of indigenous people are the poorest in the country with some 37 per cent living in poverty (World Bank, 2009).

Upheaval Following the Economic Crisis

In the year immediately before the fall of Soeharto, OPM stepped up its guerrilla activities in pursuit of independence, having gauged the weakness within the central government following the economic crisis. Unmet expectations that Wahid's government would provide them with greater latitude to pursue nationalist goals only served to strengthen OPM's resolve to increase its attacks, including targeting Muslim settlers and personnel involved in mining.

Social Contract – Mobilising Community Support for Independence

In the brief period of what became known as the 'Papuan Spring' between 1998 and 2000, a group of Papuan elites formed the *Presidium Dewan Papua* (Papuan Presidium Council – PDP). They succeeded in mobilising widespread community support for independence, rejecting the OPM's armed struggle and promoting instead 'independence through a dialogue' with the Indonesian government and the international community. In response to his own efforts to find a resolution to the conflict that did not involve independence, President Wahid facilitated the negotiations for a 'Special Autonomy Law'. This made numerous concessions to PDP, including allowing a greater return of natural resource wealth to the province, greater recognition of Papuan *adat* (customary law), establishment of a *Majelis Rakyat Papua* (Papuan People's Council – MRP), the restoration of the name of the province to Papua and legalisation of the use of the 'Morning Star' symbol (as long as it was positioned lower than the Indonesian flag).

Although the Special Autonomy Law was eventually ratified in 2002 during Megawati's administration, it was undermined by the passing of a 'Presidential Instruction' in January 2003 to divide Papua into three provinces, West Irian Jaya, Central Irian Jaya and the existing province of Papua. The ruling sparked violent protests. After the province of West Irian Jaya (West Papua) was established, the attempt to establish the third province of Central Irian Jaya in August 2003 sparked more violence, causing the government to decide to maintain the status quo of only two provinces. The failure to implement fully the Autonomy Law remains a focal point for the ongoing conflict in Papua, a situation that contrasts sharply with the implementation of the MoU in Aceh.

CAUSES OF TERRORISM IN PAPUA: ORGANISATIONAL FACTORS

Group Affiliation – Animosity within the OPM

OPM was established in 1965, two years after Indonesia assumed control over the administration of the province. Unlike GAM, OPM has lacked the necessary momentum to pose a serious threat to local control by the central government. Its members have had difficulty forming a united front, due to traditional animosities between the province's tribes.[8] It is also difficult to estimate OPM's strength due to the inaccessibility of areas in which it has operated. It is believed to be organised around local commanders with small but loyal followings. OPM claims to have between 35,000 and 50,000 men, but the Indonesian military's estimate is no more than several hundred, with a peak of up to 650 men in 2005 (McGibbon, 2006).

Fractured Leadership of the Independence Movement in Papua

The original ideologue of the separatist movement was Aser Demotekay, a devout Christian who in 1963 began to preach independence through non-violent means. A second faction arose in 1964, led by Terianus Aronggear, who believed that the Papuans would only succeed in the struggle against Indonesian colonialism through armed struggle and international support (Vermonte, 2007). OPM was established the following year. Today there remain two levels of the organisation, OPM, which is based inside Papuan territory, and the OPM Revolutionary Council, which is based in Madang, in neighbouring Papua New Guinea. Although the former conducts the armed resistance to Indonesian occupation, the latter conducts diplomatic efforts throughout the region and at the United Nations (Vermonte, 2007). Frequently targeted by the Indonesian military, OPM's leadership remains fractured and weak.

Ideology – Divided Policy Positions

Beyond the identification of historical injustices, and the daily economic exploitation and human rights abuses carried out by the Indonesian government, OPM members remain divided over policy positions (Vermonte, 2007). However, one symbol of Papuan independence that continues to provide unity across all factions is the Papuan flag, the *Bintang Kejora* (Morning Star), which was raised for the first time in 1961. In the post-Soeharto period, flag raising ceremonies have been the scene of violent clashes with the military, in which many Papuans have lost their lives, including Muslim settlers caught up in the fighting.

Recently, tensions between indigenous Christians and Muslim settlers are reported to be on the rise in Papua, fuelled by Islamist ideologues on the one side, and Christian evangelical groups one the other, preaching their own version of 'exclusivist truth' (ICG, 2008, p. 7). Although the potential thus exists for religion to provide a legitimising ideology for using terrorism to achieve political ends, to date no act of terrorism has been recorded in direct relation to religious tensions.

CONCLUSION

From the perspective of the Indonesian Government, GAM's separatist campaign in Aceh was by far a greater threat to the integrity of the Republic than the OPM's campaign. This was due largely to the size and relative unity of the former's organisation and leadership, and widespread support from the local population. The greater number and effectiveness of its terrorist attacks reflect these same factors. Like OPM, the inequitable re-distribution of natural resource rents was a contributing factor to the causes and specific targets of GAM's terrorist attacks.

More than a decade after the chaotic turn of events that accompanied Soeharto's resignation, the conflict in Aceh has ended, and with it, GAM's terrorist campaign. This is in direct response to the success to date of the 2005 MoU that set in place a new social contract between the Acehnese and the central government. However, the peace remains uneasy as grievances persist, mostly driven by local socio-economic factors. Conversely, in Papua fundamental local grievances remain unaddressed, suggesting that terrorist incidents will continue due to unmet political aspirations and ongoing socio-economic discrimination. Indeed, terrorist incidents might increase if mounting tension between indigenous Christians and Muslim settlers polarise the society along ethnic, religious, and in turn nationalist lines.

NOTES

1. The literature differentiates between domestic and transnational terrorism, the latter referring to incidents 'where indigenous terrorists attack a foreign target (kidnapping foreign tourists), where terrorists launch an attack against a target in another country (the 11 September attacks), or when a foreign country is used because it is convenient' (Hizballah attack on a Jewish community centre in Argentina) (Lutz & Lutz, 2007). In this chapter, domestic terrorism will refer to attacks that occur in conflicts that are contained within the territory of a single State and carried out by local groups whose actions are directed at that State's government at whom their grievance is directed.
2. Islamist is used here to refer to adherents of Islamism, a political ideology that seeks to implement a conservative system of Islamic values and law in all spheres of life, and includes those who seek the radical transformation of society into an absolute theocracy in the form of an Islamic state or caliphate. Jihadi-Islamists are those that support the use of violence to promote their literalist version of Islam and to achieve their political objectives.
3. The crisis was precipitated by the forced devaluation of the Thai baht, which set in motion a general run on regional currencies throughout Southeast Asia.
4. Terrorists' incident reports for Aceh and Papua are recorded in the *Global Terrorism Database* (http://www.start.umd.edu/gtd/) and the *Worldwide Incidents Tracking System* (http://wits.nctc.gov/RunSearchQuick.do;jsessionid = LQhCfb MlG2S81JRMG2BnJxjFqLrLn9GZrVGz6plTv9Lx2JjTW8QK!-1876769549).

5. For a detailed analysis of the reasons for the intensity of GAM's resurgence in the post-Soeharto period and the successes of its renewed propaganda campaign (see Schulze, 2004).

6. Referred to by non-indigenous Indonesians as Irian Jaya.

7. For details see Chauvel and Bhakti (2004).

8. See, for example, Makur (2007).

REFERENCES

Aspinall, E. (2002). Sovereignty, the successor state, and universal human rights: History and the international structuring of Acehnese nationalism. *Indonesia*, *73*, 1–24.

Aspinall, E. (2005). *The Helsinki agreement: A more promising basis for peace in Aceh?* Washington: The East-West Center.

Chalk, P., Rabasa, A., Rosenau, W., & Piggott, L. (2009). *The evolving terrorist threat to southeast Asia: A net assessment* (pp. 87–103). Santa Monica: RAND Corporation.

Chauvel, R. (2005). *Constructing Papuan nationalism: History, ethnicity, and adaptation.* Washington: The East-West Center.

Chauvel, R., & Bhakti, I. N. (2004). *The Papua conflict: Jakarta's perceptions and policies* (pp. 5–21). Washington: The East-West Center.

Crenshaw, M. (1981). The causes of terrorism. *Comparative Politics*, *13*(4), 379–399.

Derin-Güre, P. (2009). *Does terrorism have economic roots?* Boston University Working Paper, May.

Gurr, T. R. (1970). *Why men rebel.* Princeton, NJ: Princeton University Press.

Gurr, T. R. (2006). Economic factors. In: L. Richardson (Ed.), *The roots of terrorism* (pp. 85–101). New York: Routledge.

Humphreys, M. (2005). Natural resources, conflict, and conflict resolution. *Journal of Conflict Resolution*, *49*(4), 508–537.

International Crisis Group. (2001a). Aceh: Why military force won't bring lasting peace. *Asia Report No. 17*, ICG, Jakarta/Brussels.

International Crisis Group. (2001b). Aceh: Can autonomy stem the conflict. *Asia Report No. 18*, ICG, Jakarta/Brussels.

International Crisis Group. (2008). Indonesia: Communal tensions in Papua. *Asia Report No 154*, ICG, Jakarta/Brussels.

Intriligator, M. D., & Coissard, S. (2008). The economics of terrorism. In: J. Fontanel & M. Chatterji (Eds), *War, peace and security* (Vol. 6, pp. 161–172). Bingley, UK: Emerald Group Publishing Limited.

Lutz, B., & Lutz, J. (2007). Terrorism. In: A. Collins (Ed.), *Contemporary security studies* (p. 295). Oxford: Oxford University Press.

Makur, M. (2007). Tribal violence kills eight in Papua. *The Jakarta Post*, 18 October.

McGibbon, R. (2006). *Pitfalls of Papua: Understanding the conflict and its place in Australia-Indonesia relations.* Sydney: The Lowy Institute for International Policy.

Murshed, S. M. (2009). Conflict as an absence of contract. *The Economics of Peace and Security Journal*, *4*(1), 31–38.

Padden, B. (2009). Fragile four-year peace prevails in Indonesia's Aceh province. *Voice of America*, 13 August.

Post, J. M. (2006). The psychological dynamics of terrorism. In: L. Richardson (Ed.), *The roots of terrorism* (pp. 17–28). New York: Routledge.

Ross, M. L. (2003). *Resources and rebellion in Aceh, Indonesia.* Paper prepared for the Yale-World Bank project on 'The Economics of Political Violence'. Available at http://www.aceh-eye.org/data_files/english_format/analisys/analysis_others/analysis_others_2003_06_00.pdf

Schulze, K. E. (2003). The struggle for an independent Aceh: The ideology, capacity, and strategy of GAM. *Studies in Conflict & Terrorism*, *26*(4), 241–271.

Schulze, K. E. (2004). The Free Aceh Movement (GAM): Anatomy of a separatist organization. In: *Policy studies 2.* Washington: East-West Center.

Stepanova, E. (2008). Terrorism in asymmetrical conflict: Ideological and structural aspects. *SIPRI Research Report No. 23*, Oxford University Press, Oxford.

Stewart, F. (2002). *Horizontal inequalities: A neglected dimension of development, WIDER annual lectures 5.* Helsinki: UNU World Institute for Development Economics Research.

Tadjoeddin, M. Z. (2002). Anatomy of social violence in the context of transition: The case of Indonesia, 1990–2001. *Politics Administration and Change*, *38*, 1–35.

Tadjoeddin, M. Z., & Chowdhury, A. (2009). Socioeconomic perspectives on violent conflict in Indonesia. *Economics of Peace and Security Journal*, *4*(1), 38–47.

Tempo (2001). Violence at multinationals: When will the violence stop? *Tempo*, Jakarta, 26 March.

Vermonte, P. J. (2007). Separatism in Papua. In: A. T. H. Tan (Ed.), *A handbook of terrorism and insurgency in Souteast Asia* (pp. 279–292). Cheltenham: Edward Elgar.

World Bank. (2008). *Aceh poverty assessment.* Jakarta: World Bank.

World Bank, E. (2009). *Spending for development in Papua: Social, economic and fiscal trends.* Jakarta: World Bank.

CHAPTER 7

GREAT EXPECTATIONS: PROSPECT THEORY AND OIL PRICE VOLATILITY IN IRAN

Jennifer S. Hunt

ABSTRACT

Purpose – *This chapter examines the impact of oil price volatility on domestic political stability in a key supplier state.*

Methodology – *This chapter uses prospect theory to analyse socio-political instability based on significant changes in a supplier state's largest revenue source. Prospect theory posits that decisions are framed around a pivotal reference point which may or may not correspond to the status quo, but which nonetheless directly affects risk appetite. This analysis uses Iran as a case study, and relative oil price as the reference point to analyse risk-acceptant decision-making surrounding the 2009 Presidential election.*

Findings – *Dramatic economic context could be a contributing factor to risk-acceptant behaviour in domestic politics. Specifically, volatile price swings in Iran's main source of income, oil, which contributes over 80 per cent in direct and indirect revenue, and perceived external decline therein, may have been a destabilising factor. Combined with loss aversion, this context may have facilitated measures beyond those dictated by rational utility calculus to secure conservative rule in the 2009 election, and in the ensuing unrest.*

Economics of War and Peace: Economic, Legal, and Political Perspectives
Contributions to Conflict Management, Peace Economics and Development, Volume 14, 107–122

ISSN: 1572-8323/doi:10.1108/S1572-8323(2010)0000014011

Research Limitations – *Prospect theory is difficult to test outside of carefully framed laboratory experiments. Although its insights have been applied to investment behaviour, management and domestic politics, in conflict studies, robust empirical support remains underdeveloped. Moreover, since prospect theory is an individual model of decision-making, difficulties arise when dealing with nation states with multiple centres of power.*

Implications – *Prospect theory may be a useful analytic tool for analysing risk-acceptant decision-making in the context of dynamic economic situations.*

Originality – *Although this analysis complements research on rentier state theory, prospect theory integrates recent developments in behavioural economics and political psychology that may offer a new way to conceptualise the role of expectations and choice framing in decision-making which drives political stability.*

INTRODUCTION

Political decision-making research has tended to focus on the characteristics of individual leaders (such as personality, judgemental heuristics and cognitive biases), structural constraints (including government type and institutional norms) or rational choice frameworks (such as cost–benefit analysis, etc.). This chapter analyses decision-making in light of a key contextual economic factor, oil price. Although economic considerations are part of any decision calculation, this chapter uses prospect theory to analyse socio-political instability based on significant changes in a supplier state's largest revenue source, using Iran as a case study. Though analysis of decision-making in Iran is not without its limitations, the effort is crucial in addressing issues of international import. Though oil has been a major source of government revenue for the past four decades, this percentage has continued to increase and with it, vulnerability to oil price fluctuations. This chapter analyses the impact of oil price volatility on decision-making in Iran using insights from rentier state theory and prospect theory that may offer a new way to conceptualise the role of expectations and choice framing in decision-making.

Iran is a key supplier state in the world oil economy, but even more crucial is the importance of oil to Iran which directly contributes 60 per cent of its revenue (International Monetary Fund [IMF], 2008). A history of poor financial management makes Iran vulnerable to price fluctuations of its main source of income, whereas the lack of reinvestment in extraction technology makes Iranian oil production more costly and inefficient compared to other producer states, requiring an estimated USD 70–90 per barrel to break even (compared to USD 12 for Qatar) (Dow Jones, 2008). Iran uses oil rents to fund large subsidies which constitute billions of dollars and consume more than a quarter of GDP (IMF, 2007). In fact, the windfall of high oil prices up to mid-2008 was largely devoted to servicing such subsidies, especially gasoline. When the government attempted to curtail payments and ration gas, Tehran witnessed violent rioting (*Failed States Index*, 2008). Iran thus provides a case study that is both dependent on oil profit margins to maintain subsidies and internal order, and extremely sensitive to changes in those margins.

Investigating the impact of oil price volatility on decision-making in this context is not limited to heads of state or legislature such as the Supreme Leader, Ayatollah Ali Khamenei, or President Mahmoud Ahmadinejad. Though Constitutional power has remained concentrated in the hands of the Supreme Leader since the State's inception as an Islamic Republic, cracks in the establishment are visible. Political factions jockey to claim themselves inheritors of the Revolution's ideals with potential challengers in the Assembly of Experts, the religious capital of Qom, and other powerful semi-independent groups such as the Iranian Revolutionary Guards Corps, a large paramilitary force that has been steadily gaining influence, affluence and independence from official dictate through lucrative state contracts and ownership of diverse industries from telecommunications to transportation. Moreover, decision-makers in this analysis are not limited to political leaders. Citizens also make decisions that impact the socio-political stability of a state, such as the decision to participate, protest or actively overthrow.

Analysing citizenry and political leadership, this chapter argues that oil price volatility potentially impacts the context and framing of political questions and courses of action. Specifically, prospect theory suggests that steep oil price declines place decision-makers in a domain of losses which encourages risk-taking. Though prospect theory also considers the impact of gains, this will receive only cursory attention in this chapter, as losses are more pertinent to the study of instability. Though not a formal test of the theory, this chapter probes how oil price declines potentially shape, without determining in the strictest sense, policy choices and reactions.

RENTIER STATE: VALUABLE TO A POINT

In the study of oil-producing states, or at least those that derive a significant percentage of government revenue from oil sales, rentier state theory has proven somewhat inescapable (see Mahdavy, 1970; Delacroix, 1980; Beblawi & Luciani, 1987; Chaudhry, 1997; Karl, 1997; Ross, 2001). The theory postulates that a preponderance of external rent derived from exploiting a single source (usually a finite natural resource) flowing directly into state coffers tends to distort government, social and economic institutions (Mahdavy, 1970). Rentier state theorists contend that oil profits maintain petro-state stability through patronage, subsidies, and the illusion of prosperity (and when all else fails, state-funded repression) to the detriment of productivity, representation and sustainable development. Those theorists paint a dire picture for state stability when confronted with a decline in rentier supply sources or prices (Karl, 1997).

The value of rentier state theory is that it suggests that the rentier industry has a pervasive impact on all facets of state function. It has a detrimental influence in weakening government, social and economic institutions that would otherwise serve as a stabilising force to absorb price fluctuations. Of course, like all theories, rentier state theory is not without its detractors. Revision of the theory has included analysis of historical or institutional legacies, or expansion of key concepts such as clientelism (Alamardi, 2005). Some who have used statistical research assess the relationship between rent and development, or have rejected outright that low prices have impacted negatively on petro-state stability (Smith, 2002). Moreover, rentier theory deals only broadly with the impact of rentier prices, offering little about how dramatic price volatility might impact supplier political stability. This is where prospect theory may prove useful.

PROSPECT THEORY: EXPECTATIONS ARE EVERYTHING

Prospect theory posits that decision-making is based around a reference point which classifies choices as either gains or losses, with the latter overweighted relative to comparable gains. This 'loss aversion' has been applied to political contexts, with research demonstrating that states frequently extend greater efforts to guard the status quo against threatened loss than to improve their position by the same amount, for instance they are sometimes 'willing to fight to defend the same territory that they would not have been willing to fight to acquire' (Levy, 1996, p. 186). Prospect theory posits a positive connection linking loss aversion and risk appetite, and empirically demonstrates a propensity for risk-aversion in the domain of gains, and risk-acceptance in the domain of losses (ostensibly to reverse the losses entirely) (Kahneman & Tversky, 1979). This is illustrated in Fig. 1, whereby the value function is S shaped and steeper for losses than for gains. Developed using a body of experimental research, prospect theory incorporates reference dependency, framing effects and probability calculus, to suggest that individuals are more sensitive to *changes* in wealth than to *overall* levels of wealth.

As noted, reference points are key to decision-making because they determine how change and choices will be interpreted, but they are not always simple or obvious. Usually the reference point is the status quo however *expectation* levels may also serve the same function, particularly when the status quo is in flux (Levy, 2003, p. 218). This complexity is compounded by the fact that reference points are asymmetrically updated to account for recent changes, that is, there is a lag time between losses and

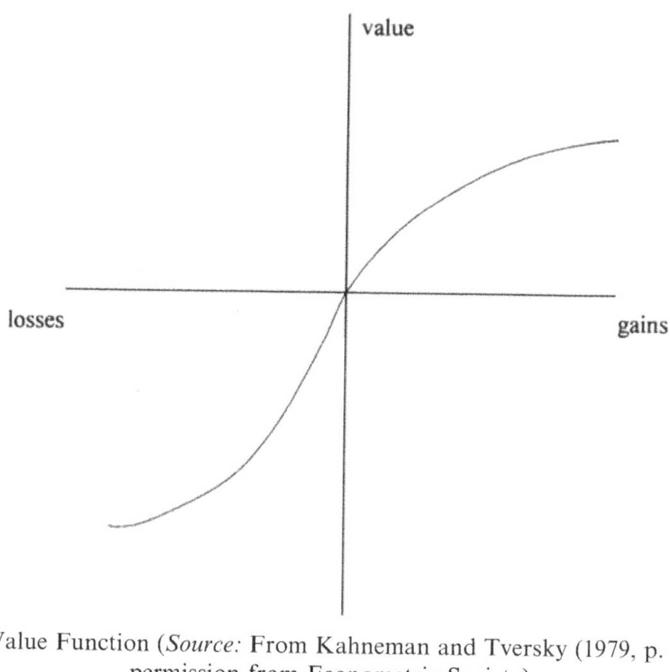

Fig. 1. Value Function (*Source:* From Kahneman and Tversky (1979, p. 279) with permission from Econometric Society).

normalisation of that loss, as opposed to gains which are absorbed instantly. In the case of expectations, this may happen even before they are achieved. Jervis' (1992) research in loss aversion suggests that gains are more quickly assimilated than losses:

> In international politics- and in life in general ... we rapidly, if not effortlessly, adjust to good fortune and any improvement in our lives ... Neither individuals nor nations are so accepting of losses, however. We remain unhappy, unreconciled, and often bitter for a prolonged period. (p. 200)

Levy (2003) notes the potential implications of this 'instant endowment effect':

> after a series of gains, an individual will renormalize her reference point around the new status quo, regard any subsequent setback as a loss rather than as a foregone gain, overweight that loss, and engage in risk-seeking behaviour to maintain her new asset position against that loss. After a series of losses, however, an individual will not adjust to the new status quo but rather continue to use the status quo ante as her reference point. She will perceive any chance of 'improving' her position to a point that still falls short of the original reference point as reducing a loss rather than making a gain, and she will gain in risk-seeking behaviour to eliminate that loss and return to the reference point. (p. 218)

A second concept, framing, pre-dates prospect theory and its effects have been studied in public policy, political science, finance and international political economy (see Cobb & Elder, 1972; Jervis, 1992; Stone, 1989; Elms, 2008). Framing is unconscious, involuntary (even when professionals are trained against it) and open to manipulation. The concept is best is illustrated by an example. In this experiment, participants were confronted with an imaginary disease that if left untreated would be expected to kill 600 people in a city (Fig. 2).

Depending on the framing, subjects responded differently when decisions were presented referring to how many people die, compared to when decisions were presented in terms of how many people would live (Tversky & Kahneman, 1981, p. 453). Even more striking, cancer patients made different real-life decisions to pursue surgery or radiation when the options were framed in terms of survival or mortality rates. Astonishingly, so did their doctors (McNeil, Pauker, Sox, & Tversky, 1982). This preference reversal stands in stark contrast to the invariance concept in rational choice theory, which insists that identical strategies should yield identical choice selection, regardless of how they are presented. As Schattschneider (1957) wrote, 'the definition of alternatives is the supreme instrument of power' (p. 937).

Combined with reference dependency and framing effects, probability calculus is the final component of the theory. Experimental evidence

Strategy 1 (Survival Frame)
Program A: 200 people will be saved
Program B: 1/3 probability that 600 will be saved; 2/3 probability that no one will be saved.
Strategy 2 (Mortality Frame)
Program C: 400 people will die.
Program D: 1/3 probability that no one will die; 2/3 probability that 600 will die.

Fig. 2. Framing Experiment.

demonstrates that humans are consistently poor deferential machines, with low probabilities overweighted and medium to high probabilities underweighted. Kahneman and Tversky (1984) found when low-probability occurrences are overweighted, the value of risky moves and long shots is improved (p. 345).

As Kahneman (2002) eloquently stated when accepting the Nobel Prize for his work on Prospect Theory, 'these are not parlour-game demonstrations of human stupidity'. Rather the research suggests that decision-makers systematically violate the tenets of rational choice frameworks (net utility-maximisation and invariance), particularly in dynamic situations which may place decision-makers in the domain of losses, despite overall gains. Moreover, expectations are potent, risk is rationalised, and context proves more important than the individual decision-maker. However, the individual is an inherent limitation to generalising this theory widely. As prospect theory is an overwhelmingly individual theory of choice selection and decision-making, it does not easily lend itself to the complex world of politics and international relations with multiple centres of power, institutions and interests. However, it is currently the most developed alternative to rational utility theory, and one that potentially illuminates decision-making much more realistically. The theory has been explored in relations such as bargaining (Kanner, 2004), coercion and loss aversion (Levy, 1997), deterrence (Schaub, 2004) crisis decision-making (McDermott, 1998; Farnham, 1992) and rebellion participation (Masters, 2004).

This chapter, in particular, builds on Levy's (1992) work on the combination of perceived external decline and internal insecurity as particularly conducive to risk-seeking (p. 287). He notes that if a 'state perceives itself to be in a deteriorating situation it may see the status quo as a certain loss, overweight that loss, and therefore be willing to take excessively risky actions in order to maintain that status quo against further deterioration or perhaps to recover recent losses', even if standard probability calculus based on expected value would lead to a preference for restraint (Levy, 1998, p. 109; 1992, p. 286). Although Robinson (2006) warns against reifying the state as 'fictitious macro-agents', this chapter's analysis will attempt to extend beyond the traditional head of state to competing groups and the citizenry to more accurately portray the state as 'historically changing constellations of social forces operating through multiple institutions' (p. 530). Using the 2009 Presidential election, this chapter uses prospect theory's tenants to examine the impact of oil price volatility on risk-acceptance in the Islamic Republic.

2009 ELECTIONS

The elections in June 2009 were anticipated to be a close contest between a decorated Revolutionary-turned-Reformer, Mousavi and the populist incumbent, Ahmadinejad. Mousavi was backed primarily by the young and the urban, a substantial voting bloc as the average age in Iran is 27 (compared to 37 in Australia and the United States). Ahmadinejad was backed by rural voters, the influential and increasingly commercial Revolutionary Guards, and importantly, the Supreme Leader, Grand Ayatollah Khamenei himself. Though political opinion polling in Iran is underdeveloped and considered somewhat unreliable, a national poll conducted just days before the election (Iranian Students' Polling Agency [ISPA], 10 June 2009) indicated Ahmadinejad leading Mousavi, 47–31 per cent respectively. Analysts including Karim Sajadpour, an Iran expert at the Carnegie Endowment for Peace (Ignatius, 2009), as well as the chief editor of Iran-based *Siyasat-e Ruz* (Politics of the Day) newspaper Mohammad Pirali (Xinhua, 2009) also predicted a legitimate, albeit closely contested, Ahmadinejad re-election. However, additional measures were taken to secure a wide (perhaps incontestable) margin of victory, including repressing dissent, invoking an external enemy, and vote rigging.[1]

In the run-up to the election, there was increasingly tight security, surveillance and press restriction. Authorities installed street cameras in major cities under the pretence of crime control (*Fars News,* 19 March 2009), and abruptly closed Human Rights Centres (Amnesty International,

23 December 2008), subtly discouraging public dissent. In addition, the incumbent president and official mouthpieces worked hard to invoke an external enemy to distract attention, and engaged in 'electronic warfare' by jamming foreign media signals and limiting access to Facebook, Twitter and opposition websites. And though it is debatable whether Iran has ever held truly fair and free elections, the 2009 election was a far cry from the 'sophistication and elegance' that normally accompanies the exercise (Alfoneh, 2009). Irregularities plagued the collection, counting and verification processes. Results from the Interior Ministry showed an unusual uniformity across regions, two to one in favour of Ahmadinejad, and all three challengers lost in their own hometowns. In an effort of Herculean proportions, 40 million handwritten votes were tallied within hours, with turnout in several provinces surpassing 100 per cent of eligible voters (Ansari, 2009). Though the Election Commission is charged to wait three days to confirm the results, the landslide was announced 1 h after the polls had closed, with Khamenei immediately pronouncing the victory a 'divine decree' and warning the opposition to avoid 'provocations' (Islamic Republic News Agency [IRNA], 14 June 2009). The close connection between the supreme leader and incumbent was not unnoticed in the ensuing unrest with slogans directed at both the President and the Supreme Leader. These protests continued for months, frequently hijacking Regime holidays. On National Students Day, nearly six months after the election, thousands of protestors in cities around the country waved Iranian flags stripped of the Islamic Republic's emblem and burned pictures of the Supreme Leader and the President, an unprecedented event, and chanted 'Khamenei is a murderer, his rule is illegitimate' along with 'Down with the Dictator' (*The Australian*, 9 December 2009).

Although the leadership establishment as a whole might have been divided about the election outcome, Khamenei's swift intervention on behalf of his loyalist pre-empted constitutionally provisioned electoral reviews by the Assembly of Experts, as well as subtle machinations by other political figures to change course. Khamenei's approval came ahead of the Guardian Council's 10-day deadline to certify the results, pre-emptively assuring that the Council would uphold the victory despite a cursory recount.

The measures, which established a wide victory margin and incontestable results, could be considered risky behaviour, and economic context could be a contributing factor to its use. Specifically, dramatic price swings in Iran's main source of income, oil which contributes over 80 per cent in direct and indirect revenue together with perceived external decline, potentially could have been a destabilising factor. The application of Prospect theory suggests that the leadership in Iran used high oil prices as their reference point, setting expectations (manifest in official budgets) of continued high revenue. Though triple-digit prices persisted for only two months, the instant endowment effect explains how such prices were normalized so quickly, setting the stage for future expectations. This 'loss' was evident in official decrees. Predictions of $200/barrel still painfully fresh, Iranian officials complained in early 2009 that anything less than $75 barrel was 'unreal and unfair', even though the resettled prices were nearly the same prices as when Ahmadinejad took office in 2005 (UPI, 17 March 2009; see Fig. 3). This loss was also reflected in popular polling. Ahmadinejad's approval ratings dropped over the same period. In October 2007, the first poll since his election two years earlier, 47 per cent of those who voted for him in the past election said they would vote for him again (ISPA, 2007). A year later, just after high oil prices began to tumble, this support was down to 13 per cent.

Kahneman and Tversky's (1979) finding that 'losses loom larger than gains' suggests that leading up to the elections in June of 2009, Iranian leadership was operating in the domain of losses, perhaps partly predicated on unsatisfied expectations of future revenue. This could have facilitated

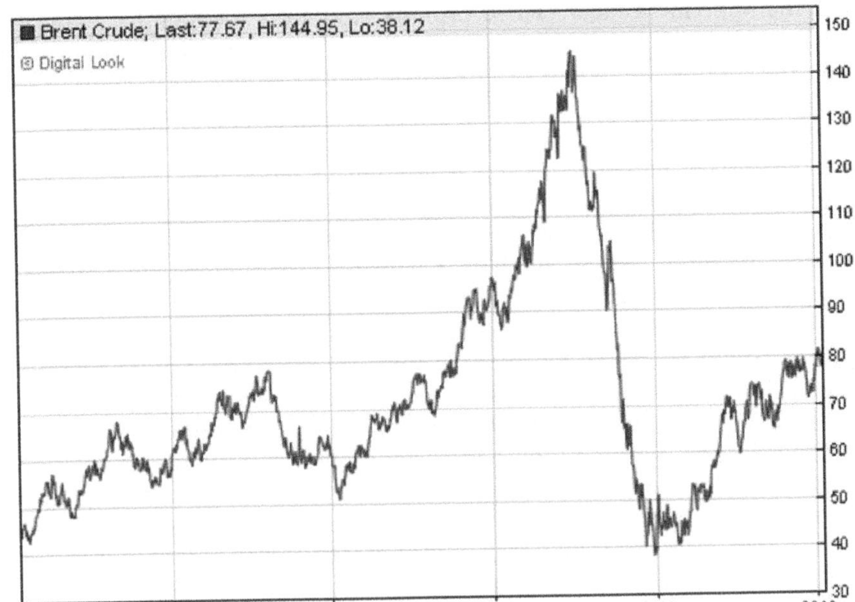

Fig. 3. Oil Prices.

risk-acceptant behaviour to guard against future losses. This behaviour included measures which far exceeded those necessary for victory, for example by precluding a run-off and using escalation. On the first point, the margin of victory (70 per cent) was far in excess of that needed to declare Ahmadinejad the winner (51 per cent), and was risky far beyond what rational utility calculus would predict (a crucial test of the theory). Indeed, disproportionate risk has been studied in relation to casualty losses in determining military combat duration, empirically demonstrating prospect theory's tenets (Bauer & Rotte, 1997). Though an Iranian presidential election has yet to be determined by one round (the candidate must secure 50 per cent of the vote to preclude a runoff), the uniformity of results across regions, speed of results release and roll irregularities indicate the haste and risk-acceptance of such measures. The risk element is enhanced as analysts both inside and outside Iran predicted a legitimate Ahmadinejad re-election. Therefore, it would appear that in line with prospect theory, even the relatively low probability that this would not eventuate, facilitated risk-seeking behaviour to secure the desired result.

Of course, application of prospect theory need not be confined to political leadership. Indeed the opposition and demonstrations could also be framed in the domain of losses after vote fraud became clear. The opposition expected to win, or at the very least, secure a run-off. This optimism was based in part on the sharp reversal of historically high oil prices (and the squandering of the 2008 windfall by Ahmadinejad's administration), and declining international standing. Suspicious of a stolen election, the widespread protests following the results perhaps demonstrated risk-acceptance in the domain of loss. In particular, opposition groups risking harsh consequences including harassment, arrest or imprisonment if identified suggests risk-acceptance in the domain of loss. With unprecedented chants directed towards the regime itself such as 'Where's my vote?' and 'Ahmadinejad is not my President', this risk was further enhanced as government media and judiciary labelled protestors 'terrorists' and connected them to 'imperialist meddling', which resulted in the expulsion of the BBC and two British diplomats (CNN, 22 June 2009). Karroubi (2009), one of the three reformist candidates, recognised the desperate move and wrote a bold letter to the Guardian Council

> You no doubt remember that on the eve of the Islamic revolution Mohammad Reza Pahlavi described the uprising of the people in Tabriz as a conspiracy by outsiders. He called his opponents, namely you and me, red and black reactionaries and accused the BBC of being behind the Islamic revolution.

The unrest, involving more than three million people, continued for months despite mass arrests and harsh sentencing (even for former high-level officials) were charged with counter-revolutionary activity. This domain of loss was not influenced by poor economic conditions. Oil prices, though depressed from the $147/barrel record the following year, and had already resettled at nearly the same price as when Ahmadinejad took office. In this way, the application of prospect theory to the Iranian protests is bolstered by research regarding relative deprivation. Scholars such as Davies (1962) contend that political stability is a state of mind or mood in society, in that it is the 'dissatisfied state of mind rather than the tangible provision of adequate or inadequate supplies of food, equality, or liberty' (p. 6). Similarly, Gurr's (1970) theory of Revolution, *Why Men Rebel*, predicts that violence is more likely in times of relative deprivation, (such as unmet expectations), rather than in times of absolute deprivation or greatest hardship. However, prospect theory has its limitations

1. Empirical pitfalls of measuring the effect of such intangible indicators (such as reference points and expectation levels).
2. Structural complexity of decision-making in modern nation-states where a multitude of uncontrolled economic and political variables operate.
3. Difficulties in interpreting actions in relation to risk-appetite when in fact nearly all political decisions are risky, the differences being degree.

Moreover decisions may be shaped by the framing effects of volatile oil prices as the application of prospect theory would suggest, but they may also be affected by idiosyncratic, ideological, culture or other variables, including the type of political system.

Further, while the unitary actor assumption has long characterised the study of international conflict, problems emerge in domestic contexts. In Iran, power is weighted heavily towards one office, the Supreme Leader. According to the revised Constitution of 1989, Khamenei commands the military and Revolutionary Guards, has the sole authority to declare war or peace, appoints the highest posts in the judiciary, police and the media, and is empowered to dismiss elected officials and overturn parliamentary legislation. Although it may be argued that very little is done, or continued, without Khamenei's blessing, his influence is not without competition (see Sadjapour, 2008; Alamardi, 2005) as subtle signals from within the government, clerical and military circles affirm. These theory-testing limitations may be viewed as directions for future research, rather than insurmountable challenges, however.[2]

CONCLUSION

The application of prospect theory provides some evidence that it is a viable analytical tool to demonstrate the relationship between economic factors and political instability. Though this complements rentier state theory research, prospect theory potentially expands conceptual boundaries to encompass recent developments in behavioural economics and political psychology. Using evidence from the case study suggests that economic contexts may facilitate domains of loss which encourage risk-taking. Thus, oil price volatility may have been a contributing factor to risk-acceptant measures surrounding and responses to the 2009 Iranian election.

Despite limitations inherent in testing prospect theory, some political science scholars continue to redirect decision-making research from its focus on individuals or institutional constraints to key contextual factors and framing effects. In analysing risk-appetite, Elms (2008) writes that, 'the relative riskiness of options comes from the situation, not the decision-makers ... the frame becomes so embedded in the choice problem that individuals cannot separate the two' (p. 12). There is preliminary evidence that prospect theory can be applied to group situations, particularly those with a strong leader, or groups composed of individuals who share similar goals such as the preservation of power (Berejikian, 2002, p. 783). Yet the theory could be improved by work that expands the applicability of group interaction (McDermott, 2004, pp. 294–297). In the absence of further theory development, alternative explanations that target inter-institutional power-struggles or (as 70 per cent of the Iranian population is under age 30) generational political change may prove more persuasive in illuminating current events in Iran.

NOTES

1. One widely cited poll (Ballen & Doherty, 2009) predicted a large margin of victory similar to the 2-1 margin of the official results. This poll, conducted one week into election campaigning, was later criticised (Langer, 2009) for the large percentage of participants (42%) who expressed no opinion or refused to answer the question, and the inclusion of responses by participants (11%) who indicated that they did not intend to vote.

2. Senior political members were noticeably absent at Khamanei's formal endorsement of Ahmadinejad's victory, including former presidents Akbar Hashemi Rafsanjani and Mohammad Khatami, former vice president for parliament and legal affairs, Mohammaad Ali Abtahi (due to his trial and six year prison sentence for

participation in the post-election demonstrations on charges of election conspiracy, propaganda against the government, and insulting the president), and Hassan Khomeini, the grandson of Ayatollah Khomeini.

ACKNOWLEDGMENTS

The author wishes to thank Dr. Leanne Piggott who was instrumental in the development of this chapter.

REFERENCES

Alamardi, K. (2005). The power structure of the Islamic Republic of Iran: Transition from populism to clientelism, and militarisation of the government. *Third World Quarterly*, *26*(8), 1285–1301.

Alfoneh, A. (2009). Four more years of Ahmadinejad. *Forbes,* June 14.

Amnesty International. (2008). Authorities close the Human Rights Centre in Tehran. December 23.

Ansari, A. (Ed.) (2009). *Preliminary analysis of the voting figures in Iran's 2009 presidential election*. Chatham House: London. Available at http://www.chathamhouse.org.uk

Ballen, K. & Doherty, P. (2009). Results of new nationwide public opinion survey of Iran before the June 12 Presidential elections terror free tomorrow. *Center for Public Opinion*, New America Foundation, May.

Bauer, T. & Rotte, R. (1997). Prospect theory goes to war: Loss aversion and the duration of military conflict. *Sonderforschungsbereich* 286, Paper 97.

Beblawi, H. & Luciani, G. (Eds) (1987). Introduction. In: *The Rentier State* (pp. 1–21). London: Croom Helm.

Berejikian, J. (2002). Model building with prospect theory: A cognitive approach to International relations. *Political Psychology*, *23*(4), 759–786.

Chaudhry, K. (1997). *The price of wealth: Economies and institutions in the Middle East*. Ithaca: Cornell University Press.

CNN. (2009). Riot police confront protestors. June 22.

Cobb, R., & Elder, C. (1972). *Participation in American politics: The dynamics of agenda-building*. Boston: Allyn & Bacon.

Davies, J. C. (1962). Toward a theory of revolution. *American Sociological Review*, *27*(1), 5–19.

Delacroix, J. (1980). The distributive state in the world system. *Studies in Comparative International Development*, *15*(3), 3–20.

Dow Jones Newswires. (2008). September 21.

Elms, D. (2008). New directions for IPE: Drawing from behavioral economics. *International Studies Review*, *10*(2), 239–265.

Failed States Index. (2008). The fund for peace and the Carnegie Endowment for International Peace. *Foreign Policy*. July/August.

Farnham, B. (1992). Roosevelt and the Munich crisis: Insights from prospect theory. *Political Psychology*, *13*, 205–235.

Fars News. (2009). Crime-Control Cameras Appear in Tehran. March 19.

Gurr, T. R. (1970). *Why men rebel.* Princeton, NJ: Princeton University Press.
Ignatius, D. (2009). Iranian elections: Change in the air. *Ya Libnan*, May 31.
International Monetary Fund [IMF]. (2007). Islamic Republic of Iran, Country Report No. 07/101, March 8.
IMF. (2008). Islamic Republic of Iran: Selected issues. June 23.
Iranian Students' Polling Agency [ISPA]. (2007). Available at http://www.ispa.ir [Persian], 21 October. Cited in Kuchaki, M, (2007) Reformers gear up for polls. *Mineah*, 7 November.
ISPA. (2009). Available at http://www.ispa.ir [Persian], 10 June.
Islamic Republic News Agency [IRNA]. (2009). Khamenei Approves Election Results. 14 June.
Jervis, R. (1992). Political implications of loss aversion. *Political Psychology*, *13*(2), 187–204.
Kahneman, D. (2002). Autobiography. Nobel Prize Press Release. Available at http://nobelprize.org/nobel_prizes/economics/laureates/2002/kahneman-autobio.html
Kahneman, D., & Tversky, A. (1979). Prospect theory: An analysis of decision under risk. *Econometrica*, *47*(2), 263–292.
Kahneman, D., & Tversky, A. (1984). Choices, values and frames. *American Psychologist*, *39*, 341–350.
Kanner, M. (2004). Framing and the role of the second actor: An application of prospect theory to bargaining. *Political Psychology*, *25*(2), 213–239.
Karl, T. (1997). *The paradox of plenty: Oil booms and petro states.* Berkeley, CA: University of California Press.
Karroubi, M. (2009). Cited in F. Jahanpour "Iran's supreme leader silences the opposition". *The Transnational Foundation for Peace and Future Research (TFF)*, 21 June.
Langer, G. (2009). Iran's election: The odds of fraud. *ABC News*, June 15.
Levy, J. (1992). Prospect theory and international relations: Theoretical applications and analytical problems. *Political Psychology*, *13*(2), 283–310.
Levy, J. S. (1996). Loss aversion, framing and bargaining: The implications of prospect theory for international conflict. *International Political Science Review*, *17*(2), 179–215.
Levy, J. S. (1997). Prospect theory, rational choice, and international relations. *International Studies Quarterly*, *41*, 87–112.
Levy, J. S. (1998). Loss aversion, framing and bargaining: The implications of prospect theory for international conflict. In: F. P. Harvey & B. D. More (Eds), *Conflict in World Politics* (pp. 96–115). New York: St. Martin's Press.
Levy, J. S. (2003). Applications for prospect theory to political science. *Synthese*, *135*(2), 215–241.
Mahdavy, H. (1970). The pattern and problems of economic development in rentier states: The case of Iran. In: M. Cook (Ed.), *Studies in the economic history of the Middle East* (pp. 428–467). London: Oxford University Press.
Masters, D. (2004). Support and nonsupport for nationalist rebellion: A prospect theory approach. *Political Psychology*, *25*(5), 703–726.
McDermott, R. (1998). *Risk-taking in international politics: Prospect theory in American foreign policy.* Michigan: Michigan University Press.
McDermott, R. (2004). Prospect theory in political science: Gains and losses from the first decade. *Political Psychology*, *25*(2), 289–312.
McNeil, B. J., Pauker, S. G., Sox, H. C., & Tversky, A. (1982). On the elicitation of preferences for alternative therapies. *New England Journal of Medicine*, *306*, 1259–1262.
Robinson, W. (2006). Reification and theoreticism in the study of globalisation, imperialism and hegemony: Response to Kiely, Pozo-Martin and Vallada. *Cambridge Review of International Affairs*, *19*(3), 529–533.

Ross, M. (2001). Does oil hinder democracy? *World Politics*, *53*(3), 325–361.
Sadjapour, K. (2008). Reading Khamenei: The world view of Iran's most powerful leader. *Carnegie Endowment for International Peace*. Washington DC: Oakland Street Publishing.
Schattschneider, E. E. (1957). Intensity, visibility, direction and scope. *American Political Science Review*, *51*(4), 933–942.
Schaub, G. (2004). Deterrence, compellence, and prospect theory. *Political Psychology*, *25*(3), 389–411.
Smith, B. (2002). *Hard times in the land of plenty: Oil politics in Iran and Indonesia*. New York: Cornell University Press.
Stone, D. (1989). Casual stories and the formation of policy agendas. *Political Science Quarterly*, *104*(2), 281–300.
The Australian. (2009). Students taunt leaders as Iran erupts. December 9.
Tversky, A., & Kahneman, D. (1981). The framing of decisions and the psychology of choice. *Science*, *21*, 453–458.
UPI. (2009). Iran complains about Price of Oil. March 17.
Xinhua. (2009). Iran's Ahmadinejad to win second term in office: Newspaper chief editor. June 1.

CHAPTER 8

DOES FISCAL POLICY DIFFER BETWEEN SUCCESSFUL AND UNSUCCESSFUL POST-CONFLICT TRANSITIONS? LESSONS FROM AFRICAN CIVIL WARS

Fabrizio Carmignani and Adrian Gauci

ABSTRACT

Purpose – *The chapter studies the impact of fiscal policy on the stabilisation of peace in the aftermath of a civil war.*

Methodology – *We use data from African war-torn countries and study the issue of post-conflict stabilisation from an empirical perspective. We employ probit analysis to formally estimate the effect of fiscal policy on the probability of maintaining peace in the post-conflict period.*

Findings – *The success of post-conflict transition does not require downsizing the government. On the contrary, successful post-conflict transitions are on average characterised by an increase in the size of the government. However, both expenditures and revenues increase at a comparable pace. Moreover, in successful post-conflict transitions, the increase in government size involves an increase in the incidence of capital expenditure relative to government consumption. On the revenue side,*

Economics of War and Peace: Economic, Legal, and Political Perspectives
Contributions to Conflict Management, Peace Economics and Development, Volume 14, 123–145

ISSN: 1572-8323/doi:10.1108/S1572-8323(2010)0000014012

budgetary grants appear to strengthen the chances of success. A heavier debt burden does not seem to compromise the probability of successfully completing the post-conflict transition.

Research limitations/implications – *Future research should (i) extend the sample to non-African countries, (ii) extend the analysis to other macroeconomic policy variables and (iii) supplement cross-country analysis on the role of fiscal policy with country case studies. A potential application of the findings of this chapter is the construction of a model to predict the evolution of currently ongoing post-conflict transitions.*

Social implications – *The findings bear implications on how governments should conduct fiscal policy in the aftermath of a conflict. They also provide guidelines for the international community on how best to assist post-conflict economies.*

Originality – *Papers concerned with the determinants of peace in the post-conflict period do not generally look at the potential contribution of fiscal policy. This chapter is the first attempt, to the best of our knowledge, to provide econometric evidence on the role of fiscal policy as a possible driver of peace stabilisation in the aftermath of a conflict.*

INTRODUCTION

Conservative estimates suggest that in the five decades following the end of World War II, the total death toll generated by civil wars is five times higher than the interstate death toll. More than 70 countries (roughly one-third of the total membership of the United Nations system) experienced episodes of large-scale civil violence, most of which produced massive refugee flows and economic devastation (Fearon & Laitin, 2003). Given these figures, it is not surprising that the causes of civil war have become the object of a recent, lively literature at the intersection of economics and political science (see, inter alia, Collier & Hoeffler, 1998; Collier, Hoeffler, & Rohner, 2008a; Miguel, Satyanath, & Sergenti, 2004; Lujala, Gleditsch, & Gilmore, 2005; Humphreys, 2005). Within this avenue of research, specific attention is now being devoted to the aftermath of a conflict.[1] As empirically shown by Collier and Hoeffler (2004), the risk of a civil conflict decreases with the time elapsed since the last civil conflict. The implication is that the post-conflict period is particularly risky, and hence, it is important to study the conditions for the consolidation of peace in the aftermath of a conflict.

The available empirical evidence indicates that maintaining peace during the post-conflict transition critically hinges upon the interaction of political and economic factors. Among the latter, the literature gives prominent relevance to the level and growth of per capita gross domestic product (GDP) and the degree of dependence on natural resources (see Collier, Hoeffler, & Soderbom, 2008b). Not much attention has been instead devoted to the role of macroeconomic policies, particularly fiscal policy. The case studies reported in Boyce and O'Donnell (2007) emphasise the importance of public finance in rebuilding state institutions following a civil conflict. Collier (2009) discusses reforms and strategies that post-conflict economies ought to undertake to increase revenues and to strengthen the effectiveness of spending. However, cross-country evidence on how different dimensions of fiscal policy affect the probability of successfully completing the post-conflict transition is still missing. In other words, from the perspective of a policymaker in a post-conflict country, it would be important to be able to answer questions such as: Should governments focus more on government consumption or public investment? Should governments worry about the stabilisation of public finance (eventually downsizing government) or expand the public sector? Is the burden of debt going to be a cause of post-conflict failure? What is the contribution of budget grants to peace stabilisation? However, the existing research leaves these (and related) questions largely unanswered.

The purpose of this chapter is to fill in the void through an econometric analysis of the links between fiscal policy and post-conflict peace in African countries. The focus on Africa is justified on two grounds. First, about half of all civil wars have taken place in Africa, and even today, several countries on the continent are torn by civil conflicts and/or go through a difficult post-conflict stabilisation. In this sense, one can argue that Africa is a good case study for researchers interested in the dynamic interaction between economics and conflict. Second, an econometric analysis of the type we have in mind requires sufficiently comprehensive fiscal policy data, and these are often not available for many post-conflict countries. However, for the specific case of Africa, the Africa Development Database of the World Bank provides a valuable source of information. Combining this database with country sources we collected from national statistical offices, we have been able to construct a panel dataset of fiscal policy variables for all of the post-conflict countries in Africa covering the period 1965–2008. Of course, the dataset has several missing observations, especially at the beginning of the sample. Still, it contains enough data points for us to be able to apply formal regression analysis tools.

The theoretical prior of our analysis draws on the game-theoretic analysis of international relations and military interactions (see, for instance, O'Neill, 1994). In the aftermath of a conflict, the stability of peace depends on whether or not the fighting parties will stick to the peace agreement. This peace agreement can be represented as the allocation of a peace payoff between the contending parties. The larger the payoff and the more equitable the distribution, the longer peace will be maintained. Our argument is that fiscal policy is one of the key determinants of the size of the peace dividend. At the same time, it is through fiscal policy that the 'winner' (the government) can make the allocation of the dividend more or less equitable. The size and scope of government expenditure, the incidence of taxation and the burden of debt are, therefore, likely to be important drivers of peace stabilisation. To test this hypothesis, we will be looking at how fiscal policy variables affect the probability of a country to successfully complete 10 years of continued peace after the end of a conflict. We will also study how the dynamics of fiscal policy variables differ between successful and unsuccessful post-conflict stabilisations.

Our main findings can be summarised as follows. The success of post-conflict transition does not require downsizing the government.[2] On the contrary, successful post-conflict transitions are on average characterised by an increase in the size of the government. However, this increase occurs in such a way that the overall stability of public finances is not heavily compromised: both expenditures and revenues increase at a comparable pace. Moreover, in successful post-conflict transitions, the increase in government size involves an increase in the incidence of capital expenditure relative to government consumption (whose contribution to horizontal redistribution is questionable). On the revenue side, budgetary grants appear to strengthen the chances of success. At the same time, and perhaps contrary to common sense and intuition, a larger burden of debt does not seem to compromise the probability of successfully completing the post-conflict transition.

In the rest of the chapter, we present first a few simple empirical regularities concerning fiscal variables during the post-conflict transition. We then provide econometric evidence from the estimation of a probit model of post-conflict peace. Subsequently, we discuss the difference in the dynamics of fiscal policy between a successful and an unsuccessful post-conflict episode. Finally, we formulate some conclusions and policy recommendations. The appendix reports the full chronology of conflicts in Africa and the description of the variables used in the analysis.

SOME PRELIMINARY EMPIRICAL REGULARITIES

For the purpose of this chapter, the post-conflict period is identified with the first 10 years that follow the end of a conflict.[3] The chronology of civil wars for the African continent is based on Gleditsch (2004) and updated to 2008 (using the information available up to the end of 2009). The full chronology is reported in the appendix.

A post-conflict transition can be successful or unsuccessful. Success occurs when the country effectively stays at peace for the whole of the 10 years. A failure instead occurs whenever a new war goes off within less than 10 years from the end of the previous conflict. In the rest of the chapter, we refer to *SPC* as the successful post-conflict and *UPC* as the unsuccessful post-conflict. In the case of African countries, we count 15 SPC and 15 UPC transitions. There are also nine countries that at the cutoff date of 2008 were still at peace, but had not yet completed the 10 years spell. These are regarded as 'ongoing' post-conflict transitions. All in all, the unit of observation in the dataset is a post-conflict episode and we include a total of 33 episodes.[4] For each episode, data are reported on an annual basis. Fiscal data fully cover 21 of the 33 episodes (11 SPC and 10 UPC). Another two episodes (notably Algeria SPC 1964–1973 and Burundi SPC 1973–1982) are covered only partially. For the remaining 10 episodes, no fiscal data are available (see appendix for details about the availability of fiscal data by country).

As a way to gauge some simple empirical regularities on the behaviour of fiscal policy variables in post-conflict situations, Table 1 reports some basic summary statistics. For each of 24 fiscal policy indicators (see appendix for a full list of variables), the table reports the average (μ) and the standard deviation (σ) in UPC and SPC. To better appreciate the differences between successful and unsuccessful post-conflicts, the table also reports the standardised mean difference of each variable. This is equal to the average of the variable in SPC minus the average of the variable in UPC divided by the standard deviation of the variable in the full sample. Finally, the table also reports average and standard deviation of the fiscal variables in states of war and peace as references to compare the statistics computed for UPC and SPC. Note that by periods of peace, here we mean the years of peace that follow the end of successful post-conflict transition until the beginning of a new war (or until 2006, in case no new war has begun since the conclusion of the last one).

Focusing on the differences between UPC and SPC, there are indeed a few variables that exhibit a rather large (positive or negative) standardised mean

Table 1. Summary Statistics of Fiscal Variables.

	UPC		SPC		Standardised Mean Difference	War Periods		Peace Periods	
	μ	σ	μ	σ		μ	σ	μ	σ
Government size									
rev	0.221	0.921	0.209	0.403	−0.130	0.178	0.554	0.229	0.420
exp	0.270	0.594	0.254	0.339	−0.115	0.254	0.523	0.314	0.356
gov	0.116	0.707	0.097	0.392	−0.308	0.124	0.618	0.118	0.411
wages	0.054	0.678	0.056	0.488	0.037	0.060	0.792	0.069	0.540
Government scope									
exp_c	0.163	0.735	0.164	0.415	0.009	0.188	0.617	0.194	0.418
exp_k	0.095	0.711	0.088	0.457	−0.098	0.068	0.685	0.112	0.831
exp_c_p	0.674	0.270	0.644	0.203	−0.168	0.745	0.203	0.656	0.301
gov_p	0.477	0.249	0.398	0.325	0.581	0.525	0.233	0.392	0.328
wages_p	0.290	0.364	0.392	0.730	−0.567	0.319	0.393	0.358	0.339
def	0.056	1.416	0.026	0.888	−0.911	0.044	0.814	0.011	1.145
health	–	–	0.020	0.514	–	0.017	0.588	0.021	0.373
edu	0.024	0.565	0.032	0.378	0.475	0.041	0.329	0.038	0.498
Sources of revenues									
grt_k	0.014	2.063	0.009	7.099	0.353	0.014	2.621	0.008	5.342
grt_c	0.006	3.351	0.017	1.737	0.322	0.006	2.429	0.006	4.694
rev_ntx	0.027	1.134	0.043	0.977	0.442	0.028	1.149	0.042	1.383
rev_ntx_p	0.154	1.060	0.214	0.835	−0.105	0.186	0.886	0.186	1.149
Debt									
debt	0.559	0.926	1.313	0.581	1.003	0.997	0.687	0.678	1.055
int_p	0.161	0.573	0.206	0.788	0.346	0.140	0.701	0.195	0.672
Fiscal balance									
bal_ov_grt	−0.049	−4.353	−0.043	−1.922	0.057	−0.072	−1.068	−0.082	−1.225
bal_ov	−0.062	−3.473	−0.072	−1.319	0.442	−0.081	−0.983	−0.091	−1.284
bal_c_grt	0.031	6.556	0.038	2.018	0.079	−0.015	−4.767	0.031	2.927
bal_c	0.018	11.287	0.012	7.429	−0.090	−0.023	−3.101	0.021	4.384
bal_prim_grt	0.034	2.714	0.065	1.076	0.262	0.018	3.669	0.060	1.165
bal_prim	0.016	5.728	0.035	2.282	−0.066	0.008	8.096	0.046	1.617

Notes: Difference means that the variable is on average higher in SPC than in UPC. See appendix for variables' definition.

difference. Both the level of debt (debt) and the incidence of interest payments on total expenditure (int_p) are much higher in SPC than in UPC. In fact, the standardised mean difference of debt is the largest of all variables. The positive sign implies that on average SPC is characterised by higher debt levels (and a larger incidence of interest payments on total expenditure) than UPC. This is indeed quite surprising as it suggests that the burden of debt might not be an obstacle to the maintenance of post-conflict peace. SPC is also characterised by a significantly larger level of current grants (grt_c). Therefore, it seems that providing post-conflict countries with budgetary grants is more conducive to peace than granting debt relief. We will return on this important policy conclusion later on, also addressing the issue of possible reverse causality.

A large mean difference is also observed with respect to defence expenditure (def): in SPC, defence and military expenditure is effectively much lower than in UPC. This observation is coherent with previous findings by Collier and Hoeffler (2006). Two issues are worth noting, however. First of all, the sample of observations is quite small. The variable def is not available for several of the episodes of unsuccessful post-conflict transition and hence, we have to be careful in making generalisations. Second, reverse causality might be particular strong in this case: it is not necessarily a large military expenditure that causes the failure of the post-conflict transition, but rather, it might be that the expectation of a failure (possibly already evident in the first years of post-conflict transition) leads the government to spend more on the military.

SPC is also characterised by larger levels of public expenditure on education (edu). Unfortunately, nothing can be said about health expenditure, as we have no observations on health for the countries in UPC. Bearing in mind that also for edu the number of actual observations in each state is small, the positive association between higher education expenditure and post-conflict success is coherent with the idea that the stabilisation of peace requires a larger provision of public goods.

Government size appears to be on average higher in UPC, but differences between successful and unsuccessful post-conflicts are relatively small. The only exception is represented by public sector wages (wages), which are larger in SPC. In fact, as it will be discussed later on, the critical difference between UPC and SPC with respect to government size is not related to average levels, but rather to dynamics in the first years of the post-conflict transition. With respect to composition of expenditures and revenues, we observe a rather larger incidence of government consumption on total expenditure (gov_p) in UPC. On the contrary, nontax revenues (rev_ntx and rev_ntx_p) are generally larger in SPC than in UPC. Reflecting the small differences in average government size across the two states, indicators of fiscal balance also do not differ much between UPC and SPC. If anything, SPC tends to display better balances than UPC when grants are included.

LOOKING BEYOND AVERAGES: EVIDENCE FROM PROBIT ANALYSIS

We now move beyond period averages to estimate the effect of fiscal policy variables on the probability of successfully completing the post-conflict transition. Our statistical framework is the standard binary choice model. Let $Y=0$ denote the SPC state and $Y=1$ the UPC state. Given a set of country characteristics $\mathbf{x}$, we can write the probabilities of being in each state as

$$\text{Prob}(Y=1|\mathbf{x}) = F(\mathbf{x}, \boldsymbol{\beta}) \tag{1}$$

$$\text{Prob}(Y=0|\mathbf{x}) = 1 - F(\mathbf{x}, \boldsymbol{\beta}) \tag{2}$$

where $\boldsymbol{\beta}$, the parameters to be estimated, represent the impact of changes in $\mathbf{x}$ on the probability of each state (see Greene, 2008, pp. 772–774). Estimation of $\boldsymbol{\beta}$ parameters then requires the specification of a functional form for the distribution on the right-hand side of Eqs. (2) and (3). Either the normal distribution or the logistic distribution is used in the literature. We experimented with both of them and noticed that results are basically the same. We report and comment on results obtained using the normal distribution:

$$\text{Prob}(Y=1|\mathbf{x}) = \int_{-\infty}^{\mathbf{x}'\boldsymbol{\beta}} \Phi(\mathbf{x}'\boldsymbol{\beta}) \tag{3}$$

where $\Phi(\cdot)$ denotes the standard normal distribution.

The vector $\mathbf{x}$ includes, for each country in each period, a set of socio-economic characteristics plus the fiscal policy variables. More specifically, we control for the quality of country's polity (polity), the timing of elections (elections), the degree of ethnic fragmentation (ethnix) and the level and growth rate of per capita GDP (gdp_pc and growth, respectively). Level and growth of per capita GDP and fiscal policy variables are all lagged to reduce the risk of reverse causality.[5]

Table 2 reports the estimated marginal effects of models (2) and (3). The marginal effects are formally defined as $f(\mathbf{x}'\hat{\boldsymbol{\beta}})\hat{\boldsymbol{\beta}}$, where $\hat{\boldsymbol{\beta}}$ are the maximum likelihood estimates of $\boldsymbol{\beta}$. Because of the way in which we have coded the binary dependent variable, a positive sign indicates that higher values of the variable reduce the probability of a successful post-conflict transition.

Before discussing the role of fiscal policy variables, it is worth taking a look at the impact of other socioeconomic controls. Elections and a better polity increase the chance of a successful post-conflict transition. This intuitive result is, however, hardly statistically significant. Ethnic fragmentation also reduces the risk of returning to violence in the post-conflict period. Both findings are consistent with the results reported by Collier et al. (2008b). The role of per capita income is instead ambiguous. The sign of the marginal effect of per capita GDP changes across different specifications of the **x** vector. However, when it is statistically significant, the marginal effect is positive, thus suggesting that richer economies are at higher risk of failure. This effect is, however, counter-balanced by the effect associated with the growth of per capita GDP. The estimated coefficients on growth are again hardly significant in statistical terms. However, their negative sign indicates that the quicker the per capita GDP returns to its post-conflict level, the more likely it is that the post-conflict transition will end up successfully.

We now turn to the estimated marginal effects associated with the fiscal policy variables. In the attempt to reduce multicollinearity, we employ a smaller group of variables than the original 24. In particular, we build on the evidence of the previous subsection to see whether the largest mean differences documented in Table 1 correspond to statistically significant effects on the probability of success/failure of the post-conflict transition.

In column I of Table 2, we look at expenditure variables. A higher level of total expenditures (exp) increases the probability of successfully completing the post-conflict transition. We suggest the following interpretation. A larger government implies a larger (and possibly more equitably distributed) peace dividend, thus making it optimal for both contending parties to maintain peace. The proportion of government consumption on total expenditure (gov_p) instead has a negative effect on the probability of successful post-conflict transition. Our idea is that for any given size of the government, the value of the peace dividend increases faster if more resources are allocated to productive expenditure. In this sense, a greater incidence of consumption relative to investment is not beneficial to peace stabilisation. However, public wages do help promote peace (as indicated by the negative coefficient on wages_p) as they make rebellion a less attractive option for a larger number of people.

In column II, we consider revenue variables. Total revenues (rev) do not play any statistically significant role, even though the negative sign is broadly in line with the idea that a larger government helps maintain post-conflict peace. A larger proportion of nontax revenues (rev_ntx_p) instead reduces the probability of SPC. We believe that this effect is related to greed: nontax revenues might capture the depth of fiscal exploitation of natural resources and hence, they represent a rent that parties would like to appropriate with violence at some point in time during the post-conflict phase. Finally, more grants (grt_p_c) increase the probability of SPC. The

Table 2. Probit Analysis of Successful and Unsuccessful Post-Conflict Transitions.

	I	II	III	IV
polity	−0.002	−0.010	−0.011	−0.014***
elections	−0.044	−0.044	−0.068	−0.008
ethnix	−0.044**	−0.137	−0.073	−0.101**
gdp_pc	0.079**	0.062	−0.087	−0.021
growth	−0.038	−0.050	−0.426*	−0.117
exp	−0.010**	–	–	–
gov_p	0.004*	–	–	–
wages_p	−0.008**	–	–	–
rev	–	−0.002	–	–
rev_ntx_p	–	0.005*	–	–
grt_p_c	–	−0.949**	–	–
debt	–	–	−0.003***	–
int_p	–	–	0.083	–
bal_prim_grt	–	–	–	−0.010**
Number of observations	94	96	74	89
Wald chi	20.800***	16.7**	26.3***	19.92***
Pseudo R^2	0.2213	0.105	0.328	0.319

Notes: The table reports marginal effects estimated from models (2) and(3), see text. The base outcome is SPC (= 0). All fiscal variables, gdp_pc and growth are all lagged by one period to control for possible endogeneity effects. See appendix for variables definition.
*, **, *** denote statistical significance at usual confidence levels.

effect is statistically large, meaning that grants significantly contribute to increasing the peace payoff of the contending parties.

We consider the impact of the burden of debt in column III. As expected from the analysis of mean differences, a higher debt to GDP ratio (debt) does not seem to be an obstacle to successful post-conflict transition. In fact, in our sample, SPC is characterised by a systematically higher level of debt than UPC. Higher debt levels are, therefore, associated with a higher probability of SPC. At the same time, the fact that higher debt levels also involve a larger amount of resources to be used for interest payments (int_debt_p) does not seem to matter much in terms of probability of success of the post-conflict transition.

Finally, in column IV we look at the impact of the overall stability of the fiscal position. In fact, we tried all six different definitions of fiscal balance, and only bal_prim_grt happens to be statistically significant. A better primary balance (inclusive of grants) helps complete the post-conflict transition successfully. Our interpretation is that the enlargement of government size in the post-conflict phase is conducive to peace only if it involves both the expenditure side and the revenue side of the budget. On the contrary, if only expenditures are expanded (especially government consumption) than the chances of success do not necessarily increase.

DYNAMIC COMPARISONS

We now turn to the analysis of the dynamic evolution of fiscal policy variables during the post-conflict transition. For this purpose, we compute averages of fiscal policy variables in each state as follows. Let w_{ijt} be the generic fiscal policy variable w observed at time t in country i in state j (where j = SPC, UPC). Then, the average taken over all is in state j at time t is $w_{jt} = \sum_{i=1}^{n} w_{jit}/n$, where n is the total number of countries in state j at time t. For each period t, the average of fiscal policy variables is defined as $w_{j(t)} = \sum_{t=1}^{T} w_{jt}/T$, where $T = 1, 2, \ldots, 10$ (if j = SPC) or the start of a new conflict (if j = UPC). The sequence of $w_{j(t)}$ values, therefore, offers a dynamic representation of how the fiscal policy variable evolves over time in each state.

To highlight differences in the dynamic evolution, in Table 3 we report the difference $w_{\mathrm{SPC}(t)} - w_{\mathrm{UPC}(t)}$ for $t = 1, 2, \ldots, 5$. The entire series of $w_{\mathrm{SPC}(t)}$ and $w_{\mathrm{UPC}(t)}$ are reported in Tables 4 and 5, but we limit our investigation to the first five years of post-conflict transition, because the number of countries in UPC is very small after the fifth year. The trends of some of the key fiscal policy variables are also depicted in Fig. 1.

It appears from the table that SPC is initially characterised by lower revenues (rev) and lower expenditures (exp) than UPC. Revenues and expenditures grow during the first five years of transition in both SPC and UPC. However, although the average growth rate of expenditure is roughly the same in the two states (1.8 per cent per year in UPC and 1.7 per cent per year in SPC), the growth rate of revenues is significantly faster in SPC (2.7 per cent per year versus 0.45 per cent per year on average in UPC, see panel A of Fig. 1). Therefore, a distinctive feature of successful post-conflict stabilisations is that the expansion of government size is matched by the increase in revenues, so that the overall fiscal position is not significantly destabilised.

At the beginning of the post-conflict transition, SPC is also characterised by lower levels of capital expenditure (exp_k), current expenditure (exp_c) and government consumption (gov) than UPC. However, the evolution of these components of expenditure in the first few years of transition is

Table 3. Differences Between Successful and Unsuccessful Post-Conflict Transition Year-by-Year.

	Years of Post-Conflict Transition				
	1	2	3	4	5
Government size					
exp	−0.050	−0.051	−0.063	−0.060	−0.042
rev	−0.019	−0.004	−0.015	−0.007	0.006
gov	−0.015	−0.037	−0.048	−0.051	−0.042
wages	−0.005	−0.005	−0.009	−0.010	−0.009
Government scope					
exp_c	−0.012	−0.032	−0.039	−0.044	−0.030
exp_k	−0.045	−0.020	−0.007	−0.002	−0.005
exp_c_p	0.044	−0.002	0.005	−0.015	−0.020
gov_p	−0.036	−0.074	−0.081	−0.093	−0.085
wages_p	0.136	0.142	0.125	0.131	0.112
def	−0.072	−0.025	–	–	–
health	–	–	–	–	–
edu	0.077	–	–	–	–
Sources of revenues					
grt_k	−0.004	0.001	0.004	0.002	−0.009
rev_ntx	0.002	0.007	0.008	0.010	0.016
grt_c	0.004	0.008	0.008	0.010	0.012
rev_ntx_p	0.046	0.040	0.042	0.061	0.085
Debt					
debt	0.437	0.674	0.870	0.905	0.911
int_p	0.049	0.060	0.087	0.062	0.071
Fiscal balance					
bal_ov_grt	−0.072	−0.002	0.017	0.031	0.032
bal_ov	−0.078	−0.014	0.005	0.015	0.013
bal_c_grt	−0.094	−0.009	−0.002	0.016	0.024
bal_c	−0.097	−0.018	−0.011	0.003	0.007
bal_prim_grt	−0.027	0.028	0.021	0.037	0.042
bal_prim	−0.028	0.024	0.015	0.026	0.025

Notes: The table reports the difference between the levels of fiscal variables in SPC and UPC in the first five years of post-conflict transition (see text for details). The statistics in the table are computed as the simple difference between the corresponding SPC and UPC values reported in Tables 4 and 5. A positive value indicates that the variable is higher in SPC than in UPC.

Table 4. Average of Fiscal Variables in Successful Post-Conflicts, Year-by-Year.

	1	2	3	4	5	6	7	8	9	10
grt_k	0.016	0.015	0.016	0.015	0.006	0.007	0.007	0.008	0.009	0.010
rev_ntx	0.033	0.040	0.039	0.039	0.041	0.043	0.044	0.046	0.044	0.042
grt_c	0.014	0.018	0.018	0.018	0.018	0.019	0.019	0.019	0.018	0.017
Rev	0.167	0.181	0.186	0.188	0.193	0.202	0.208	0.211	0.210	0.209
rev_ntx_p	0.216	0.229	0.221	0.219	0.222	0.227	0.226	0.225	0.217	0.208
exp_c	0.140	0.151	0.155	0.154	0.157	0.159	0.162	0.165	0.166	0.165
gov	0.086	0.088	0.089	0.088	0.089	0.090	0.092	0.095	0.098	0.099
exp_k	0.062	0.070	0.073	0.072	0.075	0.078	0.081	0.085	0.088	0.090
wages	0.046	0.048	0.049	0.049	0.051	0.052	0.053	0.055	0.056	0.056
exp	0.208	0.224	0.231	0.228	0.234	0.240	0.245	0.252	0.256	0.257
exp_c_p	0.714	0.696	0.684	0.679	0.674	0.666	0.661	0.653	0.645	0.639
gov_p	0.431	0.410	0.402	0.397	0.395	0.391	0.392	0.394	0.398	0.400
int_p	0.240	0.237	0.254	0.257	0.251	0.243	0.226	0.208	0.194	0.193
wages_p	0.446	0.429	0.421	0.416	0.404	0.393	0.390	0.392	0.395	0.395
debt	1.281	1.347	1.471	1.481	1.466	1.420	1.382	1.339	1.298	1.260
def	0.029	0.035	0.031	0.029	0.026	0.024	0.023	0.025	0.026	0.026
health	1.543	1.526	1.559	1.606	1.679	1.863	–	–	–	–
edu	3.495	3.533	3.651	3.434	3.237	3.063	2.961	3.040	3.018	3.105
bal_ov_grt	−0.037	−0.039	−0.040	−0.035	−0.035	−0.032	−0.032	−0.038	−0.044	−0.047
bal_ov	−0.059	−0.067	−0.070	−0.064	−0.065	−0.064	−0.063	−0.069	−0.073	−0.074
bal_c_grt	0.024	0.028	0.028	0.030	0.033	0.039	0.042	0.040	0.037	0.037
bal_c	0.004	0.002	0.002	0.004	0.006	0.011	0.013	0.011	0.010	0.011
bal_prim_grt	0.045	0.053	0.057	0.059	0.061	0.070	0.072	0.068	0.063	0.062
bal_prim	0.023	0.025	0.028	0.031	0.031	0.038	0.040	0.036	0.033	0.033

Notes: Average of fiscal policy variables at years 1, 2, ..., 10 of successful post-conflict transitions. All averages are computed over the total of 13 successful post-conflict episodes for which fiscal data are available.

quite different across the two states. In the UPC state, the expansion in total government expenditure mostly takes the form of an increase in government consumption, while capital expenditure in proportion of GDP declines. On the contrary, in the SPC state, all of the three components increase, but capital expenditure increases faster than the other two (2.9 per cent per year against an increase of 1.4 per cent a year of current expenditure and 0.3 per cent a year of government consumption). As a result of these trends, the incidence of government consumption in total expenditure (gov_p) grows fast in UPC, whereas it declines in SPC state (see panel B of Fig. 1).

Table 5. Average of Fiscal Variables in Unsuccessful Post-Conflicts, Year-by-Year.

	1	2	3	4	5	6	7	8	9
grt_k	0.020	0.014	0.012	0.013	0.015	0.016	0.016	0.014	0.012
rev_ntx	0.031	0.033	0.032	0.029	0.024	0.021	0.019	–	–
grt_c	0.010	0.010	0.010	0.007	0.006	0.005	0.004	0.004	0.003
rev	0.185	0.186	0.201	0.194	0.187	0.170	0.159	–	–
rev_ntx_p	0.169	0.189	0.179	0.159	0.137	0.126	0.119	–	–
exp_c	0.153	0.183	0.194	0.198	0.187	0.169	0.157	0.146	0.138
gov	0.101	0.125	0.137	0.139	0.131	0.121	0.115	0.107	0.102
exp_k	0.107	0.090	0.079	0.074	0.080	0.090	0.096	0.098	0.102
wages	0.051	0.053	0.058	0.059	0.060	0.053	0.049	–	–
exp	0.258	0.275	0.294	0.288	0.276	0.261	0.247	–	–
exp_c_p	0.670	0.698	0.679	0.694	0.693	0.658	0.642	–	–
gov_p	0.467	0.484	0.483	0.490	0.480	0.467	0.470	–	–
int_p	0.190	0.178	0.167	0.195	0.181	0.170	0.159	0.162	0.161
wages_p	0.311	0.286	0.296	0.286	0.292	0.279	0.279	–	–
debt	0.844	0.673	0.601	0.576	0.556	0.536	0.513	0.481	0.456
def	0.101	0.060	0.053	–	–	–	–	–	–
health	–	–	–	–	–	–	–	–	–
edu	0.034	–	–	–	–	–	–	–	–
bal_ov_grt	0.035	−0.036	−0.057	−0.067	−0.067	−0.073	−0.073	–	–
bal_ov	0.018	−0.053	−0.074	−0.079	−0.077	−0.082	−0.080	–	–
bal_c_grt	0.118	0.037	0.030	0.014	0.009	0.007	0.006	–	–
bal_c	0.101	0.020	0.013	0.001	−0.001	−0.002	−0.001	–	–
bal_prim_grt	0.073	0.025	0.036	0.022	0.019	0.018	0.017	–	–
bal_prim	0.051	0.001	0.012	0.005	0.005	0.006	0.007	–	–
Number of episodes	10	8	5	4	4	3	3	2	1

Notes: Average of fiscal policy variables at years 1, 2, … , 9 of unsuccessful post-conflict transitions. The bottom line of the table reports the number of episodes over which averages are computed.

The dynamic pattern of current grants (grt_c) is also quite interesting. The difference between SPC and UPC is quite small at the beginning of the transition. But then, the difference grows quickly during the first four years: whereas SPC is characterised by a steady increase in the flow of grants, UPC displays the opposite trend (see panel C of Fig. 1). The fact that immediately at the beginning of the post-conflict transition grants are higher in the SPC state might suggest that the international community 'picks-the-winner': among all post-conflict countries, some are chosen and receive a larger initial endowment of grants, which, in turn, puts them in the condition to

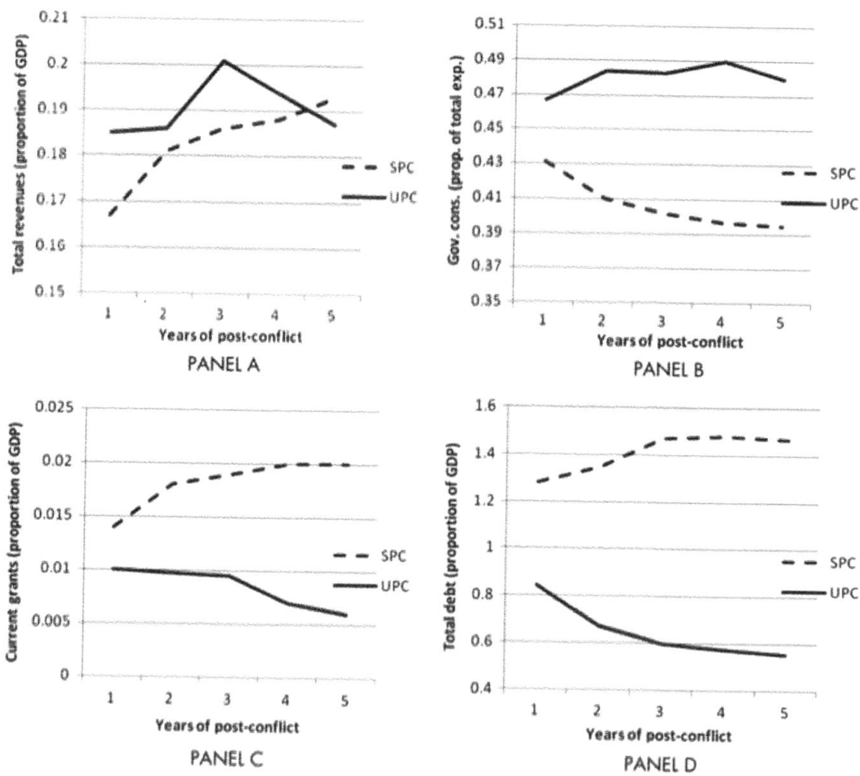

Fig. 1. Dynamics of Selected Fiscal Policy Variables in SPC and UPC. *Source:* Author's computations from data in Tables 3–5.

sustain peace over the post-conflict period. However, the fact that over time the gap in the level of grants between the two states widens might indicate some endogeneity in the behaviour of the international community: grants tend to go to those countries that show more promising progress towards peace, whereas countries that initially struggle in maintaining peace receive less and less support. This sort of 'disengagement' of the international community then leads to the failure of the post-conflict transition process.

The data in the table also confirm our previous findings on the role of debt. Not only total debt (debt) is initially significantly higher in SPC (see panel D of Fig. 1), but the difference also grows over time. In SPC, the level of debt moderately increases in percent of GDP over the first five years of transition (1.4 per cent per year), whereas in the UPC state it decreases.

The proportion of resources devoted to interest payments (int_p) is systematically and persistently higher in SPC than in UPC. These findings might seem at odds with the evidence recently reported by UNDP (2008) on the contribution of debt relief to post-conflict recovery. However, we stress that there are two important differences between our analysis and UNDP's (2008). First of all, we look at different samples of post-conflict episodes. Second, UNDP is mainly concerned with the correlation between debt service and post-conflict growth, whereas we look at how, after controlling for growth, debt affects the probability of stabilising peace. In other words, we look at the role of debt from a sharply different angle to UNDP.

Finally, the analysis of the dynamics of military, education and health expenditure is once again severely affected by the lack of data. The dynamic comparison must indeed be limited to the very first years of transition. It appears that SPC is effectively characterised by lower military expenditure (def). This expenditure also declines steadily (more than 8 per cent per year) throughout the first five years of post-conflict transition. The decline seems, however, to be even faster in the UPC state in the first two years of transition. However, we have to stress that much of this decline is driven by the variations in the size of the military in Angola. Most of the other countries in UPC increase, albeit only marginally, their military expenditure between the first and the second year of post-conflict transition.

CONCLUSIONS

In this chapter, we have studied the role of fiscal policy in determining the success or failure of post-conflict transition. Our idea is that fiscal policy is relevant because it can significantly affect the payoffs of the conflicting parties, thus strengthening (or weakening) their commitment to the peace agreement. We have then looked at the issue from an empirical perspective. Using a large collection of fiscal policy variables for the group of war-torn African countries, we have found that the fiscal dimension does matter, even after controlling for other possible determinants of war and peace. With respect to the specific case of the post-conflict transition, our key results can be summarised as follows. The success of post-conflict transition does not require downsizing the government. On the contrary, successful post-conflict transitions are on average characterised by an increase in the size of the government. However, this increase occurs in such a way that the overall stability of public finances is not heavily compromised: both expenditures and revenues increase at a comparable pace. Moreover, in successful post-conflict transitions, the increase in government size involves an increase in the incidence of capital expenditure relative to government consumption (whose contribution to horizontal redistribution is questionable). On the revenue side, budgetary grants appear to strengthen the chances of success. At the same time, and contrary to common sense intuition, a larger burden of debt does not seem to compromise the probability of successfully completing the post-conflict transition.

From our results, we can draw a few policy recommendations that we believe are also relevant to non-African post-conflict countries. First of all, countries in post-conflict transition should not pursue fiscal stability through a reduction in the size of government. On the contrary, there is need for a larger government in the first years after a war, so government expenditure should increase. However, this increase should not significantly exceed the rate of expansion of revenues. With the end of the conflict, the potential for tax collection will increase and government ought to strengthen their efforts in this direction. A balanced expansion of revenues and expenditures is likely to be more conducive to the success of the post-conflict transition than government downsizing.

Second, while expanding the overall size of the government, countries should also adjust the scope of the government. In this context, it appears to be important to promote capital expenditure, which is expected to strengthen the peace dividend over time.[6] The proportion of government consumption in total expenditure should correspondingly decrease and possibly more space should be given to targeted forms of redistribution to address horizontal inequalities between the fighting parties. Unfortunately, we have limited data on education and health expenditure, but the little evidence we presented seems to suggest that the reallocation of resources from the military to the provision of public education and health will strengthen peace through two complementary effects: (i) a larger peace dividend and (ii) dynamically efficient redistribution.

Third, financial assistance in the form of budgetary grants might be more important than debt relief in the first years of post-conflict transition, at least from the perspective of maintaining peace. Because the debt burden does not appear to affect the chances of success, whereas grants do, the international community should consider a new approach in assisting post-conflict economies: in the immediate aftermath of a war, debt cancellation ought to be replaced by direct budgetary assistance to compensate the weak capacity of governments to mobilise domestic resources. Of course, in the medium term, debt cancellation will remain important to improve the development prospects of the country.

NOTES

1. See for instance the recent special issue of the *Journal of Peace Research*, *45*(4), 2008.

2. Government downsizing has been for long a common practice in reforming the public sector of developing economies. This view was still implicit in the Washington Consensus of the mid 1990s. However, it has since then progressively changed (see USAID, 2005 and UNDESA, 2005 for a discussion of different approaches). Our results suggest that from the perspective of peace stabilisation, a reform of the public sector that involves government downsizing might be particularly risky.

3. This is a standard approach in the literature. An empirical justification for this choice comes from the observation that the post-conflict risk sharply decreases after ten years from the end of the previous war (see Collier & Hoeffler, 2004 and Collier et al., 2008b). The results of our analysis change somewhat when we define post-conflict as the five (rather than ten) years after the end of a conflict, but the main qualitative implications and recommendations concerning the use of fiscal policy remain the same.

4. We include the 15 completed *SPC* and the 15 *UPC*, but we exclude the ongoing post-conflicts. We make, however, an exception for the three ongoing post-conflicts that started in 2001 (Sierra Leone, Algeria and DRC). As of 2009, these countries are entering the ninth year of consecutive peace and all available information suggest that peace is likely to last for an additional year. We, therefore, include these three ongoing stabilisation episodes as *SPC*. The results of our empirical analysis are not qualitatively different when the three episodes are excluded.

5. The alternative approach is to instrument the potentially endogenous variables. We reran our model using lagged values of the potentially endogenous regressors, as instruments and results are not qualitatively different from those reported in the text. Instrumental variable estimates are available from the authors upon request.

6. We stress the complementary between this recommendation and Boulding's (1946) advice to rebuild assets as peace stabilisation tool in the aftermath of World War II.

ACKNOWLEDGMENTS

We would like to thank Oumar Diallo, the editors Jurgen Brauer and Ben Goldsmith, participants at the Third Australasian Conference on the Economics and Politics of War and Peace (Sydney, 26–27 June, 2009), and participants at the 32nd Conference of the African Studies Association of the Australasia and Pacific (Brisbane, 30 September–2 October, 2009) for very helpful comments. The authors are solely responsible for any remaining errors and inconsistencies. The views expressed in this chapter are those of the authors and do not necessarily represent the official position of the United Nations Economic Commission for Africa or any other agency of the United Nations System.

REFERENCES

Beck, T., Clarke, G., Groff, A., Keefer, P., & Walsh, P. (2001). New tools in comparative political economy: The database of political institutions. *World Bank Economic Review, 15*, 165–176.

Boulding, K. E. (1946). *The economics of peace*. New York: Prentice Hall.

Boyce, J. K., & O'Donnell, M. (2007). *Peace and the public purse*. Centre on International Cooperation Studies in Multilateralism. London: Rienner Publishers.

Collier, P. (2009). Post-conflict recovery: How should strategies be distinctive? *Journal of African Economies, 18*, i99–i131.

Collier, P., & Hoeffler, A. (1998). On economic causes of civil war. *Oxford Economic Papers, 50*, 563–573.

Collier, P., & Hoeffler, A. (2004). Greed and greviance in civil war. *Oxford Economic Papers, 56*, 563–595.

Collier, P., & Hoeffler, A. (2006). Military expenditure in post-conflict societies. *Economics of Governance, 7*, 89–106.

Collier, P., Hoeffler, A., & Rohner, D. (2008a). Beyond greed and grievance: Feasibility and civil war. *Oxford Economic Papers, 61*, 1–27.

Collier, P., Hoeffler, A., & Soderbom, M. (2008b). Post-conflict risks. *Journal of Peace Research, 45*, 461–748.

Fearon, J., & Laitin, D. (2003). Ethnicity, insurgency, and civil war. *American Political Science Review, 97*, 75–90.

Gleditsch, K. (2004). A revised list of wars between and within independent states, 1816–2002. *International Interactions, 30*, 231–262.

Greene, W. (2008). *Econometric analysis* (6th ed.). Upper Saddle River, NJ: Pearson Prentice Hall.

Humphreys, N. (2005). Natural resources, conflict and conflict resolution. *Journal of Conflict Resolution, 49*(4), 508–537.

La Porta, R., Lopez-de-Silanes, F., Shleifer, A., & Vishny, R. (1999). The quality of government. *Journal of Law, Economics, and Organizations, 15*, 222–279.

Lujala, P., Gleditsch, N., & Gilmore, E. (2005). A diamond curse? Civil war and a lootable resource. *Journal of Conflict Resolution, 49*, 538–562.

Miguel, E., Satyanath, S., & Sergenti, E. (2004). Economic shocks and civil conflict: An instrumental variables approach. *Journal of Political Economy, 112*, 725–753.

O'Neill, B. (1994). Game theory models of peace and war. In: R. Aumann & S. Hart (Eds), *Handbook of game theory* (Vol. 2, pp. 996–1053). New York: Elsevier Science.

UNDESA. (2005). Unlocking the Human Potential for Public Sector Performance. World Public Sector Reform 2005. United Nations Department of Economic and Social Affairs, New York. Available at http://unpanl.un.org/intradoc/groups/public/documents/un/unpan0216161.pdf

UNDP. (2008). Post-conflict recovery: Enabling local ingenuity. United Nations Development Programme, New York. Available at http://www.undp.org/cpr/we_do/eco_recovery.shtml

USAID. (2005). Reforming public administration in post-conflict societies. U.S. Agency for International Development, Washington, DC Available at http://pdf.usaid.gov/pdf_docs/PNADG326.pdf

APPENDIX. VARIABLES DEFINITION

Name	Code	Definition
Fiscal variables in percent of GDP[a]		
Total expenditure	exp	Total expenditure and net lending include both current and capital (development) expenditures and includes lending minus repayments
Total revenues	rev	Total revenue and grants equal the sum of government revenue and grants. Revenue includes all nonrepayable and nonrepaying government receipts other than grants. Grants are defined as unrequited, nonrepayable, noncompulsory receipts
Government consumption	gov	Current expenditure on goods and services comprises payments of wages and salaries in cash to employees (including the armed forces) before deduction of withholding taxes and employees' contributions to social security and pension funds, as well as employers' contributions to superannuation schemes outside government, and other purchases of goods and services (wages and salaries in kind, office supplies and maintenance charges, etc.)
Wages and salaries	wages	Wages and salaries consist of all payments in cash, but not in kind, to central government employees in return for services rendered, before deduction of withholding taxes and employees contributions to social security and pension funds
Current expenditure	exp_c	Total current expenditure includes requited payments other than for capital assets or for goods or services to be used in the production of capital assets, and unrequited payments for purposes other than permitting the recipients to acquire capital assets
Capital expenditure	exp_k	Expenditure for acquisition of land, intangible assets, government stocks and nonmilitary and nonfinancial assets; also for capital grants and lending minus repayments
Defence expenditure	def	Data generally cover expenditures of the Ministry of Defence (excluded are expenditures on public order and safety, which are classified separately)
Health expenditure	health	Public health expenditure consists of recurrent and capital spending from government (central and local) budgets, external borrowings and grants (including donations from international agencies and nongovernmental organisations) and social (or compulsory) health insurance funds

APPENDIX. (*Continued*)

Name	Code	Definition
Education expenditure	edu	Total public expenditure is current and capital public expenditure on education plus subsidies to private education at the primary, secondary and tertiary levels by local, regional and national government including municipalities (household contributions excluded)
Nontax revenues	rev_ntx	Receipts from sources other than the tax system, like property income, fees, fines and contributions to government employee pension funds within government
External capital grants	grt_k	Grants are unrequited, nonrepayable, noncompulsory receipts of government from other governments or international institutions. In determination of the deficit/surplus, grants are grouped with revenue and expenditure rather than with financing
Total current grants	grt_c	Grants include grants from other foreign governments, international organisations and other government units
Total government debt	debt	Debt is the entire stock of direct government fixed-term contractual obligations to others outstanding on a particular date. It includes domestic and foreign liabilities such as currency and money deposits, securities other than shares and loans. It is the gross amount of government liabilities reduced by the amount of equity and financial derivatives held by the government (end year)
Overall budget balance including current grants	bal_ov_grt	Defined as total revenue including current grants minus total expenditure and net lending (author's definition)
Overall budget balance excluding current grants	bal_ov	Defined as the overall budget balance including current grants minus total current grants (author's definition)
Current budget balance including current grants	bal_c_grt	Defined as total current revenues including grants minus total current expenditure (author's definition)
Current budget balance excluding current grants	bal_c	Defined as the current budget balance including current grants minus total current grants (author's definition)
Primary budget balance including current grants	bal_prim_grt	Defined as total revenue including grants minus current expenditure net of interest on debt (both domestic and external) (author's definition)

APPENDIX. (*Continued*)

Name	Code	Definition
Primary budget balance excluding current grants	bal_prim	Defined as the primary budget balance including grants minus total current grants (author's definition)
Fiscal variables in proportion of revenues and/or expenditures[a]		
Current expenditure	exp_c_p	Current expenditure in proportion of total expenditures
Government consumption	gov_p	Government consumption in proportion of total expenditure
Wages and salaries	wages_p	Wages and salaries in proportion of current expenditure
Interest on debt	int_p	Interest accrued on outstanding domestic and external debt in proportion of current expenditure
Nontax revenues	rev_ntx_p	Nontax revenues in proportion of total revenues
Other variables		
Per capita GDP	gdp_pc	GDP per capita is gross domestic product divided by midyear population. Data are expressed in constant US dollars and log-transformed[b]
Growth	growth	Annual percent change of per capita GDP[b]
Ethnic fractionalisation	ethnix	Probability that two randomly selected individuals are not of the same ethnic group[c]
Quality of the polity	polity	Quality of the polity defined in terms of democracy and autocracy. The variable takes values between −10 (absolute autocracy) and +10 (perfect democracy)[d]
Time of elections	legelec	Dummy variable taking value 1 in years when a legislative election was held[e]

[a] *Source:* African Development Indicators, World Bank and National Statistical Offices.
[b] *Source:* World Development Indicators (World Bank).
[c] *Source:* La Porta, Lopez-de-Silanes, Shleifer, and Vishny (1999).
[d] *Source:* Polity IV database.
[e] *Source:* Database of Political Institutions (Beck, Clarke, Groff, Keefer, & Walsh, 2001).

Chronology of civil wars in African countries and availability of fiscal data

	War	Successful Post-Conflict Episodes (SPC)	Unsuccessful Post-Conflict Episodes (SPC)	Ongoing Post-Conflict Episodes (OPC)	Fiscal Data Available Since
Chad	1966–1971	1991–2000	1972–1979		1983
	1980–1988				
	1990		1989		
Nigeria	1967–1970	1985–1994	1971–1979		1985
	1980–1981		1982–1983		
	1984				
Rwanda	1963–1964	1965–1974	1995–1997		1980
	1990–1994	1999–2006			
	1998				
Mozambique	1979–1992	1993–2002			1980
Liberia	1989–1990		1991	2004–	2001
	1992–1996		1997–1999		
	2000–2003				
Guinea-Bissau	1998	1999–2008			1984
Sierra Leone	1991–1996		1997	2001–	1980
	1998–2000				
South Africa	1989–1993		1994–1998	2003–	1973
	1999–2002				
Sudan	1965–972	1973–1982	1993–1994	2006–	1984
	1983–1992				
	1995–2006				
Zimbabwe	1972–1979	1980–1989			1980
Algeria	1962–1963	1964–1973		2001–	1967
	1992–2000				
Angola	1975–1994		1995–1997	2002–	1985
	1998–2001				
Burundi	1972	1973–1982	1989–1990	2002–	1980
	1988				
	1991–1998		1999		
	2000–2001				
Cameroon	1959–1961	1962–1971			1980
Democratic Rep. of Congo	1965	1966–1975	1994–1995	2001–	1996
	1993				
	1996–2000				
Congo	1997–1999	2000–2009			1984
Uganda	1966	1967–1976	1989–1995	2002–	1984
	1980–1988				
	1996–2001				
Ethiopia	1974–1991	1992–2001			1981

Sources: Gleditsch (2004) and CIA World Factbook (2009 issue). Fiscal data are taken from the African Development Database of the World Bank.

CHAPTER 9

THE COLLIER CHALLENGE: HOW CAN RELIABLE TRANSITIONAL FINANCING SYSTEMS BE CREATED IN 'BARELY FUNCTIONAL' STATES?

Andrew Ladley and Jessie Williams

ABSTRACT

Purpose – *This chapter uses the work of Oxford economist Paul Collier to explore the conditions under which financing systems can be created to support the governance and economies of fragile states. This support is especially needed in the immediacy of a crisis or as a practical strategy to potentially change the dynamics of a particularly vulnerable state. The focus is on his 2008 proposal for Haiti, for a partnership of domestic and international financial institutions. Central to the proposal is the establishment of an Independent Service Authority (ISA) to fund and implement government policy, especially in delivery of basic services. Representatives from aid donors, Haitian expatriates or diaspora and members of the government would sit on the ISA board, sharing responsibility for effectively administering public funds. This model was proposed to the United Nations in late 2008 to stabilise and transform the government and economy of Haiti (Collier, 2008, 2009b).*

Economics of War and Peace: Economic, Legal, and Political Perspectives
Contributions to Conflict Management, Peace Economics and Development, Volume 14, 147–165

ISSN: 1572-8323/doi:10.1108/S1572-8323(2010)0000014013

Methodology – *The chapter explores the issues raised in the model using a case study of the Regional Assistance Mission in the Solomon Islands (RAMSI).*

Findings – *"The work concludes that the RAMSI process worked well to stabilise financial systems and survived significant political challenge due to a framework of local agreements, regional or international resolutions, treaties, statutes and contracts. This suggests that such a framework will help to 'buttress' any mixed local–international financial institutions in the event of domestic political or legal contest in Haiti (or wherever else this model is considered).*

Limitations – *The chapter does not compare Haiti and the Solomon Islands as societies or economies, or go into the details of how the proposed financial institutions would operate and transition to other arrangements. Space also prevents consideration of the other international partnership models applied in Haiti from 2006–08 (e.g. the Haiti Economic Governance Reform Operation or EGRO; see the case study on Haiti by Bradford and Scott (forthcoming), 76–84). After the earthquake in January 2010, Collier re-visited Haiti and stressed the importance of longer-term economic transformation (a Haiti Marshall plan) as well as emergency relief.* A key element of the international community's assistance will be finding mechanisms to handle finances. However the details of the new proposals are yet to be made public, hence this chapter focuses solely on Collier's 2008 proposals.*

INTRODUCTION

This chapter explores one key aspect of the governance and service delivery proposals in the development model put forward by Oxford economist Professor Paul Collier for Haiti in 2008 (well before the current earthquake crisis), which suggests a radical approach to service delivery using an alliance of donors, expatriates and government. This is intended to provide reliable financial receipt and delivery mechanisms at a time when the state's

*Collier, P., & Warnholz, J.-L. (2010a). Haiti earthquake: Social and economic fabric must be rebuilt too. The Guardian, Sunday, 17 January. Available at http://www.guardian.co.uk/world/2010/jan/17/haitiearthquake-social-fabric-rebuilt; Collier, P., & Warnholz, J.-L. (2010b). We need a Marshall plan for Haiti. Globe and Mail, 13 January. Available at http://www.theglobeandmail.com/news/opinions/we-need-amarshall-plan-for-haiti/article1430309/

systems are either broken or untrustworthy to citizens and donors. To this end, this chapter:

- identifies the fundamentals found by Collier to support economic development in the world's poorest nations and in post-conflict states;
- explains the structure and function of the Independent Service Authority model proposed for Haiti;
- outlines the way in which compacts or codes and charters could be used as a form of shared sovereignty between the international community and a government to reduce conflict, and;
- discusses the use of security guarantees by external forces.

The chapter then compares the Collier proposals with the Regional Assistance Mission in the Solomon Islands (RAMSI) from 2003, arguing that the mission provided a governance model analogous to the institutions proposed for Haiti. It outlines the structure and function of the RAMSI intervention, the use of domestic internationalised financial institutions (DIFIs), and domestic political opposition to these institutions. It concludes that a range of local agreements, regional or international resolutions treaties, statues and contracts is needed to buttress DIFIs and protect them from political and legal challenges.

FUNDAMENTALS OF REBUILDING FRAGILE STATES

Collier contends that it is possible (indeed essential) to assist fragile or 'post-conflict' states by engaging a range of domestic and international partners to re-build the financial and service delivery systems. He argues that an innovative approach to service delivery is needed at a time when the state's systems are either broken or untrustworthy to citizens and donors. A partnership approach, essentially bypassing government service delivery in fragile states, would seem logical. On the one hand, citizens want peace, along with rapid delivery of goods, services, infrastructure and jobs. On the other hand, donors want reliable spending of substantial funding essential for that delivery and the transformation that should reduce the risks of further instability and conflict.

Collier's proposal, made at the invitation of the UN Secretary General in 2008, forms the basis of a comprehensive package to stabilise and transform the government and economy in Haiti (Collier, 2008). Haiti seems an appropriate candidate for this kind of innovation. Its problems appear to have grown more intractable, not less, including systemic instability, weakness of institutions, population bulge, urban slums, organised crime and violence. Rated one of the poorest and most corrupt countries in the Western Hemisphere (Transparency International, 2008), at least six separate UN missions have sought to promote governance reforms since the early 1990s, with little success. The country's dire circumstances were compounded by a series of hurricanes in 2008 and a world food crisis. Further challenges confronted it in 2009 including the global recession and relational impact on remittances. Yet Collier (2008) argues that it is not only possible to launch economic development initiatives in Haiti, but it is an 'imperative' (p. 1).

He identifies a number of fundamentals that support economic development in Haiti (Collier, 2008, p. 5):

- security is being provided by Brazilian peacekeepers under the auspices of the UN who are undaunted by Cité Soleil (the shanty town in the capital city);
- a favourable trade deal has been struck with the United States (albeit short-term) and a fledgling garment manufacturing industry is developing, and;
- political leadership is 'good by the standards of most post-conflict situations', providing an important change in a country known for leaders seeking to serve themselves rather than the people.

Collier argues that the 'youth tsunami' coming down the demographic track means an immediate combined US and Canadian (and UN) drive for a rapid transition out of fragility and towards longer-term transformation is an imperative. He estimates that the UN mission in Haiti (MINUSTAH) will cost around USD 5 billion, which, if there is no change, would be more like humanitarian than development assistance (i.e. without any transformation). Economic security, he asserts, must supersede the temporary establishment of UN military security. Otherwise any social order created will be temporary.

This plan must be seen in the context of Collier's recent work, including particularly *The Bottom Billion* (2007) and *War, Guns and Votes* (2009). His essential argument is the need for evidence to drive new approaches to bridge effective governmental failure, especially for states of the 'bottom billion' (people in abject poverty). Developed states and a good bulk of middle-income states, are broadly doing ok. But, left alone, the bottom billion states will be unable to escape from a series of 'development traps' (Collier, 2007a, 2008, 2009a, 2009b). Failure to address these issues is not acceptable in humanitarian as well as economic terms. Hence in his data-driven suggestions, Collier argues that the assumptions of traditional peace-building, state-building, development and electoral systems in these places, need to be reconsidered and effective alternatives developed.

Collier's proposals to the United Nations (UN) regarding Haiti in December 2008 produced work on implementation by the UN mission, local authorities, key regional states, some major international investors and donors from early 2009. Yet by the end of 2009, no final form had emerged, not least because of the collapse of the government that had been the principal backer of the proposals. However, the proposals remain on the table for the new government.[1]

The Haiti plan is outlined below and then compared with another post-conflict state-building case, the Regional Assistance Mission in Solomon Islands (RAMSI). The entire RAMSI exercise, starting from 2003 and including the current adapted version six years down the track, appears to have been conducted without reference to Collier's work. And in turn, Collier makes no apparent reference in his work under review, to RAMSI. Despite the obvious differences, we think this 'blind' practical example is a real-world opportunity to reflect on the Collier model of building financial institutions. Our conclusion is that there is considerable work to be done on what we call the *Collier challenge*. In particular, it is questionable whether the proposal for a coalition of donors and citizens to deliver services and a stable financial system is feasible. We suggest that conflict within the government is likely to limit the longevity of such a model. We stress the importance of a wide range of mechanisms to 'buttress' any such financial institutions against the inevitable political challenges that they will face.

SUPPORTING GOVERNANCE IN FRAGILE STATES: THE INDEPENDENT SERVICE AUTHORITY MODEL

Collier's key proposal is to establish an Independent Service Authority (ISA) to counter the 'deep-seated' weaknesses of the public sector. This would pave the way for the plan's export and investment initiatives, along with infrastructure development and service delivery – all of which require financial intervention from the government, supported by donors and the contracting of NGOs.

As 'a public agency outside the civil service, somewhat analogous to an independent central bank or an Independent Revenue Authority, which implements government policy but does not set policy', the ISA would have three functions:

- receiving funds from donor governments and any other potential sources (which would be included in the national budget process);
- channelling such funds to NGO and private service providers by entering into contracts with them, and;
- monitoring the performance of such providers in a way that is comparable and could generate 'yardstick competition', and shield service delivery from the patrimony and corruption that is common within the target states (Collier, 2008, p. 14).[2]

A board would oversee the ISA with the majority of members from the government, as well as representatives from the donors and other pertinent actors (such as the Haitian diaspora, to also attract funding from them). As a result, donors would be 'co-responsible for the honest and efficient operation of funding for basic social services ... once donors saw that the system was effective, they would then have the reassurance necessary for funding to be increased' (Collier, 2008, p. 15). The 'solid base of evidence' would help Haiti tap new funding sources, such as the Gates Foundation. Donors would gradually channel current funding of NGOs through the ISA to get it up and running. Rather than being a short-term fix, the ISA may, if successful, become a permanent institution with appropriate scrutiny.

As for implementation, Collier invited the Haitian Government to examine the package to decide if it would be useful. If not, the whole idea would be 'quietly forgotten'. Speed would be essential if the government wanted to take the ideas forward (Collier, 2008, p. 18). By the end of 2009, it had become clear that despite some dramatic early indications of support from the UN, surrounding states, donors, investors and the government of Haiti, fragility of the government itself was a major stumbling block. At the time of writing, the proposals await the buy-in of the new Prime Minister Jean-Max Bellerive, who was confirmed in November 2009 after Michele Pierre-Louis was fired by the Senate for allegedly failing to improve the country's economy.

In terms of the receipt and expenditure of funds for public purposes (not private investment), the ISA aspect of the proposal can be seen as the lynchpin – no ISA, no funding, no plan and no investment on the back of the promised political and financial stability. The logic behind the financing system proposal is simple: the need for a reliable mechanism of receiving and distributing public funds.[3] Such reliability would give confidence to both investors and donors. The ISA proposal would by-pass core functions of the state as traditionally conceived (centralising funds for public expenditure). Indeed, this is the precise purpose, based on the argument that the state was in this respect (and in others) essentially dysfunctional.

Collier proposed that both donor money and government money could be handled through the ISA, which would be responsible for writing contracts, scrutinising contractor performance, reallocating money according to performance. Rather than assuming that the state had to perform these functions itself, it was preferable to rely on systems that work, regardless of whether they are public, private or the non-profit sector. The central premise, supported by the OECD's Fragile States Group (2008), states that the contracted-out services or functions should enable the state to strengthen its capacity and legitimacy over time. For voters/citizens some effective delivery and improvements seemed to be a key to the legitimacy of the state itself.

COMPACTS TO PRODUCE SHARED GOVERNANCE BETWEEN NATIONAL AND INTERNATIONAL STAKEHOLDERS

In his wider work, Collier is enthusiastic about negotiating codes, standards and charters for everything from managing natural resource revenue to budget transparency and for democracy generally. Simplifying the arguments, he proposes compacts at the international level and with local actors and authorities (the best available), for transitional arrangements with shared governance to establish the conditions for longer-term stability and state functioning without major violence. Core arrangements would include, for example, a voluntary code of electoral accountability in return for international security guarantees against coups; regional cooperation in reducing military expenditure; and ISA-like institutions, or what we call DIFI.[4]

These post conflict compacts would better protect service delivery from future war and conflict-related problems. Donors would commit to a long period of substantial aid to rebuild the economy and the Security Council or bi-lateral body would agree to long-term security provision. In return for this pledge of money and security, the government would commit not to cross a series of red lines. In a post-conflict context, it is unlikely that any government would be more than transitional. Therefore, parties to the particular conflict would need to sign formal agreements to create the DIFI, to respect its integrity, to refrain from disturbing its activities and from trying to misuse the institution or affiliated service delivery institutions for their own strategic purposes, and potentially to protect it. These parties would be incentivised to enter such compacts for a range of advantages, including showing their supporters that foreign funds will be transferred to deliver services (e.g. education and health). In bringing parties together in dialogue around such compacts, the process would be part of peace and reconciliation objectives.

HOW SECURITY MIGHT BE DELIVERED IN FRAGILE STATES

The UN states that half of the countries emerging from violent conflict revert to conflict within five years (Secretary General, 2005). Reflecting on this tendency, Collier argues that foreign commitment to long-term security should entail occasional armed interventions. These would not only be to restore law and order, but provide the necessary space for governance reforms to cement. In the event that an elected government, abiding by agreed 'compacts' (including compliance with the code of electoral conduct), was overthrown by a military coup, requests by the host government would trigger military intervention by capable states (or combinations of states). Mostly, these would be 'over the horizon' guarantees, meaning states would airlift forces to put down local military takeovers.

This would require much longer commitments, such as a decade of peace enforced by external military force. In this context, national sovereignty issues are less relevant than efficacy: 'to be effective, an external presence requires troops with a mandate to fight to preserve the peace, as well as contributing governments willing to accept causalities' (Collier, 2007a, p. 177). Collier points to the former French colonies in Africa that were (until the guarantees were withdrawn) less likely than other comparably poor countries to experience civil war because the French gave informal security guarantees to governments (Collier, 2007b, p. 16767). Such external security guarantees would allow for the downsising of the state's own army (e.g. seen in Mozambique). In his analysis, the military forces of weak states are often extortion rackets largely responsible for leaking donor money.

Thus Collier's proposals are starkly in the mould of 'get-over-all-that-post-colonial-blame' economic realism. His writing is driven by statistics, research, stories of what-actually-happens-to-the-money and, wherever possible, by local voices demanding more from their feuding warlords, corrupt leaders, dysfunctional governments and misled electorates. Risk management (not risk elimination) is a key feature. So is the probing consideration of *incentives*, both for the economy and for political participation by all concerned. In this respect, his work is classic political economy as he builds an evidence-based case for the application of economic theory to raw politics. What are the incentives, for example, that structure decisions to resort to violence in government, or incentives for corruption, and how might these be changed? It is possible, he argues, to reduce post-conflict governance risks by a combination of mutually reinforcing steps aimed at economic recovery, external guarantees of peacekeeping, fairer elections and internationally supported public service delivery – all sustained at least over a 10-year period. In this context, the international community is required to pay for the transition of the 'bottom billion' and the process must be sustained by restructured incentives that hold the players to a non-violent *shared governance*.

There are of course critics. Most obviously, some cite sovereignty issues, paternalism or even neo-colonialism. Collier's approach seems to emphasise initial local consent, and then to search for something that might work to change things, including strategies to support local reformers overwhelmed by corruption, nepotism, populist (and often racist) slogans and militarism.

BUTTRESSING

The categories of states under discussion by definition need financial support for almost every state function. But even if funds are available (from taxes or donors), it is an important requirement to have reliable mechanisms to ensure proper receipt and delivery. Major 'leaks', including corruption, military 'capture' and inadequate systems/expertise impede development strategies in these fragile states. Hence, the proposal for DIFIs are a hybrid mixture of international of domestic systems for the collection and delivery of funds.

Although, DIFIs are proposed as a development strategy for the 'bottom billion' states (generally poor, fragile, institutionally weak, partly democratic with major problems of violence, corruption, etc.) the ideas may be relevant to a host of other situations. For example, electoral and governance incentives are almost always at risk of being 'skewed' in states with substantial national resource revenues (e.g. Libya, East Timor). Perversely, having lots of oil, diamonds, logs, fish or uranium, seems to fuel rather than reduce conflict.

The logic for DIFIs applies particularly to the critical period between war and consolidated peace. A major goal in that period is to get people busy, re-establishing infrastructure, state and economic institutions, state services like schools, getting work for demobilised soldiers, rebuilding homes, getting markets functioning, etc. But without reliable financial systems, it is extremely difficult to manage with probity large amounts of foreign aid or domestic revenues (assuming availability), especially in the golden window when good spending could add most value.

Focusing on the application of this thinking to any specific example, we can return to the general question of why any domestic political competitors/ incumbents might agree to set up a DIFI. And if they did agree initially, what happens when key leaders tire of the shared arrangements? These simple questions are not idle, as the discussions in Port au Prince in 2009 over Collier's proposals make clear. Other examples show the same tensions – a partly internationalised mechanism to manage the oil money of Chad fell over once the incumbents fully grasped the possibilities of diverting the revenue for militarisation (Kroslak, 2009). The relevant implementing legislation was amended and the country toppled into an ongoing conflict.

Collier's Haiti ISA proposal invites *shared sovereignty* in a compact between the international community and the government – and, effectively, with the people of Haiti. Of course, 'government' in Haiti does not always speak with one voice in its executive or legislative branches. Also, in Haiti and elsewhere, constitutional challenges may have to be faced in the courts. We therefore argue that even if there is initial agreement to these sorts of financial arrangements, they need to be supported by as much 'buttressing' as possible. There is a substantial array of possible supporting arrangements. For Haiti, the list could include:

- UN or Organisation of American State resolutions, treaties (with major regional states);
- domestic legislation;
- constitutional amendments;
- arrangements for international personnel to staff the ISA and relevant agencies;
- contracts and monitoring arrangements (to generate the evidence on which the whole delivery of services by contract depends);
- some means of connecting directly with the public;
- some clear means of dispute resolution (involving the ISA, donors and government), and;
- implementation of systems for settling investment disputes.

All these arrangements will buttress the proposal for DIFIs. Such buttressing can be seen as staking and anchoring fragile new plants against wind damage, along with regular watering and some protection from goats and rabbits that might eat the plants. Collier stresses speed to capture momentum and outpace recidivists. Speed would indeed get the plant into the ground. Our stress is on buttressing for making the proposals durable against opposition.

In some societies emerging from conflict it is difficult to find plausible and legitimate negotiating partners to give the consent necessary for shared arrangements. This will especially be the case if the systems are intended to be put into place as part of peace processes, often before elections. Who would genuinely 'consent' for Somalia, for example? Which voices could one rely upon in the current post-'global political agreement' Zimbabwe?

The proposal for shared sovereignty arrangements and an independent financial institution to implement the development strategy should add new dimensions to peace negotiations. On the one hand, it could complicate the processes in seeking agreements from protagonists (often, combatant leaders) about shared sovereignty arrangements in advance of elections or any clear system of government. On the other hand, looking for such agreements at a time when all might benefit might be the best time to get such agreement. Again, we would stress the need not only for initial agreement, however complex this might be, but also for buttressing, right from the start.

COMPARING THE MODEL WITH THE RAMSI

We argue that the RAMSI intervention in Solomon Islands (2003 onwards) can be seen as an interesting test of the Collier thesis, albeit in very different (and more favourable) circumstances than in Haiti. The widespread social unrest that broke out in 1999 between the indigenous inhabitants of Guadalcanal and settlers from the adjacent island of Malaita developed into a low-level armed conflict between opposing ethnic militias and continued after the signing of the Townsville Peace Agreement in 2000 with a complete breakdown of law and order. What Patrick Chabal and Jean-Pascall Daloz (1999) refer to as the 'instrumentalisation of disorder' whereby criminality becomes a key political instrument, culminated in the effective capture and ransacking of the state by a relatively small cohort of corrupt leaders, ex-militants and renegade police officers. Government could not meet debt obligations or supply basic services. In addition, the central government could not fund provincial governments for service provision (health, education, agricultural extension, etc.), which resulted in the collapse of those services (Frankel, 2004).

An independent authority – the Solomon Islands Rehabilitation Authority (SIRA) – was initially proposed to take over government in the areas of law and order and financial management (Wainwright, 2003). The government would have continued to run the remaining policy areas, with substantial input from SIRA (Fullilove, 2006). This plan, however, was regarded by Australia as too intrusive of sovereignty and the approach eventually adopted and deployed in July 2003 was a unique kind of authority. RAMSI was not a transitional administration but a regional framework for assistance. The official aim outlined in the framework document stated that 'strengthened assistance will address the most serious specific threats to security and economic recovery in Solomon Islands' (Solomon Islands Government, 2003).

The package came with security. RAMSI was a police-led operation, backed by (the unused threat of) military force. Officers of RAMSI's participating police force were not *advisors*, but investigators with full domestic police powers under Solomon Islands law. The results were dramatic. Law and order was quickly restored. Security also meant a functioning judiciary, restorative justice projects and facilities such as prisons. RAMSI funded prosecutors, lawyers, judges, magistrates and court administration and logistics personnel, not just the police. In addition to re-establishing law and order, the plan established the Budget Stabilisation Program. The priority of the Solomon Islands Government (SIG), with the assistance of RAMSI, was to provide greater fiscal and economic management of the Solomon Islands' haemorrhaging public finances.

RAMSI's economic governance pillar focused on providing advisors and in-line personnel to work with the government (mainly through the Ministry of Finance and Treasury) to stabilise government finances. The short-term objectives of controlling expenditure and stabilising the budget were again quickly met. In addition RAMSI:

- delivered a realistic 2004 budget that directed resources to meet basic social services and infrastructure maintenance needs;
- prepared a comprehensive debt management strategy to prioritise and find solutions to the large public debt and related arrears;
- cleaned up the public sector payroll;
- strengthened revenue collection through agencies like Customs and Inland Revenue, and;
- re-established scrutiny of proper payment systems (AusAID, 2004).

Public servants were paid on time and audit reports submitted to Parliament. In addition, an Australian Accountant General was appointed to approve payments from the public purse. RAMSI also worked with the government to reopen enterprises such as the Gold Ridge mine and the Guadalcanal plains palm oil plantation.

Overall coordination of RAMSI was exercised by a Special Coordinator's Office in Honiara headed by a senior Australian diplomat, and through a high-level inter-departmental committee in Canberra (Dinnen & Firth, 2008). The speed and peaceful manner in which RAMSI restored law and order and essential services and stabilised government finances attracted considerable praise (Fullilove, 2006). These achievements provide a welcome contrast with other international interventions. RAMSI was commended as 'a model for future deployment' (Watson, 2005). As well as delivering a fully funded budget in 2008, other recent initiatives include:

- developing the capacity of staff and systems in the Ministry of Finance and the Treasury;
- implementing anti-corruption measures which have reduced leakages particularly in Treasury and Inland Revenue;
- implementing accountability processes in Customs;
- providing foreign direct investment legislation and management, and;
- transparency of tax and duty exemptions.

The backlog of central government financial statements was eliminated and debt interest and trade creditor arrears were paid off (AusAID, 2008; George, 2008; Pacific Islands Forum, 2005; Winter, Schofield, & Duituturaga, 2008). Australia committed finances and resources to RAMSI until the end of 2013 (Osifelo, 2009b). The World Bank and Asian Development Banks have supported the process showing their trust in the accountability structures (Osifelo, 2009a).[5]

For our purposes, RAMSI established something analogous to the proposed institutions for Haiti. In-line international staff initially ran the budget process, accountability improved, donors approved, funds flowed (both from local revenue sources and donors) and a functioning state was quickly re-established. The example thus suggests that a DIFI-like arrangement worked essentially as Collier hoped. But we also need to appreciate the buttressing supports, without which RAMSI would have been kicked out the country some time ago.

HOW RAMSI WON AGREEMENT

A comprehensive legal framework underpins RAMSI. A prior regional framework under the auspices of the Pacific Islands Forum was central to these arrangements. In the Biketawa Declaration of 2000, the Forum heads of government and foreign ministers endorsed principles of good governance, democracy, the rule of law and human rights, and a security recognition of 'the need, in time of crisis or in response to members' request for assistance, for action to be taken on the basis of all members of the Forum being part of the extended Pacific Islands family' (Biketawa Declaration s.3).

RAMSI's mandate was also explicitly agreed between the SIG and the countries of the Pacific through the Pacific Islands Forum, at the time of the mission's deployment in 2003. The mandate sought to address the challenges that faced the Solomon Islands, including civil unrest and lawlessness, economic decline and stagnation, and a dramatic decline in government standards. The mandate covers: restoration of civil order; stabilisation of government finances; promotion of longer-term economic recovery and revival of business confidence and the rebuilding of government institutions or machinery. Endorsement of the mission also came from the UN Security Council and the UN Secretary General (although not by formal resolution).

In addition to this regional agreement, RAMSI was underpinned by a specific international treaty between the SIG and Australia, New Zealand, Fiji, Papua New Guinea, Samoa and Tonga establishing the mission's deployment and reflecting the agreed mandate. Further, a legal foundation was established in the domestic law of Solomon Islands, in the form of the *Facilitation of International Assistance Act 2003* passed unanimously by Parliament in July 2003. This Act incorporated the RAMSI treaty, thus giving direct legal domestic effect to it. The Act provides powers, privileges and immunities of the type agreed to by the Solomon Islands government in the RAMSI Treaty.

It was only after all this architecture was in place that assistance was requested under section 3 formally through notice given by the Governor General to the regional governments, to establish RAMSI and intervene in Solomon Islands.

HAS RAMSI OVERSTAYED ITS WELCOME?

To provide ongoing evaluation of this architecture, RAMSI established a Performance Framework in 2005 to enable its work to be assessed against publicly stated objectives. The evaluation process included:

- a People's Survey undertaken by an independent contractor with Solomon Islands survey staff to obtain information on the views of locals on issues of relevance;

- a performance report prepared by an independent group of experts (essentially representing the Forum);
- self-assessment mechanisms, and;
- oversight by the Solomon Islands Government/RAMSI Performance Assessment Working Group.

This process thus envisaged a direct appeal to the population, as well as close re-engagement of the region. It also came in a rapidly changing context after 2006. It is useful to summarise these events, simply because they illustrate what we regard as inevitable, that 'shared arrangements' will challenge local incumbents. The most dramatic evidence of trouble was in the major riots and arson in the capital Honiara that followed the general election and the apparent victory of one faction in securing office. In the wake of the riots, Prime Minister Sogavare took office and promptly attempted to set up a commission of inquiry into the cause of the riots. This was against RAMSI legal advice that an inquiry would prejudice immediate criminal legal action against two MPS facing charges for inciting the riots. Both of these MPs were strong supporters of the Prime Minister and hence essential for him to retain office (AusAID, 2008). There was also concern that the RAMSI police had failed to anticipate or control the riots (Moore, 2006). In September 2006 the SIG declared the Australian High Commissioner persona non grata, claiming he was interfering in domestic politics (Sogavare, 2006). A further concern was the SIG decision to appoint Julian Moti as its new Attorney General in 2006. In that position, Moti would have been responsible for the proposed inquiry. Moti was at the time wanted under Australian anti-paedophile legislation. Another link in the chain of strained relationships was the SIG attempt to rearm its local police, which saw the Australian Foreign Minister publish an open letter in a Solomon Islands newspaper defending RAMSI's achievements and warning of a 'deliberate push to undermine' it. Prime Minister Sogovare replied, accusing Australia of trying to run a 'parallel government' (Jones, 2007). But the population of Solomon Islands was strongly against re-arming police, since it was looted police weaponry that had plunged the country into crisis before 2003.

From 2006 onwards, thus, there were growing threats from the SIG to repeal the 2003 founding legislation, thus revoking consent and forcing RAMSI's removal. These threats failed, indeed, they backfired. A majority of MPs was needed to revoke the legislation – but Prime Minister Sogovare's government was toppled from office in a parliamentary vote of no confidence. RAMSI also faced constitutional legal challenge in the Solomon Islands courts but this also was unsuccessful.

Put simply, the Solomon Islands Prime Minister's administration lost office at least in significant measure due to its attempts to govern without the restrictions resulting from RAMSI's role in the administration. For our purposes, we highlight the 'buttresses' that had been comprehensively agreed by a predecessor parliament, by the region and, arguably, by the population itself. When the political context changed these original arrangements held, not least because the general public saw RAMSI's presence as crucial for security. A 2008 People's Survey reconfirms this as 86 per cent of respondents interviewed supported RAMSI's continued presence in the country (ANU Enterprise, 2008).

It is hard to find a more compelling case for 'buttressing' – including for some mechanisms of reaching directly to the people (surveys, in this case). In the event, the local government determined to oust RAMSI lost office itself. We note that this happened in a parliamentary system, which allowed a change of government by a confidence vote in Parliament.

CONCLUSION

In no way are we comparing Haiti and Solomon Islands as societies and economies, but on one topic at least – a role for transitional financial institutions – we think that the RAMSI experience offers some lessons. There may be different institutional ways of achieving reliable financial management, operating separately from weak or damaged institutions of government in fragile or post-conflict situations. We cannot explore the full spectrum of possibilities here but note that a combination of agreements, contracts and existing corporate bodies might work. Collier's challenge is to think differently and practically about solving problems, not keep working with sieves to handle funds. And his thesis is so full of 'real politik-economik' that he would be well aware that local politicians would inevitably at some point try to out-game the 'new treasury'.

In Haiti, and indeed anywhere the *Collier challenge* is taken up, an internationalised role in receiving and distributing funds provides an implicit challenge to the role of national government. As such, one should expect contest. Hence, arrangements made in a vulnerable period, may be renegotiated; compacts may be undone, contracts may be broken. These contests will be in politics, parliament, the courts, the region and, perhaps, in elections. For DIFIs to survive in these 'political kitchens', they have to 'prepare for the heat'. An extremely important aspect of the planning for DIFIs should therefore be gradual processes by which transitions can be made into reformed and fully domestic institutions. In this regard, recent case studies for the World Bank on fragile states set out particularly useful lessons for building carefully negotiated (with host governments) and appropriate public sector reforms into the transitional arrangements (Bradford & Scott, forthcoming).

In this context, *buttressing* for both crisis and transitional arrangements appears to be essential. In peace processes, a comprehensive framework of local agreements, regional or international resolutions, treaties, statutes and contracts will not exempt DIFIs from the inevitable political or legal challenge – but it should substantially improve the chances of durability. Collier argues that the space for transforming Haiti is a departing train – it needs to be caught or the opportunity will be missed. We do not disagree, but suggest that there should always be time for buttressing. The RAMSI buttressing was done in a remarkably short time – weeks. However, it was well-signposted, the region was prepared and ready, the Solomon Islands government was exhausted and hence willing to legislate, and the people were determined that the past should remain just that. In Haiti, and elsewhere, the conditions might not be so propitious. It would still be brave to launch a domestic international financial institution without the sort of buttressing set out in this chapter.

NOTES

1. One visible outcome of the reconstruction and development plan for Haiti occurred in September 2009 when Brazilian Foreign Minister Celso Amorim and US Trade Representative Ron Kirk agreed that Brazilian and US companies operating in Haiti will be able to export products to both countries duty-free under the terms of the US Haitian Hemispheric Opportunity (HOPE) programme.
2. The two models of aid distribution currently operating lack accountability, that is, aid given by donors to the respective government's budget (monopoly supply) and that given directly to NGOs for particular projects (project-based).
3. Contracting out and use of interim international personnel have occurred elsewhere and the DAC/OECD Fragile States Groups have had discussions on parallel cabinets for coordinating service delivery where local state structures are inadequate (OECD, 2006). Yet no full-fledged agency of this kind has been established (World Bank, 2002).
4. Similar to Collier's ISA, but with potentially wider application.
5. Criticisms have been made, many of which are heard in other interventions. Most of these call for adaptation of the mission rather than withdrawal. There are a number of inherent weaknesses and reforms that are ongoing to address issues of accountability and transparency, including addressing concerns over spending special funds like the Tsunami Disaster Relief Fund (see Petorius, Lokay, & Arumae, 2008). A number of other initiatives remain outside this process, including regional

and bi-lateral programmes. Concerns revolve around the fact that RAMSI advisers are perceived by local bureaucrats as contractors who are essentially working for private sector interests, rather than for the public service. Australia has also been criticised for using the programme to promote overseas business interests and private sector growth (see Anderson, 2008).

REFERENCES

Anderson, T. (2008). *The limits of RAMSI*. Sydney: AID/WATCH.

ANU Enterprise. (2008). *People's survey 2008*. Honiara: RAMSI.

AusAID. (2004). *Solomon Islands: Rebuilding an island economy*. Canberra: Commonwealth of Australia.

AusAID. (2008). *Annual program performance report for Solomon Islands 2007–08*. Canberra: Commonwealth of Australia.

Bradford, M., & Scott, G. (forthcoming). Developing robust economic governance systems – A project for the World Bank MDTF for Research and Knowledge Work on Fragile States.

Chabal, P., & Daloz, J. (1999). *Africa works: Disorder as political instrument*. Oxford: James Currey and Indiana University Press.

Collier, P. (2007a). *The bottom billion: Why the poorest countries are failing and what can be done about it*. Oxford: Oxford University Press.

Collier, P. (2007b). Poverty reduction in Africa. *Proceedings of the National Academy of Sciences of the USA*, *104*(43), 16763–16768.

Collier, P. (2008). *Haiti: From natural catastrophe to economic security. A report for the secretary general of the United Nations*. Oxford: Oxford University.

Collier, P. (2009a). *War, guns and votes: Democracy in dangerous places*. New York: Harper Collins.

Collier, P. (2009b). Beyond the begging bowl. *The Guardian*. Available at http://www.guardian.co.uk/commentisfree/2009/apr/03/haiti-security-aid-hope. Retrieved on Friday 3 April.

Dinnen, S., & Firth, S. (Eds). (2008). *Politics and statebuilding in the Solomon Islands*. Canberra: Asia Pacific Press, The Australian National University.

Frankel, J. (2004). *The manipulation of custom: From uprising to intervention in the Solomon Islands*. Sydney: Pandanus Books.

Fullilove, M. (2006). *The testament of Solomons: RAMSI and international state-building*. Sydney: Lowy Institute for International Policy.

George, T. (2008). *Submission by regional assistance mission to Solomon Islands special coordinator to the foreign relations committee, national parliament of Solomon Islands*. Honiara: RAMIS.

Jones, L. (2007). Calls to end Solomon Islands assistance. *The Australian*, 12 February.

Kroslak, D. (2009). Chad: The oil effect? *openDemocracy*. Available at http://www.opendemocracy.net/article/chad-the-oil-effect. Retrieved on 18 September.

Moore, C. (2006). 'Helpem Fren' the Solomon Islands and RAMSI 2003–2006. *National Presidents Forum 14 July 2006*, Australian Institute of International Affairs, Sydney.

OECD. (2008). *State building in fragile situations: How can donors do no harm and maximise their positive impact*. Paris: OECD.

OECD Fragile States Group. (2006). Room document 9: Workstream on service delivery. Prepared for the 7th meeting of the Fragile States Group in the World Bank Headquarters 17–18 October, OECD, Paris.

Osifelo, E. (2009a). Gov't-RAMSI pack takes a new stop. *Solomon Star*, Saturday 16 May.

Osifelo, E. (2009b). Donor banks pledge to support our budget. *Solomon Star*, Saturday 16 May.

Pacific Islands Forum. (2005). *Mission Helpem Fren – A review of the regional assistance mission to Solomon*. Suva: Pacific Islands Forum Eminent Persons Group.

Petorius, C., Lokay, P., & Arumae, H. (2008). *Solomon Islands: Public financial management – Performance report*. Rotterdam: ECORYS Nederland BV.

Secretary General. (2005). *In larger freedom: Towards development, security and human rights for all*. New York: United Nations.

Sogavare, M. (2006). *Address to the nation by the prime minister*. 18 February 2007.

Solomon Islands Government. (2003). *Framework for strengthened assistance to the Solomon Islands*. Honiara.

Transparency International. (2008). *Corruption perception index*. Berlin: Transparency International.

Wainwright, E. (2003). *Our failing neighbour: Australia and the future of the Solomon Islands*. Barton: The Australian Strategic Policy Institute.

Watson, J. (2005). *A model pacific solution? A study of the development of the regional assistance mission to Solomon Islands*. Canberra: Land Warfare Studies Centre, Department of Defence.

Winter, J., Schofield, K., & Duituturaga, E. (2008). *Annual performance report 2007/2008: A report on the performance of the regional assistance mission to Solomon Islands*. Honiara: RAMSI.

World Bank. (2002). *World Bank group work in low-income countries under stress: A task force report*. Washington: World Bank.

PART III
TRADE, LAW, INSTITUTIONS AND INTERNATIONAL CONFLICT: NEW PERSPECTIVES ON ENDURING DEBATES

CHAPTER 10

PEACE THROUGH TRADE? ECONOPHORIA IN NORTHEAST ASIA

Brendan Howe

ABSTRACT

Purpose – *This chapter assesses the extent to which 'Econophoria' (all problems seen as surmountable though development and economic growth) is justified with regard to the maintenance of peace in Northeast Asia where, despite ongoing tensions, outright war has been averted for half a century. Given that peace talks, international organisations and democratic dyads (alternative explanations for the absence of war) are in short supply, and in the context of regional economic 'miracles', the various economic peace mechanisms are addressed through analysis of Northeast Asian data.*

Design/methodology/approach – *The impact of economic development in relation to war and peace is seen to operate at both the macro-level between states (trade, interdependence) and at a micro, transformative level within them. This chapter applies Northeast Asian data to each of the theoretical traditions of economic peace to assess whether there is sufficient fit to provide grounds for optimism and therefore econophoria.*

Findings – *Owing to the limitations of socio-economic transformation and interdependence the impact of the spread of commerce is felt more at*

Economics of War and Peace: Economic, Legal, and Political Perspectives
Contributions to Conflict Management, Peace Economics and Development, Volume 14, 169–184

ISSN: 1572-8323/doi:10.1108/S1572-8323(2010)0000014014

a socially constructed rather than rational cost–benefit level. Peace in Northeast Asia has not come through trade, but trade has facilitated improved conditions for the construction of a peaceful regional community.

Originality/value – *This chapter offers grounds for cautious optimism with regard to the relative stability of the peace regime in a region considered one of the most dangerous in the world. However, it also warns levels of economic development and interdependence which are insufficient to take an econophoric determinist stance.*

INTRODUCTION

Authoritarian regimes and realist analysis during and after the inter-war 20-year crisis have seemingly condemned the notion of peace through trade to the dustbin of history, along with the rest of the liberal internationalist social engineering project. Nonetheless, the concept may be seen as a paradigm born before its time, the tenets of which hold increasing relevance in a modern and interdependent world. This is particularly the case in the security environment of Northeast Asia. Here there are few successful examples of diplomatic success in securing peace (the repeated collapse of the Six Party Talks on North Korea's nuclear and missile weapons programs, the failure of Japan and South Korea and Japan and China to resolve historic tensions and geographical borders, and the impasse over the status of Taiwan being just some of the high-profile failures). The other sides of the virtuous triangle (democracy and international organisation) seem in particularly scant supply. Yet a remarkable econophoria, where all problems are seen as surmountable through development and growth, has emerged alongside the dynamic economic success stories of most states in the region (Buzan & Segal, 1998). This econophoria may even be seen as empirically justified given that war has been absent from the subregion for 50 years despite ongoing tensions and insufficient democratic dyads and regional international organisations. However, we must not be too quick to jump to causal conclusions regarding the source of regional peace.

To paraphrase Richard Cobden (leader of the Anti-Corn Law League, known as the 'Apostle of Free Trade'), this chapter addresses the limitations of the 'labour of cabinets and foreign offices' in securing peace in Northeast Asia. It first traces the intellectual origins of the link between trade and peace. The chapter also assesses the extent to which the 'spread of commerce' contributes to peace as a result of unit-level (state-level) transformation, and the transformation of a regional operating environment (system) for a part of the world described by specialists as the most dangerous places on earth (Calder, 2001). Yet it concludes that due to the limitations of socio-economic transformation and interdependence in the region, the impact of the spread of commerce is felt more at a socially constructed rather than rational cost–benefit level, alongside the socialisation effects of other forms of interaction.

TRACING THE ORIGINS OF LIBERAL THOUGHT ON TRADE AND PEACE

The intellectual heritage of liberal thought on trade and peace can be traced to Emmanuel Kant. Indeed, Russet and O'Neal describe the liberal internationalist premises of peace through trade, the spread of democracy and international organisation, as the three sides of the Kantian triangle and have demonstrated the independent pacific effect of each, albeit with significantly less confidence regarding the systemic effects of international governmental organisations (O'Neal & Russet, 1999; Russet & O'Neal, 2001).

The belief in peace through trade reached a false dawn with Normal Angell's 'Great Illusion', in which he outlined how an *intertwining of interests*, or complementary interests resulting from a division of labour (specialisation), the cobweb structure of monetary interests and the complex relations between finance and trade, made war for profit an irrational undertaking (Angell, 1913, 1938). Angell's work has been largely discounted due in the main to some unfortunate timing, with the first version published in 1913 on the eve of the First World War, and the second in 1938 on the eve of the Second World War (Papayoanou, 1999). However, it is important to note that he did not claim that war had become impossible, only that in economic terms it was no longer a rational enterprise, and that man can, since he makes war, also make wars to cease (Angell, 1935). Angell's hypothesis therefore is not deterministic as such, but rather probabilistic. That is to say, economic considerations are but one of the calculations involved in the decision to go to war, and mutual interdependence through trade can cause this set of calculations in a rational decision-maker to be added to the peace side of the ledger during any cost–benefit analysis.

In addition, increased economic interactions also contribute to a socialising effect. Human beings have a natural tendency to fear the unknown. Fear of the unknown, as the common usage of the term xenophobia indicates, has the potential to generate hostility, or at the very least, worst-case scenarios conducive to a realist or neorealist interpretation of international relations. According to such power-based political models, the rational position assumes a struggle of all against all, the urge of others to dominate, and at least the possibility of war breaking out. Realist models become self-fulfilling prophesies through the security dilemma in which states and statesmen resort to self-help in a hostile, anarchic environment and arm for self-defence even though this poses a threat to others.

Yet increased economic interaction often requires face-to-face meetings and at the very least requires repeated interaction with the same opposing players (essentially an iterated game), allowing each side to come to understand (if not agree with) the underlying motivations and interests of the other, thereby reducing fear of the unknown, uncovering shared interests and possible mutual gains and reducing another of the causes of war.

The impact of economic development in relation to war and peace is seen therefore to operate at both the micro-level within states in the region and at the macro-level between them. The next section considers the transformative effect of economic development within state actors in the region whereas the section following addresses the international component of peace through trade.

UNPACKING THE LINKS BETWEEN DEVELOPMENT, DEMOCRACY AND PEACE

The relationship between economic development, democracy and peace is complex, with considerable disagreement as to whether development stimulates democracy or vice versa. In fact, the processes of economic development and democratisation are probably mutually reinforcing. It is important at this juncture to consider the role of democratisation as an intervening variable between trade and peace. Although democracies are not inherently more peaceful than authoritarian regimes, that democracies do not fight each other is as close to a natural law as we come in political science. In addition, economic growth in the region could stimulate not only political evolution towards democracy, but also the social evolution of middle classes. The middle classes may be wary of hostile words and actions by their government towards those of neighbouring states, fearing that these could be detrimental to their bank balances and investments.

So economic development can promote the emergence of a socio-political class which on the one hand is war-averse (as a result of personal financial cost-benefit calculations), and on the other is likely to push for political rights – even to the extent of transforming polities in the region into democracies. This thereby contributes promotes democratic dyads and a regional democratic peace. Thus if trade promotes economic growth, and economic growth creates war-aversion, trade can be seen to contribute to peace in the region.

The great liberal hope for the region is that as China continues its phenomenal economic progress, a natural and inevitable bi-product will be the emergence of a true Chinese civil society that in turn will press for political liberalisation. Lowell Dittmer predicts 'under such circumstances, previous experience suggests that a full-blown civil society – albeit still with distinctive Chinese cultural characteristics – is apt to emerge as quickly as bamboo shoots after a spring rain'. Zbigniew Brzezinski agrees: 'It is impossible to envision a long-term process of increasing economic pluralism without the appearance of civil society in China that eventually begins to assert its political aspiration' (Nau, 2002).

Modernisation is also expected to transform China's foreign policy objectives, along with those of its neighbours. As Edward Morse (1970) contends 'Foreign policy has been radically transformed by the revolutionary process of modernization not only in the societies composing the Atlantic region, but wherever high levels of modernization exist'. There is no doubt that high levels of modernisation are being achieved throughout East Asia, with first Japan, then the Asian Tigers, (South Korea, Hong Kong, Taiwan and Singapore) and finally China itself and the Asian Tiger Cubs (Thailand, Malaysia, Indonesia and, debatably, the Philippines) becoming increasingly developed and integrated into the international economy. The hope that even North Korea could be encouraged to liberalise politically through being helped to develop economically underpinned South Korean President Kim Dae-jung's 'Sunshine Policy' and also the proposals for Northeast Asian energy cooperation.

Liberal optimism about the eventual pacific effects of modern capitalist development models is perhaps most famously summed up by Francis Fukuyama (1989) in his 'End of History' hypothesis, whereby a liberal victory in both the economic and political realms has led to a situation where there is no more ideological conflict. The notion of democratic contagion from the West provides further support for this hypothesis (although given the geopolitical progression it should perhaps be called contagion from the East). In a similar manner to that feared by Western

Cold War strategists about the spread of communism, countries in the communist bloc have toppled like dominos to the liberal economic and political transition (Whitehead, 1996). Democratic values have spread from America through Japan to Korea and Mongolia, and have even affected China.

The peoples of many post-totalitarian countries are increasingly 'westernised' in their outlook, even to the extent of claiming that were not for 'the system', they would have been like the West (Przeworski, 1991). They, and the regimes representing them, have allowed considerable penetration of their societies by western media, cultural and economic organisations. Private organisations (from satellite television operators to car manufacturers), foreign state operations (from the BBC to overseas aid) and multi- and non-governmental organisations (from the World Bank to Save the Children) suggest the advantages of belonging to the Western political and economic club, and put pressure on transitional regimes to move in a direction acceptable to this club.

However, in some ways economic development is serving to restrict democratic pressures in China by strengthening the hand of the central government and channelling the enthusiasm of the most dynamic elements of society into getting rich rather than getting rights. In a similar way, as pointed out by Haggard and Noland, in a country such as North Korea, even nominally private economic exchanges can be monopolised by the state and military sector to provide fungible resources to support the regime (2008). At the very least, both countries have a long way to go before the populations feel the beneficial effects of economic liberalism. North Korea remains an economic basket case and one reason for China's prolonged double-digit economic growth is that it was starting from such a low base. Given energy consumption and electricity consumption per capita figures, China barely rates as an industrial economy, let alone a post-industrial one (International Energy Agency, 2009). Things are not helped by the conservative and restrictive attitude of the political old guard towards the information age and the extraordinarily low priority given to research and development when compared to OECD countries (Normile, 2005).

Many analysts are now beginning to question whether China will be able to sustain its economic growth pattern. Indeed, doubts have surfaced over Chinese economic data (Cai, 2000). Although military expenditure tends to be underrepresented, economic growth is exaggerated. An example of this is the startling conundrum of how all 31 provinces managed to beat the national average growth rate for 2002 (Spencer, 2003). Xinhua News Agency (2003) may well attribute China's economic performance in recent years to 'an effective macroeconomic control mechanism and opening up to the world', but it seems in part attributable to 'communist officialdom's tradition of currying favour by exaggerating achievements' (Spencer, 2003). In GNP per capita terms, China remains a low-income developing country, still ranked outside the top 100 in the world and has very limited resources (Wang, 2007). According to China's own strategic plans, it will take until the middle of the century before it can be called a 'modernized, medium-level developed country' (Zheng, 2005). China will face three big challenges before it gets there

1. resource shortage;
2. environmental degradation and
3. lack of coordination between economic and social development (Zheng, 2005).

A market economy, by its nature, blossoms in commercial liberalism rather than the authoritarian pseudo-communist political system of China.

On a more general level, the consensual process of liberal transition is also under threat. The Western way of life only exerts a positive attraction as long as it is perceived to be desirable and preferable to other alternatives. Should the capitalist democratic world system enter a pronounced downturn (as perhaps heralded by the 2008 global financial crisis) this may no longer be the case, particularly if increased inter-regional competition leads to a new wave of protectionism and shrinking global trade. Furthermore, the promised benefits of liberal transition policies have been slower to materialise within transitional states than many hoped. An internal expectancy gap has developed within many transitional states, and in some cases, this could lead to discontent, undermining or even reversing the liberalisation that has already occurred.

The processes of both economic and democratic transition are themselves sources of considerable uncertainty and hardship, which may derail the process of liberalisation. Some groups are bound to lose, at least in the short term. Support for transition is only generated by

- general optimism that ultimately all will benefit;
- hope that even if this is not the case, then at least the majority will do so and
- the common belief held by most, that they will form part of this majority.

The longer that people are uncertain about how democratic spoils will be distributed, the greater the chance of an authoritarian relapse (Pridham, 1991). Thus economic transition may not lead to democratic consolidation and the formation of more peaceful democratic dyads. More than any other form of government, democracy depends for its legitimacy on the consent of a majority of those governed. In order to generate and maintain such consent, democracy must provide what the majority of people want. Political perceptions vary in accordance with economic circumstances, and the inevitable costs of transition include corruption, inflation, underemployment of capital and labour, allocative inefficiencies and distributional effects (Maravall, 1997). No matter the universal aspirations, no reform makes all better off, and certainly some will benefit more than others. Any group that perceives itself worse off in relative, let alone absolute, terms is therefore likely to resist the implementation of the reform.

Despite the limitations to the links between internal economic development and international peace, economic forces operating across borders have been given even more prominence by liberal academics attempting to establish the conditions conducive for peace. Commercial interactions between states are not only potentially win–win in economic terms for the entities engaged in such practices (although again, some internal constituencies are always likely to lose), but also have the potential to reduce conflictual tendencies by increasing the cost of war and the benefits of peaceful cooperation by fostering economic interdependence. The next section explores the spread of commerce as a factor directly contributing to the development of a peaceful Northeast Asian operating environment.

HOW COMMERCE SPREADS PEACE: THE CASE OF NORTHEAST ASIA

This section outlines the ideas underpinning the interdependence peace theory and applies it to the case of Northeast Asia. According to the theory, the spread of commerce and the process of economic interdependence are seen to operate at three levels

1. Global level, whereby the various processes of globalisation have made all industrialised states interdependent.
2. Regional level, whereby certain regions of the world are seen to represent zones of economically induced peace.
3. Dyadic level, whereby mutual dependence between pairs of states is seen as reducing the likelihood, or even possibility of them going to war.

As aforementioned, Norman Angell's work is considered an early and extremely influential example of interdependence peace theory, and from his foundations we can trace the evolution of all three of these considerations. His best-known work, *The Great Illusion* sold more than a million copies, and was translated into 17 languages. He exposed as an 'illusion' the idea that military power could make a country wealthy, that the trade, territory and colonies of a defeated enemy could profitably be added to the wealth of the victor, and that international interdependence could be disrupted without damaging trade (de Wilde, 1989). He concluded that the more that countries developed and became dependent on each other, the greater the costs of war, and the smaller the benefits that could be hoped to be gained from war.

Critics of Norman Angell's hypothesis tend to be over-reliant on a single historical event, First World War where comparatively high levels of economic interdependence proved insufficient to prevent war. Yet other surveys have found many instances where interdependence did serve to restrain foreign policy decision-makers. Mark Gasiorowski and Solomon Polachek (1982) found a strong, inverse relationship between trade and conflict. Their results indicated that international conflict could be eased considerably by engaging a hostile nation in interactions that are beneficial to it. The 'anomaly' of the First World War can be explained in two ways: first that interdependency is an incremental process in the pressures on decision-makers for peace are gradually ratcheted up until in their cost–benefit rational calculations it really is illogical for them to allow things to deteriorate to open warfare. Thus what may have been idealism a hundred years ago could be realistic now. This section will apply such reasoning to Northeast Asia.

The second answer, as addressed in the introduction to this chapter, is that interdependence forms part of the operating environment within which decision-makers act, and other personal or national interests, misperceptions or miscalculations can override the rational imperative not to go to war. Given the multi-causal nature of the origins of warfare, economic interdependence does not make war impossible even if it does make it irrational from a cost–benefit analysis. However, increased economic interaction can also help to precipitate a socially constructed community within which war becomes a more unlikely and unacceptable policy option. This will be addressed in the final section on rationality and socialisation.

At the global level, a CIA publication analysing global trends at the dawn of the new millennium leading to a world vision of 2015, finds globalisation accelerating and exceeding predictions made in 1997 about 2010 (CIA, 2000). It notes international economic dynamics, including the development of the World Trade Organisation, and the spread of information technology, have had much greater influence than previously anticipated. The chapter predicts: 'The networked global economy will be driven by rapid and largely unrestricted flows of information, ideas, cultural values, capital, goods and services, and people' and that 'this globalised economy will be a net contributor to increased stability in the world' (CIA, 2000). In particular, 'Emerging Asia' is highlighted as the fastest growing region (CIA, 2000). Economic interdependence at all levels contributes to peace because

1. All are better off, so have fewer grievances, and can appreciate the benefits of cooperation rather than conflict.
2. The interdependence of vital leading sectors of the economies of the participants, particularly those related to military capacity, make mobilisation for war physically difficult and prohibitively expensive.
3. 'Spillover' (whereby repeated cooperative behaviour in one sector of public life can spill over into or replicate itself between the same actors in other areas) creates a culture of cooperation rather than conflict.
4. Integration breaks down the monolithic nature of the state encouraging cross-cutting interests, and complicating the decision to wage war.

At the regional level, the spread of trading relations between neighbours contributes to the evolution of what Spencer Thompson (1996) has termed a 'zone of peace' which in turn increases the likelihood of democratic transformation. This thereby reverses the direction of the democratic peace hypothesis. The experience of Western Europe is often presented as proof that complex interdependence (multiple channels of communication and interactions between states, combined with an absence of an issues hierarchy and an awareness of the benefits of cooperation) can prevent conflict (Keohane & Nye, 1977). After a second global war had been ignited in this region and chronically damaged the national interests of all the regional participants, attention turned to deliberately engineering interdependence as a bulwark against future conflict. Ernst Haas (1961) termed this project a functionalist theory of international peace. The functional sector of international organisation concerns those areas tentatively described as non-political or low politics, such as economic, social, technical, humanitarian, prosperity, welfare and social justice promotion. Thus the European Union was founded on the belief that functional cooperation would lead to reduced tension and greater mutual interdependence between regional powers whose mutual antagonism had played a significant role in most of the major wars of the preceding century.

At the bilateral level the rationale that interdependence leads to peace is that the costs of war in this situation are greater because markets, investments and flow of goods are disrupted. Each dependent state is much more vulnerable than it is under more autarkic conditions and, at the same time, repeated incidents and processes of cooperation between mutually dependent dyads foster a culture of communication and compromise. Furthermore, incentives for conflict are lower because 'in a relatively open liberal international economy, access to raw materials, finance and markets is obtained at less cost and on a greater scale than would be possible via military control of territory or spheres of influence' (Buzan & Segal, 1998). Thus, 'a liberal economic order divorces wealth and welfare from control over territory, and thereby removes one of the main reasons for the use of force' (Buzan & Segal, 1998). This is the logic behind the economic side of Russet and Oneal's virtuous triangle (1999, 2001).

At face value, interdependence through commerce is spreading in Northeast Asia. Not just the major modern capitalist export-driven economies of the region (Japan, South Korea, Taiwan and Hong Kong) but also the developing former socialist economies of Russia and Mongolia, the still nominally socialist economy of China and even North Korea, are driven to improve the lives of their citizens by selling what they can produce both globally and regionally. (Yet in the case of North Korea what is being traded and trafficked may be considered as inappropriate for a liberal and peaceful world order). Special economic zones are flourishing and most of the economies in the region are pressing to join global and regional economic organisations. Russia and China have long given up on autarky, and the *Juche* philosophy of North Korea is failing so clearly that even the 'Dear Leader' appears a convert to international trade. Thus Kim Jong Il has shown enthusiasm for a Buick plant near Shanghai and has shown a consistent interest in establishing special economic zones. He has shown awareness and interest in the transition of both Russia and China, expressed a desire to improve relations with the United States, and has referred to the kidnappings of Japanese citizens in the 1970s and 1980s as 'mistakes that will not be repeated' (Gregg, 2003). This would seem to be the inevitable impact of Fukuyama's end of history hypothesis – the alternatives just do not work.

Yet globalisation rankings for all countries in the region remain very low, especially when only economic indicators are considered. Therefore we need to consider the role of interdependence in the tighter, region-wide setting or between dyads, rather than in the global context (Kearney, 2003; Foreign Policy, 2007).[1] Certainly, Asian trade has risen dramatically in terms of both trade in goods as a percentage of purchasing power parity (PPP) GDP, and trade in goods as a percentage of total goods produced. Likewise, foreign direct investment as a percentage of PPP GDP has risen through the timeframe considered. Even North and South Korea have managed to initiate a joint cooperative economic project in the Gaeseong Industrial Complex, despite the ongoing obstacles and the latent state of war between them. However, these trade measurements still lag behind those found in Europe (World Bank, 2001, 2008).

Exports within the region have increased and exports within the APEC bloc now exceed the percentage of total exports of those shipped within the borders of the European Union. Yet those within the East Asian Economic Caucus (Brunei, China, Hong Kong, Indonesia, Japan, S. Korea, Malaysia, the Philippines, Singapore, Taiwan and Thailand) remain lower (if the Southeast Asian nations are excluded from these measurements the figures would be lower still). This is because the United States is absent from the EAEC while it is present in APEC. Even though this is notionally counterbalanced by the inclusion of China in the EAEC figures and its exclusion from the APEC measurements, the effect is not enough to overcome the omission of the United States from the EAEC (IMF, 2001, 2007). Thus, rather than the true mutual dependence between equals we find in Europe, Asia is faced with a much more lopsided system. For most of regional economies, trade within Asia is becoming increasingly important. However, China is a large exception. The region as a whole is faced with a lopsided system of over-reliance on the United States and Chinese markets, unequal bilateral trading relationships between industrialised and emerging Asia, and also between the Chinese mega-economy and other states. This means that

1. The pacific effects of intra-regional interdependence are not felt.
2. Relations between rapidly developing countries have the potential to deteriorate as they fight for a share of the American, Chinese and other international markets.
3. Power relations are likely to reassert themselves.

In addition, the economies of Northeast Asia may not be ideally suited in promoting interdependence. On the one hand, variance in terms of size, structure, regulations and levels of development of Northeast Asian economies may impede the free flow of trade and investment. On the other hand, Japan, China, South Korea and Taiwan may be too similar in terms of being mostly export-oriented producers of similar goods. In 2002, China and Japan managed to negotiate free trade arrangements with the Association of Southeast Asian Nations (ASEAN) countries but not with each other. Japan and South Korea have been talking about a free trade arrangement since the late 1990s, but have still to put anything of substance together. Korea has managed to negotiate an FTA with the United States, but this has yet to be fully implemented, and it does not constitute a move towards regional integration. The final impediment combines the historical and the structural. The major economies of the region have all experienced economic growth and development, largely supported by a trans-regional regime composed of the United States and international organisations with a global focus, and therefore they see little need to change. In many ways Northeast Asian countries may be seen as neither wanting nor needing regional organisation.

CONCLUSION: RATIONALISATION AND SOCIALISATION

Despite diplomatic efforts to establish cooperation in Northeast Asia, the absence of war in the region for the past 50 years seems to have come about despite the frequently collapsing peace talks and summits rather than because of them. It would also be wrong to credit liberal economic development and interdependence as the source of this phenomenon. The dramatic growth of Northeast Asian economies, so-called miracles has perhaps not surprisingly led to a degree of econophoria in the region, and the spread of commerce certainly seems to hold a great degree of promise. However, just as in inter-war Europe, it is premature to herald a Northeast Asian zone of economically inspired peace – the interdependence project still has a long way to go in the region.

Yet economic growth and at least the prospect of interdependence has contributed to a proliferation of talks and initiatives, increased contact and interaction at transnational, national and sub-state levels, and a socialisation of policy elites. For example, the former South Korean chief negotiator at the Six Party Talks used his extensive personal experience generated through inter-Korean aid negotiations to explain North Korean reasoning to other participants. This process can independently contribute to the evolution of a socialised operating environment in which peace may be more likely to endure.

Economic and strategic interaction, and recognition by ruling elites of the permanence and importance of these processes, can lead to rules evolving for avoiding conflicts and for facilitating desired exchanges. Failure to avoid conflict would mean an enormous inconvenience and, more seriously, potential loss of competitive advantage for those who failed to take this step when others had done so. So rationally, international order can evolve functionally from the logic of anarchy without pre-existing cultural bonds. So, despite lacking formal international organisation or governance, and falling short of the conditions necessary for a liberal perpetual peace, Northeast Asia appears to offer an important demonstration of Alexander Wendt's (1992) famous maxim, 'Anarchy is what states make of it'. Essentially we do not need to wait for the full spread of commerce to make war irrational, or at the very least an unacceptable policy option.

In the Northeast Asian context, as pointed out by Haggard and Noland (2008), the Six Party Talks have proven remarkably resilient, despite having little in the way of significant breakthroughs. Even North Korean nuclear and missile tests have been insufficient to prevent the resumption of talks. Despite the slow pace of negotiations, none of the parties appears willing to abandon them altogether, and all have signalled they are willing to discuss a more enduring multilateral mechanism. The size, strength and importance of the entities concerned might even act in favour of a resolution being reached. Nobody wants to be left behind, and therefore Haggard and Noland (2008) are right to identify the region as potentially ripe for deeper economic cooperation and integration. The talks are focused on security issues, but many of the solutions to the problems being considered are of an economic nature – trade, recognition, aid and development assistance in return for the scaling back of weapons programmes. Likewise from a socialisation perspective, Bill Clinton's experience in the talks and the personal political capital he generated there allowed him to secure the release of Asian-American reporters who had strayed into North Korea.

The costs of war and the benefits of peace in Northeast Asia probably already outweigh any rational calculus that could lead to hostilities resuming in the region. Integration, should it come, will further strengthen pacific tendencies and rational imperatives favouring cooperation over conflict. The main problem with Northeast Asian econophoria is that even if all are better off, misery and inequality are not the only causes of war. Sometimes individuals, groups and nations act according to a different rationality to that of economic well being, as with North Korea's military first doctrine. Advocates of economic interdependence tend to overestimate the potential for spillover into high political areas as a result of establishing a culture of 'yes-ability' or cooperation in low political fields (Fisher, Ury, & Patton, 1991). Even the European Union seems to find the problems of a common foreign and security policy insurmountable. However, when combined with the other elements of socialisation in a more complex integrative model, there are grounds for cautious optimism. Peace in Northeast Asia has not come through trade, but trade has facilitated improved conditions for constructing a peaceful regional community.

NOTE

1. The Globalisation Index is calculated through assessment of components related to economic, personal, technology, political, trade, FDI, portfolio flows, income payments, travel and tourism, telephone, transfer payments, internet users, hosts, servers, international organizations, peacekeeping and embassies considerations.

REFERENCES

Angell, N. (1913). *The great illusion*. New York: G. P. Putnam's Sons.

Angell, N. (1935). Nobel lecture university of Oslo. Available at http://nobelprize.org/nobel_prizes/peace/laureates/1933/angell-lecture.html

Angell, N. (1938). *The great illusion-now*. Harmondsworth: Penguin.

Buzan, B., & Segal, G. (1998). Rethinking East Asian security. In: M. Klare & Y. Chandrani (Eds), *World security: Challenges for a new century*. New York: St. Martin's Press.

Cai, Y. (2000). Between state and peasant: Local cadres and statistical reporting in rural China. *China Quarterly*, *163*, 783–805.

Calder, K. E. (2001). The new face of Northeast Asia. *Foreign Affairs*, *80*(1), 106–122.

Central Intelligence Agency. (December 2000). *Global trends 2015: A dialogue about the future with nongovernmental experts* (pp. 5–25). Available at http://www.cia.gov/cia/publications/globaltrends2015/index.html

de Wilde, J. (1989). Norman Angell: Ancestor of interdependence theory. In: J. Rosenau & H. Tromp (Eds), *Interdependence and conflict in world politics*. Aldershot: Avebury.

Fisher, R., Ury, W., & Patton, B. (1991). *Getting to yes: Negotiating agreement without giving in*. New York: Penguin.

Foreign Policy. (2007). Globalization index rankings for 2007. Available at http://www.foreignpolicy.com/story/cms.php?story_id = 4030

Fukuyama, F. (1989). The end of history? *National Interest* (16), 3–18.

Gasiorowski, M. J., & Polachek, S. W. (1982). Conflict and interdependence: East-West trade and linkages in the era of detente. *Journal of Conflict Resolution*, *26*(4), 709–729.

Gregg, D. (2003). My turn: Kim Jong Il – The truth behind the caricature. *Newsweek*, February 3. Available at http://stacks.msnbc.com/news/863858.asp

Haas, E. (1961). International integration: The European and the universal process. *International Organization*, *15*(3), 366–392.

Haggard, S., & Noland, M. (2008). North Korea's foreign economic relations. *International Relations of the Asia-Pacific*, *8*(2), 219–246.

IEA. (2009). International energy agency energy statistics of non-OECD countries. Available at http://data.iea.org/ieastore/product.asp?dept%5Fid = 101&pf%5Fid = 203

IMF. (2001). *Direction of trade statistics and IMF staff calculations*, Washington DC: International Monetary Fund.

IMF. (2007). *Direction of trade statistics and IMF staff calculations*, Washington DC: International Monetary Fund.

Kearney, A. (2003). Measuring globalization: Who's up, who's down? *Foreign Policy* (January/February), 60–72.

Keohane, R., & Nye, J. (1977). *Power and interdependence: World politics in transition*. Boston: Little, Brown and Company.

Maravall, J. (1997). *Regimes, politics, and markets: Democratization and economic change in Southern Europe and Eastern Europe*. New York: Oxford University Press.

Morse, E. (1970). The transformations of foreign policies: Modernization, interdependence and externalization. *World Politics*, *22*(3), 371–392.

Nau, H. (2002). *At home abroad: Identity and power in American foreign policy*. Ithaca: Cornell University Press.

Normile, D. (2005). Is China the next R&D superpower? *Electronic Business*, January 7. Available at http://www.edn.com/article/CA610433.html

O'Neal, J., & Russett, B. (1999). The Kantian peace: The pacific benefits of democracy, interdependence, and international organizations, 1885–1992. *World Politics*, *52*(1), 1–37.

Papayoanou, P. (1999). *Power ties: Economic interdependence, balancing, and war*. Ann Arbor, MI: University of Michigan Press.

Pridham, G. (1991). *Encouraging democracy: The international context of regime transition in Southern Europe*. New York: St. Martin's Press.

Przeworski, A. (1991). *Democracy and the market: Political and economic reforms in Eastern Europe and Latin America*. New York: Cambridge University Press.

Russet, B., & O'Neal, J. (2001). *Triangulating peace: Democracy, interdependence, and international organizations*. New York: Norton.

Spencer, R. (2003). A Chinese puzzle as everyone's a winner. *The Daily Telegraph*, February 7.

Thompson, W. (1996). Democracy and peace: Putting the cart before the horse? *International Organization*, *50*(1), 141–174.

Wang, Y. (2007). China's rise: An unlikely pillar of US hegemony. *The Harvard International Review*, *29*(1), 56–60.

Wendt, A. (1992). Anarchy is what states make of it: The social construction of power politics. *International Organization*, *46*(Spring), 391–425.

Whitehead, L. (1996). Three international dimensions of democratization. In: L. Whitehead (Ed.), *The international dimensions of democratization: Europe and the Americas*. New York: Oxford University Press.

World Bank. (2001). *2001 world development indicators*. Washington DC: Development Data Center.

World Bank. (2008). *2008 world development indicators*. Washington DC: Development Data Center.

Xinhua News Agency. (2003). Xinhau commentary on Chinese economy. Available at http://english.peopledaily.com.cn/200301/29/eng20030129_110899.shtml

Zheng, B. (2005). China's 'peaceful' rise to great power status. *Foreign Affairs*, *84*(5), 18–24.

CHAPTER 11

REGIONAL INTEGRATION AND MILITARISED INTERSTATE DISPUTES: AN EMPIRICAL ANALYSIS

Golam Robbani

ABSTRACT

Purpose – *This chapter aims to position regional integration in the Kantian peace tripod and to test whether regional economic integration has a significant effect in reducing militarised interstate disputes.*

Methodology – *It uses logistic regression on cross-sectional–time-series data and a generalised estimating equation.*

Findings – *The analysis shows that regional integration had a significant impact in reducing militarised interstate disputes between 1950 and 2000.*

Practical implications – *This chapter may provide a new dimension to the academic discussion on the Kantian peace proposition, and encourage policy makers in less integrated regions to integrate with their neighbouring states in a bid to minimise political tensions.*

Originality – *The chapter is based on original data on regional integration collected by the author.*

Economics of War and Peace: Economic, Legal, and Political Perspectives
Contributions to Conflict Management, Peace Economics and Development, Volume 14, 185–203

ISSN: 1572-8323/doi:10.1108/S1572-8323(2010)0000014015

INTRODUCTION

Centuries ago, Immanuel Kant (1970[1795]) sketched a philosophical view of a peaceful world with open commerce, democracy and international organisations. Considerable research shows that trading nations fight less, democracies rarely go to war and international organisations have peaceful impact (Oneal & Russett, 1999a; Russett & Oneal, 2001). Despite the fact that regional integration arrangements (RIAs) may contain all the three elements of the Kantian peace tripod, surprisingly little attempt has been made to empirically assess the impact of RIAs in shaping political relations among member states. The economic implications of regional integrations have been widely studied and fiercely debated, but analyses of their impact on political–military relations have been sparse (Mansfield & Pevehouse, 2003).

Although the unprecedented success of the European Union (EU) in making another regional war 'unthinkable' has deeply influenced policy makers throughout the world, paradoxically, regional integrations are largely considered to be an 'economic' phenomenon – ignoring their plausible political benefits. With globalisation, the world is facing ever-increasing 'problems without passports' (Annan, 2002) and nation states are no longer in a position to deal with such challenges. As long as a desired 'world government' to manage the 'global village' is not in sight, it is time to re-examine whether the political dimension of regional integration can help. This chapter investigates whether RIAs have any significant impact in reducing militarised interstate disputes (MIDs).

This study builds on empirical analyses that indicate that regional integrations reduce conflict between states. For example, Mansfield and Pevehouse (2000, p. 775) demonstrate that parties of the same preferential trade arrangements (PTA) are less prone to disputes than other states, and that hostilities between PTA members are less likely to occur as trade flows rise between them. Their study, however, is based on all the RIAs notified to the World Trade Organization (WTO) including bilateral free trade areas (FTAs). Although it is interesting to see the impact of bilateral agreements on interstate conflict, the present study excludes bilateral agreements to single out the effect of commercial intergovernmental organisations (IGOs) on interstate conflict. Powers (2004, 2006) considers alliance obligations in regional economic institutions in Africa and finds some pacifying effect, but reports that 'African dyads are more likely to fight each other if both countries are democracies, have increasing disparity in power capabilities, are allies, and trade with each other' (Powers, 2006, p. 455). Studying Asia,

Goldsmith (2007, p. 14) also indicates that 'IGOs seem to matter little for war and peace in Asia'. These studies hint to the fact that there might be some regional disparity in the effect of RIAs, although that topic is beyond the scope of this study. By considering common membership to RIAs, this study finds a significant and consistent negative relationship between RIAs and MIDs. I believe my contribution will add significant value to the existing debate over the Kantian peace proposition, and open a new avenue for discussion on the political impact of RIAs around the world.

The chapter is structured as follows. Drawing the relationship between Kantian peace proposition and RIAs, the next section elaborates on the prospect of peace through regional integration. The third section describes the research design and reports the result. The fourth section concludes that regional integration is negatively linked to MIDs.

HOW REGIONAL INTEGRATION PRODUCES PEACE

Regional integration is a form of intergovernmental cooperation on commerce and diplomacy. RIAs have a number of roles in reducing interstate conflict:

- creating an expectation of economic benefit among member states (Mansfield & Pevehouse, 2000, p. 779);
- limiting the capacity of participants to subsequently raise trade barriers, helping to attract foreign investment into the integrated region and
- demonstrating the benefits of cooperation and the costs of non-cooperation, prompting shallow integration to spill over to other areas of cooperation as neo functionalists have argued (Haas, 1958). This increase in scope and coverage creates a 'domino effect' (Baldwin, 1993) attracting more members to take part in the integration process.

In effect, closer cooperation amplifies expected economic benefits of integration and increases the opportunity cost of military disputes. Starting with the European Coal and Steel Community (ECSC), the EU integration process spilled over to other areas and attracted other states to join the integration process. Frequent interaction between leaders of neighbouring states helps to transform interstate relationship from enmity to amity. Consistent cooperation in areas of common interest may eventually create a security community of which the EU is an obvious example (Deutsch, 1957). Furthermore, RIAs can be defined as established IGOs, which routinely facilitate interaction among leaders and provide direct and indirect communication channels to solve problems before they escalate (Dorussen & Ward, 2008).

In short, the combined effect of commercial interest, institutional and networking facilities and mutual trust through frequent interaction may give rise to peaceful international relations among nations.

HOW RIAs FORM THE KANTIAN PEACE TRIPOD

The three elements of the Kantian peace proposition (i.e. trade, democracy and international organisation) are popularly described as the three legs of the Kantian peace tripod (Russett & Oneal, 2001). Although not without exceptions, in general, RIAs are trade-based IGOs and they are usually formed among democratic states (Mansfield, Milner, & Rosendorff, 2002). I demonstrate below how RIAs fit in with the Kantian peace model.

TRADE, RIAs AND CONFLICT[1]: THE FIRST LEG OF THE TRIPOD

Almost all RIAs start with trade integrations, often with states signing PTA in the initial stages. By reducing trade barriers, RIAs promote trade among integrated members – creating the first leg of the Kantian tripod (Baier & Bergstrand, 2007). Trade interdependence strengthened through RIAs helps to reduce interstate conflict in two ways. On one hand, it offers a huge trade opportunity for integrated states, and on the other hand, it increases the opportunity cost of potential conflict. Consequently, people and politicians become more accommodating of their neighbouring states and prefer to settle disputes peacefully. As a result, declaring a war against an integrated state imposes a heavy economic cost, and eventually creates domestic pressure on political leaders to use force only as a last resort. Furthermore, in the event of any trouble, fellow integrated states may stand ready to broker a deal before the conflict escalates to a point where their own interests might be at stake.

Some empirical studies demonstrate that economically important trade has statistically significant and substantial benefits for reducing interstate violence (Oneal & Russett, 2003a, 2003b; Robst, Polachek, & Chang, 2006; Polachek, 1980; Polachek & Seiglie, 2006; Russett, 2003, p. 159; Gartzke, 2005; Gelpi & Grieco, 2008).[2] As trade is a primary focus of cooperation through RIAs, I expect that integrated states will have less conflict than non-integrated states. According to my data, between 1950 and 2000, 92 per cent of the 1,245 MIDs among politically relevant dyads occurred among non-integrated dyads. This compares to only 8 per cent among integrated dyads in the subgroup. Nonetheless, it is important to note that trade integrations among European states during the first quarter of the twentieth century could not prevent the First World War.

DEMOCRATIC PEACE AND RIAs: THE SECOND LEG OF THE TRIPOD

Democracy forms the second leg of the Kantian peace tripod. There is considerable argument that 'democracies rarely fight each other' (Russett & Oneal, 2001, p. 36; Starr, 1992, 1997; see also Russett, 1993; Chan, 1997; for a critical analysis see Rasler & Thompson, 2005; Slantchev, Alexandrova, & Gartzke, 2005).[3] Following the EU model of integration, most integration arrangements tend to call for some preconditions to new membership such as democratic governance, rule of law and respect for human rights which encourage (potential) parties to improve their democracy at home before joining a RIA.[4] States founded on individual rights such as equality before the law, free speech and other civil liberties, private property and elected representation are fundamentally against war (Doyle, 1997, 2004). According to the Polity IV dataset, a polity score of 10 indicates purely democratic states and minus 10 indicates extremely autocratic states. During the period under study, the average polity score for integrated dyads was 0.71 compared to −0.71 for non-integrated dyads. As integrated states are somewhat more democratic than non-integrated states, I expect that RIA members will also be more peaceful than their non-integrated counterparts.

INTERNATIONAL ORGANISATION, CONFLICT AND RIAs: THE THIRD LEG

International organisation forms the third leg of the Kantian peace tripod. This element is also present in RIAs. All integration arrangements in this study take place among three or more sovereign states or territories and often these have separate secretariats which can be considered to be international organisations. The relationship between IGOs and peace is still a grey area (Boehmer, Gartzke, & Nordstrom, 2004); however, there are arguments that co-membership in IGOs reduces the probability of war (Russett & Oneal, 2001; Bearce & Omori, 2005; Haftel, 2007; Mansfield & Pevehouse, 2000; Shannon, 2009).[5] Pevehouse and Russett (2006) find that densely democratic IGOs contribute to peaceful resolution of conflicts by aiding credible commitments, dispute settlement and socialising states to behave peacefully. Nonetheless, they recognise that the link between IGOs and Kantian peace is less robust and more problematic than the other two elements of the peace proposition.

Noting that 'IGOs are not all created equal', Boehmer et al. (2004, p. 2) suggest that institutionalised IGOs reduce the risk of militarised disputes. IGOs with a security mandate are more effective than economic organisations in promoting peace. I should note here that the security mandated IGOs (not considered in this analysis) promote collective security for their members, but create a security dilemma for others. For instance, the recent move to extend NATO membership to Georgia has created enormous pressure on Russia. In contrast, economic organisations do not create political rivals because they are rules-based and market-driven. From a network perspective, Dorussen and Ward (2008, p. 189) point to the fact that

> IGOs create network ties between states allowing them, either individually or collectively, to intervene more effectively in latent conflicts. The IGO network also provides direct and indirect communication channels, where indirect links can act as partial substitutes for direct diplomatic ties.

Regional members can be expected to be better informed and well aware of the background and critical factors involved in a conflict. Therefore, member states are often in a better position to broker a deal before the dispute escalates. I also assume that regionally integrated states will fight less because they have other avenues to express their demand, desire or grievances, and have mediation facilities available to ease any potential tension.

COMBINED EFFECT OF THE TRIPOD LEGS IN PRODUCING PEACE

Plenty of studies consider Kantian peace elements separately, but such analysis overlooks the interactive effects of these elements. For example, 'in Kant's own view, the three legs of the tripod are not truly independent elements that are individually useful in preventing wars. Rather, they are integrally related' (Russett & Oneal, 2001, p. 157). Kant presents each of the three 'definitive articles' as necessary conditions that *together* establish a sufficient condition for establishing a pacific union (Doyle, 2004, p. 7). Due to the combined effect of the Kantian peace elements represented in RIAs, I expect integrated states to be less conflict-prone than non-integrated states.

RESEARCH DESIGN

This study used the non-directed dyad year as the unit of analysis with the temporal domain between 1950 and 2000. This time frame is chosen due to the clear development and increase in the number of RIAs in the post-war period. I collected the data on RIAs[6] and the data on other variables are assembled using the EUGene software. The sources of data on specific variables are cited in appropriate places.

I have run Logit (with and without peace years' correction) and the GEE (generalised estimating equation) on three subsets of data:

- All dyads
- Politically relevant dyads (PRDs)
- Regionally relevant dyads (RRDs)

PRDs are defined (Oneal & Russett, 1999b) as contiguous dyads, or states contiguous on land or separated by less than 150 miles of water, and dyads containing at least one major power (as defined by Small & Singer, 1982). RRDs are defined as the pair of states which are either contiguous to, or integrated with, each other. This is necessary to capture the states which are not contiguous but integrated, such as Canada and Mexico since 1994. The dataset used for this study contains 8,273 integrated dyads which are not contiguous to each other.

Dependent Variable

Onset of Militarised Interstate Disputes

The dependent variable, *MID*, is the onset of militarised interstate disputes as compiled by the Correlates of War (COW) Project (Ghosn & Bennett, 2003). The COW data record a dispute in a year if a member of the dyad has threatened to use force, made a demonstration of force or actually used military force against the other. MID is a dichotomous variable that equals

1 when a dispute between state *i* and *j* started in year *t*, and 0 otherwise. I used the option 'mark dispute/crisis onset for originators and joiners'[7] and did not drop ongoing disputes.

Independent Variables

Although RIAs are my main variable of interest, I have used some other variables which are routinely used in Kantian peace literature. Specific descriptions of the variables are as follows.

Regional Integration Arrangements

The variable RIA is assigned 1 if the states in a dyad are common members to any form of regional integration [i.e. PTA, FTA, Customs Union (CU), Common Market (CM) or Economic Union (EcU)]. I assign a 0 if dyads are not integrated.[8]

I considered only the RIAs with more than two parties and a secretariat and that are still functional in a respective year. Following Haftel (2007, p. 222), I excluded bilateral trade agreements (i.e. bilateral FTAs), non-reciprocal agreements (such as the United States-Caribbean Basin Initiative and the Lomé Convention) and framework agreements (such as the Asia-Pacific Economic Cooperation). Based on these criteria, I could finally include 16 RIAs in my data, which cover almost all countries in the world (full names are listed in the appendix).

*Trade Interdependence (*TradeDependence*)*

To assess the impact of trade interdependence on the likelihood of military conflict, I used the trade data compiled by Barbieri, Keshk, and Pollins (2009) available in the COW database. Following Barbieri (1995, 1996, 1998), I measured trade interdependence = $\text{salience}_{ij} \times \text{symmetry}_{ij}$. Here salience = $\sqrt{(\text{trade share}_i \times \text{trade share}_j)}$ and symmetry = $1 - |\text{trade share}_i - \text{trade share}_j|$ and $\text{trade share}_i = \text{trade}_{ij}/\text{trade}_i$.

*Democracy (*PolityLow*)*

To estimate democratic peace, data have been used from Polity IV (Marshal & Jaggers, 2005). The variable *PolityLow* is the lower of the polity scores in a dyad. Following the 'weak link' logic (Dixon, 1994), I assume that less democratic states have a higher probability of engaging in conflict. My analyses support earlier findings that democratic states fight less.

*Alliances (*Alliance*)*
Following the existing research tradition, I also control for the influence of alliances. The variable *Alliance* equals 1 if the states are linked by a mutual defence treaty, a neutrality pact or an entente, and 0 otherwise. The source of data is the COW Alliance dataset (Gibler & Sarkees, 2004). As expected, alliance shows a significantly negative relationship with MIDs.

*Major Powers (*MajorDyad*)*
Research shows that dyads including a major power have a positive relationship with MIDs. To test if this is also the case in my analysis, I included a variable called *MajorDyad*. COW data define major powers as described by Small and Singer (1982). My finding is consistent with earlier research that dyads containing a major power are more conflict-prone.

*Capability (*CapabilityRatio*)*
A preponderance of power is often said to inhibit overt conflict (Bremer, 1992; de Soya, Oneal, & Park, 1997; Kugler & Lemke, 1996; Maoz & Russett, 1993). Therefore, I include this variable to examine the impact of dyadic balance of power. National capability is measured by COW national capabilities index (CINC) composed (in equal weights) of a country's share of the system's total population, urban population, energy consumption, iron and steel production, military manpower and military expenditures (Singer & Small, 1995). The variable *CapabilityRatio* is the natural logarithm of the ratio of the stronger state's capability index to that of the weaker member in each dyad. My analyses support the prior findings that capability ratio has a negative relationship with MIDs.

*Contiguous States (*Contiguity*)*
Proximity increases the probability of conflict. Therefore, it is important to include contiguity in the analysis. Data on contiguity have been used from Stinnett, Tir, Schafer, Diehl, and Gochman (2002). The variable *Contiguity* equals 1 if two states are contiguous, either sharing a land boundary or separated by less than 150 miles of water. As contiguous countries are more conflict-prone (Robst et al., 2006), and countries are usually integrated in their respective geographic regions, I assume that regional integration should be able to explain conflict behaviour more clearly than any other form of IGOs. It is logical, therefore, to hypothesise that regionally integrated contiguous states would be more peaceful than non-integrated contiguous dyads, ceteris paribus. My empirical analysis supports this argument.

*Distance Between States (*Distance*)*
Following existing research practices (see Oneal & Russett, 1999b), I also control for distance between the countries in a dyad. *Distance* is the natural logarithm of the great circle distance between the capitals or major ports of country *i* and country *j*. I have used the option 'capital distance, contiguity plus war trap location change' in compiling the data. The original data source of contiguity and distance is Small and Singer (1982). *Distance* has always appeared negative as expected.

ANALYSIS AND FINDINGS

The base model that I have used here is as follows:

$$\begin{aligned} MID = {} & \beta_0 + \beta_1 RIA + \beta_2 MajorDyad + \beta_3 TradeDependence + \beta_4 Alliance \\ & + \beta_5 Contiguity + \beta_6 CapabilityRatio + \beta_7 PolityLow + \beta_8 Distance \end{aligned}$$

I have used two estimation methods: logistic regression analysis on pooled (the combination of cross-sectional and time-series) data with and without peace years correction (Beck & Tucker, 1996; Beck, Katz, & Tucker, 1998) and GEE (Bennett & Stam, 2000, p. 664; Liang & Zeger, 1986; Hardin & Hilbe, 2003; Oneal & Russett, 1999b).[9]

The result of logistic regression using the base model on all dyads, PRDs and RRDs (with and without correction for peace years) is reported in Table 1. *RIA*, the main variable of interest, shows expected signs and significance ($p<0.01$) except that it became marginally insignificant ($p<0.1$) in case of all dyads with correction for peace years. Other notable exceptions are: *Alliance* is not significant if I consider correction for peace years with any subset of data; *CapabilityRatio* is marginally insignificant ($p<0.1$) in RRDs with peace years and *PolityLow* is not significant in cases of RRDs with correction for peace years. The recurrent failure to be significant with correction for peace years may have been due to the fact that the huge number of 'irrelevant' peace years has diluted our result. Those are 'irrelevant' in the sense that, due to the long distance between them, most dyads have little interest at stake to fight for, or hardly have any capacity to fight against the other state.[10] No variable shows unexpected signs. To avoid multicollinearity, I dropped dyads with major powers and contiguous dyads from the models for PRDs and RRDs; and for the same reason, I have not used contiguity and distance simultaneously as the correlation between these two variables is very high ($\rho = -0.9922$).

Table 1. Logistic Estimates on MID Onset Based on All Dyads, PRDs and RRDs (With and Without Peace Years' Correction), 1950–2000.

Variables	(1)	(2)	(3)	(4)	(5)	(6)
	All_dyads	All_pceyrs	PRD	PRD_pceyrs	RRD	RRD_pceyrs
RIA	−0.60***	−0.32*	−0.87***	−0.54***	−0.78***	−0.38***
	(0.11)	(0.18)	(0.12)	(0.15)	(0.12)	(0.15)
MajorDyad	2.08***	2.04***				
	(0.07)	(0.19)				
TradeDependence	−0.64***	−0.55***	−0.46**	−0.32***	−3.93***	−3.23***
	(0.14)	(0.10)	(0.19)	(0.10)	(1.02)	(1.21)
Alliance	−0.25***	−0.02	−0.41***	−0.19	−0.46***	−0.19
	(0.07)	(0.15)	(0.07)	(0.13)	(0.07)	(0.13)
Contiguity	3.60***	3.13***				
	(0.06)	(0.14)				
CapabilityRatio	−0.27***	−0.26***	−0.24***	−0.23***	−0.10***	−0.09*
	(0.02)	(0.05)	(0.02)	(0.05)	(0.03)	(0.05)
PolityLow	−0.06***	−0.04***	−0.04***	−0.03***	−0.02***	−0.01
	(0.01)	(0.01)	(0.01)	(0.01)	(0.01)	(0.01)
Peace years		−0.05***		−0.07***		−0.08***
		(0.01)		(0.01)		(0.01)
Distance			−0.19***	−0.12***	−0.38***	−0.30***
			(0.01)	(0.02)	(0.04)	(0.05)
Constant	−6.28***	−5.26***	−2.12***	−1.48***	−2.14***	−1.42***
	(0.06)	(0.14)	(0.06)	(0.16)	(0.08)	(0.19)
Observations	331674	331674	42958	42958	18406	18406

Notes: Standard errors in parentheses.
$^{*}p<0.1$, $^{**}p<0.05$, $^{***}p<0.01$.

Applying GEE (see Table 2) on the same model as describe earlier, I find that RIA is strongly significant ($p<0.01$) on all dyads, PRDs and RRDs. Trade dependence is not significant in cases where there are PRDs, but significant in RRDs. This seems due to the impact of major power in a dyad because the correlation between *TradeDependence* and *RIA* in PRDs is negligible ($\rho = -0.0043$), whereas the correlation coefficient increases substantially ($\rho = -0.0586$) if I exclude major powers. Other anomalies are that the *Alliance* variable is not significant with all dyads, and *CapabilityRatio* and *PolityLow* marginally fail to be significant in RRDs ($p<0.01$).

So, with few exceptions, the estimates suggest that *RIA* had a significant impact in reducing MIDs during 1950–2000. The result is consistent in

Table 2. GEE Estimates on MID Onset Based on All Dyads, PRDs and RRDs, 1950–2000.

Variables	(1)	(2)	(3)
	All_dyads	PRD	RRD
RIA	−0.60***	−0.84***	−0.77***
	(0.20)	(0.18)	(0.19)
MajorDyad	2.07***		
	(0.20)		
TradeDependence	−0.47***	−0.23	−3.69***
	(0.16)	(0.25)	(1.31)
Alliance	−0.25	−0.41***	−0.46***
	(0.16)	(0.15)	(0.16)
Contiguity	3.59***		
	(0.15)		
CapabilityRatio	−0.27***	−0.24***	−0.11*
	(0.05)	(0.06)	(0.06)
PolityLow	−0.06***	−0.04***	−0.02*
	(0.01)	(0.01)	(0.01)
Distance		−0.19***	−0.38***
		(0.03)	(0.05)
Constant	−6.26***	−2.12***	−2.14***
	(0.11)	(0.16)	(0.19)
Observations	331419	42942	18398
Number of dyad	11286	1418	782

Notes: Standard errors in parentheses.
*$p<0.1$, **$p<0.05$, ***$p<0.01$.

politically and regionally relevant dyads. All the other variables behave as expected – no variable shows contradictory signs, although a few of them fail to be (strongly) significant. This finding may reinforce the suggestion that 'we should encourage state leaders to pursue deep integration as a way to create and foster positive commercial expectations, thus increasing the apparent cost of war' (Bearce, 2003, p. 367).

Barbieri (1998, 2005) and Barbieri and Schneider (1999) provide the main challenge to the liberal claim that trade reduces conflict. Therefore, it is interesting to note here that using Barbieri's dataset (Barbieri et al., 2008, 2009) and her specification, I did not find support for her claim that trade dependence instigates conflict. On the contrary, the variable *TradeDependence* almost always shows a significantly negative relationship with MIDs and never appears positive in any of the models.

CONCLUSION

Through this research regional integration appears to be a relevant candidate in explaining interstate relationships, as Mansfield (2003, p. 232) observed. As RIAs contain most aspects of the Kantian peace tripod, Kant's dream might become a reality through RIAs. These findings should encourage leaders in less integrated regions (such as the Middle East and North East Asia) to increase their efforts towards regional integration. Furthermore, where some regions are still locked in a 'security dilemma' (such as India and Pakistan), recognising the political benefits of regional integration may reduce mistrust among close neighbours.

This research is only a preliminary indication of the potential that regional integration provides for peace. Further research is necessary to refine the findings and check for robustness. This research should be extended with updated data to capture the impact of the RIAs which have proliferated since the 1990s, and to verify whether any other variables are responsible for a reduction in MIDs among integrated states. Further attention could be given to whether deeper integration implies a better prospect for peace, and if there is any regional variation in the effect of RIAs.

As a final point, until a 'world government' (Weiss, 2009) is in sight to manage the ever-increasing problems beyond the state boundary or capacity, attaining global peace through regionalisation remains a viable option. In this regard, only future research can verify if the South Asian Association for Regional Cooperation could be used as a way out for the coalition force in Afghanistan.

NOTES

1. The idea that free trade may reduce conflict dates back to the seventeenth century. Philosophers like Baron De Montesquieu and Immanuel Kant, British Statesman Richard Cobden, John Bright, Sir Norman Angell and Jacob Viner espoused the view that free trade reduces conflict (cited in Polachek, 2001). Former US President Woodrow Wilson also believed that 'a world open to commerce would be a world at peace' (Destler, 2005, p. 6). President Roosevelt's Secretary of State, Cordell Hull, became convinced that 'unhampered trade dovetailed with peace; high tariffs, trade barriers, and unfair economic competition, with war' (Destler, 2005, p. 15). There is also a long history of sceptics to the liberal view, for example Hamilton, List and Hirschman (cited in Schneider, Barbieri, & Gleditsch, 2003, p. 3). Critics of free markets, such as, V. I. Lenin (1970[1916]) and Patrick Buchanan (1998) argue that globalisation generates not amity, but added international

antagonism (cited in Gartzke & Li, 2003, p. 562). Kenneth Waltz (1979) also belongs to this group.

2. Barbieri (1998), for example reports that greater interdependence significantly increases the risk of militarised dispute. For other views contrary to the liberal argument, see Barbieri (2005) and Martin, Mayer, and Thoenig (2005). For a list of studies related to trade and conflict, see Table 1.2, p. 17 in Schneider et al. (2003) or Barbieri (2005, pp. 46–47).

3. On the contrary, Powers (2006, p. 460) demonstrates that the 'democratic peace proposition does not hold in Africa but, in fact, the relationship is the reverse'.

4. Critics may point to Myanmar in ASEAN. However, recent events demonstrate that the country is facing enormous pressure from the outside as well as within the ASEAN states to restore democracy in the country. See http://uk.reuters.com/article/worldNews/idUKSIN14425020071122 (accessed on 16 January 2008).

5. However, Russett and Oneal note 'Our conclusion that IGOs causally affect the likelihood of war or peace is plausible, even likely, but not conclusive' (2001, p. 212). On the contrary, Boehmer et al. (2004), Hafner-Burton and Montgomery (2006) and Dorussen (2006) all find that co-membership of IGOs is either insignificant, or may even increase the likelihood of conflict once data are corrected for length of time since a previous conflict in the dyad (cited in Dorussen & Ward, 2008, p. 190). We must note here that most, if not all, of the studies do not account for IGOs created for different purposes.

6. I am grateful to UNU-CRIS, and especially to its Director Dr. Luk Van Langenhove, for the generous support for the compilation of the dataset on RIAs.

7. There are disagreements whether one should 'mark dispute/crisis onset for originators and joiners'. Bennett and Stam (2007, p. 44) do not suggest doing so for they do not believe that 'these decisions are equivalent'. However, the author is convinced that 'researchers should be concerned with all years in which states are involved in a conflict' (Oneal & Russett, 1999b, p. 428), and hence, used dispute onset as originators and joiners. Nevertheless, I find no significant difference in results if the option 'mark dispute/crisis onset for originators and joiners' is ignored.

8. There were several complications in collecting the data on RIAs. Although the number of RIAs is amazingly high, the success in attaining their stated objective is disappointingly low. Consequently, it is not easy to ascertain the precise status of an RIA. Furthermore, multiple memberships of a single country to different RIAs represent another problem. Most countries are members of more than one integration arrangements which complicates the decision to include a country as a member. To solve multiple membership problems, I considered states only in the RIAs where they are better integrated. For instance, Pakistan is a founder member of the South Asian Association for Regional Cooperation (SAARC) as well as of the Economic Cooperation Organization (ECO – with Iran and Turkey). Considering its level of engagement and regional affinity, Pakistan has been considered in SAARC, and not in ECO.

9. Oneal and Russett (1999b, p. 427) describe: 'GEE is a quasi-likelihood method developed specifically for pooled time-series, cross-sectional analyses. A great virtue is its flexibility. GEE can be used to estimate general linear models, including analyses of dependent variables that are binomial or a count of events, as well as those with a normal distribution. Researchers can specify the function linking the

covariates to the response variable and the correlational structure of the error terms within groups'.

10. Oneal and Russett (1999b, p. 425) term these as 'false negatives'.

ACKNOWLEDGMENTS

The research project was financed by the GARNET Mobility Grant (contract no. 51330) under the EC funded Framework 6 Network of Excellence on 'Global Governance, Regionalism and Regulation: the Role of the EU', and was developed under the supervision of Professor Kristian S. Gleditsch at the Department of Government, University of Essex in Spring 2008. Thanks to Tobias Boehmelt for his help with STATA. I am very grateful to Luk Van Langenhove and Philippe De Lombaerde at UNU-CRIS for their invaluable support for my research and sponsorship for data collection on regional integration. This revised version is based on the comments by Professor Brian M. Pollins on my conference presentation at the University of Sydney (June 26–28, 2009). The comments from the editors of this book have also been very helpful. Finally, I am very grateful to two of my colleagues, Buiter and Moonen, for reading my draft to help me correct grammatical mistakes. Nevertheless, I am solely responsible for any errors of fact and interpretation.

REFERENCES

Annan, K. A. (2002). Problems without passports. Foreign Policy/Nobel Laureates. Los Angeles Times Syndicate International, a division of Tribune Media Services. Available at http://www.digitalnpq.org/global_services/nobel%20laureates/09-16-02.html. Accessed on November 27, 2009.

Baier, S. L., & Bergstrand, J. H. (2007). Do free trade agreements actually increase members' international trade? *Journal of International Economics*, *71*(1), 72–95.

Baldwin, R. (1993). *A domino theory of regionalism*. NBER Working Paper No. 4465. Available at http://papers.ssrn.com/sol3/papers.cfm?abstract_id = 252201. Accessed on September 4, 2009.

Barbieri, K. (1995). Economic interdependence and militarized interstate conflict, 1870–1985. Paper presented at the 36th Annual Convention of the international Studies Association, 20–24 February, Chicago, IL.

Barbieri, K. (1996). Economic interdependence: A path to peace or a source of interstate conflict? *Journal of Peace Research*, *33*(1), 29–49.

Barbieri, K. (1998). International trade and conflict: The debatable relationship. Paper presented at the 35th Annual Convention of the International Studies Association, 18–21 March, Minneapolis, MN.

Barbieri, K. (2005). *The liberal illusion: Does trade promote peace?* Ann Arbor, MI: The University of Michigan Press.

Barbieri, K., Keshk, O., & Pollins, B. (2008). Correlates of war project trade data set codebook. Version 2.0. Available at http://correlatesofwar.org. Accessed on August 28, 2009.

Barbieri, K., Keshk, O., & Pollins, B. (2009). Trading data: Evaluating our assumptions and coding rules. *Conflict Management and Peace Science, 26*, 471–491.

Barbieri, K., & Schneider, G. (1999). Globalization and peace: Assessing new direction in the study of trade and conflict. *Journal of Peace Research, 36*(4), 387–404.

Bearce, D. H. (2003). Grasping the commercial institutional peace. *International Studies Quarterly, 47*, 347–370.

Bearce, D. H., & Omori, S. (2005). How do commercial institutions promote peace? *Journal of Peace Research, 42*(6), 659–678.

Beck, N., Katz, J., & Tucker, R. (1998). Taking time seriously in binary time-series–cross-section analysis. *American Journal of Political Science, 42*(1), 1260–1288.

Beck, N., & Tucker, R. (1996). Conflict in space and time: time-series–cross-section analysis with a binary dependent variable. Paper presented at the 92nd Annual Meeting of the American Political Science Association, August, San Francisco, CA.

Bennett, D. S., & Stam, A. (2000). EUGene: A conceptual manual. *International Interactions, 26*, 179–204.

Bennett, D. S., & Stam, A. (2007). EUGene: Expected utility generation and data management program (V3.2 documentation). Available at www.eugenesoftware.org. Accessed on July 23, 2009.

Boehmer, C., Gartzke, E., & Nordstrom, T. (2004). Do international organizations promote peace? *World Politics, 57*, 1–38.

Bremer, S. (1992). Dangerous dyads: Conditions affecting the likelihood of interstate war, 1816–1965. *Journal of Conflict Resolution, 36*(2), 309–341.

Buchanan, P. J. (1998). *The great betrayal: How American sovereignty and social justice are being sacrificed to the gods of the global economy*. Boston, MA: Little, Brown.

Chan, S. (1997). In search of democratic peace: Problems and promise. *Mershon International Studies Review, 41*(1), 59–91.

de Soya, I., Oneal, J. R., & Park, Y. H. (1997). Testing power-transition theory using alternative measures of national capabilities. *Journal of Conflict Resolution, 41*, 509–528.

Destler, I. M. (2005). *American trade politics* (4th ed.). Washington, DC: Institute of International Economics.

Deutsch, K. W. (1957). *Political community and the North Atlantic Area: International organization in the light of historical experience*. Princeton, NJ: Princeton University Press.

Dixon, W. J. (1994). Democracy and the peaceful settlement of international conflict. *American Political Science Review, 88*(1), 1–17.

Dorussen, H. (2006). Heterogeneous trade interests and conflict: What you trade matters. *Journal of Conflict Resolution, 50*(1), 87–107.

Dorussen, H., & Ward, H. (2008). Intergovernmental organizations and the Kantian peace. *Journal of Conflict Resolution, 52*(2), 189–212.

Doyle, M. W. (1997). *Ways of war and peace*. New York: W.W. Norton.

Doyle, M. W. (2004). Liberal internationalism: Peace, war and democracy. Available at http://nobelprize.org. Accessed on August 26, 2008.

Gartzke, E. (2005). Economic freedom and peace. In: J. D. Gwartney, R. Lawson & E. Gartzke (Eds), *Economic freedom of the world: 2005 annual report*. Canada: Fraser Institute.

Gartzke, E., & Li, Q. (2003). War, peace, and the invisible hand: Positive externalities of economic globalization. *International Studies Quarterly*, *47*(4), 561–586.

Gelpi, C. F., & Grieco, J. (2008). Democracy, interdependence and the sources of the liberal peace. *Journal of Peace Research*, *45*(1), 17–36.

Ghosn, F., & Bennett, S. (2003). Codebook for the dyadic militarized interstate incident data, Version 3.10. Available at http://correlatesofwar.org. Accessed on August 8, 2008.

Gibler, D. M., & Sarkees, M. (2004). Measuring alliances: The correlates of war formal interstate alliance data set, 1816–2000. *Journal of Peace Research*, *41*(2), 211–222.

Goldsmith, B. E. (2007). A liberal peace in Asia? *Journal of Peace Research*, *44*(1), 5–27.

Haas, E. B. (1958). *The uniting of Europe: Political, social and economic forces 1950–1957*. Stanford, CA: Stanford University Press.

Hafner-Burton, E. M., & Montgomery, A. H. (2006). Power positions: International organizations, social networks, and conflict. *Journal of Conflict Resolution*, *50*(3), 3–27.

Haftel, Y. Z. (2007). Designing for peace: Regional integration arrangements, institutional variation and militarized interstate disputes. *International Organization*, *61*(1), 217–237.

Hardin, J. W., & Hilbe, J. M. (2003). *Generalized estimating equations*. USA: Chapman and Hall/CRC.

Kant, I. ([1795]1970). In: H. Reiss (Ed.), *Perpetual peace: A philosophical sketch*. Cambridge: Cambridge University Press [Reprinted in Kant's Political Writings].

Kugler, J., & Lemke, D. (1996). *Parity and war: Evaluations and extensions of the war ledger*. Ann Arbor, MI: University of Michigan Press.

Lenin, V. I. (1970[1916]). *Imperialism: The highest stage of capitalism*. New York: International Publishers.

Liang, K. Y., & Zeger, S. L. (1986). Longitudinal data analysis using generalized linear models. *Britanika*, *73*(1), 13–22.

Mansfield, E., Milner, H., & Rosendorff, P. (2002). Why democracies cooperate more: Electoral control and international trade agreement. *International Organization*, *56*(3), 477–514.

Mansfield, E. D. (2003). Preferential peace: Why preferential trading arrangements inhibit interstate conflict. In: E. D. Mansfield & B. M. Pollins (Eds), *Economic interdependence and international conflict: New perspectives on an enduring debate* (pp. 222–236). Ann Arbor, MI: University of Michigan Press.

Mansfield, E. D., & Pevehouse, J. C. (2000). Trade blocs, trade flows, and international conflict. *International Organization*, *54*(4), 775–808.

Mansfield, E. D., & Pevehouse, J. C. (2003). Institutions, interdependence, and international conflict. In: G. Schneider, K. Barbieri & N. P. Gleditsch (Eds), *Globalization and armed conflict* (pp. 233–250). Lanham, MD: Rowman and Littlefield.

Maoz, Z., & Russett, B. (1993). Normative and structural cases of democratic peace, 1946–1986. *American Political Science Review*, *87*(3), 624–638.

Marshal, M. G., & Jaggers, K. (2005). Polity IV dataset users' manual version 2004. Available at www.systemicpeace.org/polity/polity4.htm. Accessed on April 23, 2009.

Martin, P., Mayer, T., & Thoenig, M. (2005). *Make trade not war?* CEPR Discussion Paper no. 5218.

Oneal, J. R., & Russett, B. (1999a). The Kantian peace: The pacific benefits of democracy, interdependence, and international organization. *World Politics*, *52*(1), 1–37.

Oneal, J. R., & Russett, B. (1999b). Assessing liberal peace with alternative specifications: Trade still reduces conflict. *Journal of Peace Research*, *36*(4), 423–442.

Oneal, J. R., & Russett, B. (2003a). Assessing the liberal peace with alternative specifications: Trade still reduces conflict. In: G. Schneider, K. Barbieri & N. P. Gleditsch (Eds), *Globalization and armed conflict*. Maryland: Rowman and Littlefield.

Oneal, J. R., & Russett, B. (2003b). Clear and clean: The fixed effect of the liberal peace. *International Organization*, *55*(2), 469–485.

Pevehouse, J. C., & Russett, B. (2006). Democratic intergovernmental organizations promote peace. *International Organization*, *60*(4), 969–1000.

Polachek, S. W. (1980). Conflict and trade. *Journal of Conflict Resolution*, *24*, 55–78.

Polachek, S. W. (2001). Trade based interactions: An interdisciplinary perspective. Revised version of the Presidential Address delivered at the Annual Meeting of the Peace Science Society International, October 2000, New Haven, CT. Available at www.binghamton.edu/econ/wp02/WP0202.pdf. Accessed on May 11, 2008.

Polachek, S. W., & Seiglie, C. (2006). *Trade, peace and democracy an analysis of dyadic dispute*. IZA Discussion Paper no. 2170. The Institute for the Study of Labor, Bonn.

Powers, K. (2004). Regional trade agreements and military alliances. *International Interactions*, *30*(4), 373–395.

Powers, K. (2006). Dispute initiation and alliance obligations in regional economic institutions. *Journal of Peace Research*, *43*(4), 453–471.

Rasler, K., & Thompson, W. R. (2005). *Puzzles of the democratic peace: Theory, geopolitics, and the transformation of world politics*. New York: Palgrave Macmillan.

Robst, J., Polachek, S., & Chang, Y. C. (2006). *Geographic proximity, trade and international conflict*. IZA Discussion Paper no. 1988. The Institute for the Study of Labor, Bonn.

Russett, B. (1993). *Grasping the democratic peace: Principles for a post-cold war world*. Princeton, NJ: Princeton University Press.

Russett, B. (2003). Violence and disease: Trade as a suppressor of conflict when suppressor matter. In: E. D. Mansfield & B. Pollins (Eds), *Economic interdependence and international conflict: New perspectives on an enduring debate*. Ann Arbor, MI: University of Michigan Press.

Russett, B., & Oneal, J. (2001). *Triangulating peace: Democracy, interdependence, and international organizations*. New York: W.W. Norton.

Schneider, G., Barbieri, K., & Gleditsch, N. P. (2003). *Globalization and arms conflict*. Lanham, MD: Rowman & Littlefield.

Shannon, M. (2009). Preventing war and providing the peace: International organizations and the management of territorial disputes. *Conflict Management and Peace Science*, *26*(2), 144–163.

Singer, J. D., & Small, M. (1995). *National military capabilities data. Correlates of war project*. Michigan: University of Michigan.

Slantchev, B. L., Alexandrova, A., & Gartzke, E. (2005). Probabilistic causality, selection bias, and the logic of the democratic peace. *American Political Science Review*, *99*(3), 459–462.

Small, M., & Singer, J. D. (1982). *Resort to arms: International and civil wars, 1816–1980*. Beverly Hills: Sage Publication.

Starr, H. (1992). Why don't democracies fight one another? Evaluating the theory-findings feedback loop. *Jerusalem Journal of International Relations*, *14*(4), 41–57.

Starr, H. (1997). Democracy and integration: Why democracies don't fight each other. *Journal of Peace Research, 34*(2), 153–162.
Stinnett, D. M., Tir, J., Schafer, P., Diehl, P. F., & Gochman, C. (2002). The correlates of war project direct contiguity data, version 3. *Conflict Management and Peace Science, 19*(2), 58–66.
Waltz, K. N. (1979). *Theory of international politics.* New York: McGraw-Hill.
Weiss, T. G. (2009). What happened to the idea of world government. *International Studies Quarterly, 53*, 253–271.

APPENDIX. FULL NAMES OF REGIONAL INTEGRATIONS USED IN THIS STUDY

AMU	Arab Maghreb Union
ANDEAN-CAN	Andean Community
ASEAN	Association of Southeast Asian Nations
CACM	Central American Common Market
CARICOM	Caribbean Community
COMESA	Common Market for Eastern and Southern Africa
ECCAS	Economic Community of Central African States
ECO	Economic Cooperation Organization
ECOWAS	Economic Community of West African States
EFTA	European Free Trade Area
EU	European Union
GCC	Gulf Cooperation Council
MERCOSUR	Common Market of the Southern Cone
NAFTA	North American Free Trade Agreement
SAARC	South Asian Association for Regional Cooperation
SACU	South African Customs Union

Different names of the same organisation, for instance, EU and EEC, have been counted as one.

CHAPTER 12

ECONOMIC INTEGRATION, ECONOMIC SIGNALLING AND THE PROBLEM OF ECONOMIC CRISES ☆

Jedidiah Royal

ABSTRACT

Purpose – *This chapter draws on several areas of scholarship to consider the impact of economic crises on the utility of economic costly signalling theory (ECST).*

Design/methodology/approach – *The chapter introduces the problem of economic crises into the debate over ECST to better understand its practical utility. It first highlights the pacific benefits anticipated by ECST to provide a conceptual baseline. It then reviews contemporary economic and political science literature that links economic integration, economic crises and external conflict. Finally, it introduces a perspective on how the conditions created by economic crises reduce the ability and willingness of states to send economic costly signals.*

☆ Disclaimer: The words and views expressed in this chapter are the author's alone. They do not represent any official policies or views of the US Government.

Economics of War and Peace: Economic, Legal, and Political Perspectives
Contributions to Conflict Management, Peace Economics and Development, Volume 14, 205–223

ISSN: 1572-8323/doi:10.1108/S1572-8323(2010)0000014016

Findings – *The chapter finds that the value of ECST to security policy is problematic when considering the occurrence of economic crises.*

Originality/value – *This chapter advances the debate over capitalist peace theory by introducing the problem of economic crises to the discourse.*

INTRODUCTION

Does economic interdependence lead to peace? Recent scholarship has produced promising results linking interdependence with a decrease in the likelihood of military conflict (notable contributions include Oneal & Russett, 1997; Russett & Oneal, 2001; Gartzke, 2005; Gartzke, Li, & Boehmer, 2001; Hegre, 2000).[1] In accordance with this, some advocate policies expanding economic interdependence to reduce the likelihood of conflict. Theoretical arguments linking interdependence and peace have traditionally been described in terms of economic costs: economically interdependent states are less likely to go to war with one another because of the costs associated with disruption of the economic relationship during wartime. This rationale has been a long-standing feature of liberal theory, dating back at least to Immanuel Kant's writings.

More recently, some theorists have drawn from signalling theory to develop a second rationale for linking interdependence with peace. This rationale, referred to here as *economic costly signalling theory* (ECST), posits that economically integrated states can use their economic relationship to send costly signals, short of the use of force, that credibly represent their resolve, thus reducing the potential for miscalculation that could result in militarised conflict. However, the recent scholarship on ECST has not sufficiently considered the occurrence of and conditions created by economic crises. The focus of this chapter is to address this gap in the literature. It draws attention to recent economic and political science scholarship that correlates economic integration, economic crises and inter-state conflict. Furthermore, it hypothesises that economic crises tend to reduce the ability and willingness of states to undertake economic costly signals. As such, the advent of an economic crisis can undermine the general expectations of ECST theorists.

This chapter proceeds in three parts. It first reviews the expected pacific benefits of ECST to provide a conceptual baseline. Second, the chapter reviews contemporary research that correlates economic integration, economic crises and inter-state conflict. The final section considers the impact of economic crises on the ability and willingness of states to send economic costly signals. The chapter concludes that, when accounting for economic crises, ECST is unlikely to be an effective organising principle for diplomatic and security policymakers.

WHAT ARE THE EXPECTATIONS OF ECONOMIC COSTLY SIGNALLING THEORY?

The international environment is characterised by imperfect information. States are unable to fully know the capabilities, motivations and assumptions of other states. Due to the existence of imperfect information, states have incentives to misrepresent themselves by bluffing, particularly with regard to their willingness to use force, to gain diplomatic advantage. At times, this is a high-risk, high-reward strategy. The incentive to bluff combined with the existence of imperfect information results in conditions that can lead to strategic miscalculation and conflict (Bueno de Mesquita, Morrow, & Zorick, 1997).

Given this dilemma, upon what assumptions do states pursue diplomatic and security policies when faced with a potential threat? Costly signalling theory, a component of general game theory, assumes that there are avenues available for states to gain credible information about the intentions of other states, thereby reducing the risk associated with miscalculation, although not entirely (a situation characterised by perfect information is always assumed to be impossible). This reduction of risk occurs through the use of costly signals, which are signals undertaken at a cost to the sender of the signal to display its resolve on a particular matter. Fearon (1997, p. 69) defines costly signals as follows:

> A threat may be rendered credible when the act of sending it incurs or creates some cost that the sender would be disinclined to incur or create if he or she were in fact *not* willing to carry out the threat ... For a threat to increase the target's belief that the sender would be willing to fight, it must be more likely that a resolved state would make the threat than an unresolved state. Thus, to be credible, a threat must have some cost or risk attached to it that might discourage an unresolved state from making it.

Costless signals, such as privately communicated diplomatic threats, are generally ineffective in overcoming this dilemma because, as mentioned, weakly resolved states have incentives to misrepresent themselves to encourage a potential adversary to acquiesce (Walsh, 2007). In other words, talk is cheap.

Costly signals are highly valuable for inter-state relationships because they reveal the true resolve of a state with regard to the thresholds for the use of force during an escalatory phase of competition (Fearon, 1994, 1997). These signals can be delivered to indicate either a high or a low threshold for war, both of which may decrease tensions depending on the circumstances. For example, Mikhail Gorbachev's use of costly signals, including the withdrawal of military forces from Afghanistan, ratcheted down tensions and conveyed a desire for co-operation that brought a peaceful conclusion to the Cold War (Kydd, 2005; Copeland, 2000).

Liberal security theorists are increasingly looking towards signalling as a rationale for why economic interdependence might lead to a reduction in the likelihood of conflict. Interdependence here is meant to function specifically as an indicator of vulnerability (Mansfield & Pollins, 2003). High levels of vulnerability are associated with high levels of cost in the event of termination or disruption of the economic relationship. As such, higher levels of interdependence lead to higher levels of vulnerability. Elements of an interdependent relationship may include trade, financial market integration, monetary coordination and official financial holdings.

This burgeoning research topic has focused on *deliberate* signalling among integrated states, primarily through negative economic signals designed to disrupt an economic relationship. The most overt and obvious signalling tools are economic sanctions and embargos. A state's wilful agreement to undertake economic harm to signal its political intentions can be a powerful statement. Such was the case with the US embargo on Cuba following Fidel Castro's political alignment with the Soviet Union.

Much less attention has been paid to *non-deliberate* methods of economic signalling. Gartzke (2003) has noted the opportunity for signalling extends more broadly than simply negative economic statecraft. For example, markets can autonomously assess that political conditions in a foreign country do not warrant the risk of investment. Indeed, such non-deliberate signals could be considered a more credible and genuine signal than a politically driven signal, as markets are independent and are unlikely to have motives other than profit (Gartzke & Li, 2003; Gartzke et al., 2001). Diplomatically calculated signals between potential adversaries can include any number of ulterior motives.

Gartzke has described militarised disputes as bargaining problems, noting that 'if states fight because they have trouble identifying mutually acceptable bargains short of a contest, then factors that allow states to reduce uncertainty should more often allow interdependent states to avoid the need for military violence' (Gartzke, 2003, p. 102). In a slightly different variation, Stein (2003, p. 117) has described militarised disputes as information problems, writing, 'The explanation for the occurrence of costly conflict is that actors have private information about their resolve and have no credible way to signal that to others short of incurring the costs of conflict ... Such militarization can be avoided through costly signalling'.

Therefore, according to ECST, economic relationships provide states with an additional range of economic options to signal their resolve to a potential adversary. Although signalling credibly through these economic avenues comes at an economic cost, such as the loss of export markets and disruption of financial markets, the cost would be considered less than the combined economic, political, social and human costs borne by both sides as a result of military conflict. In accordance with this approach, signalling should be more efficient and effective as levels of economic interdependence grow (Morrow, 1999, 2003). That is, the likelihood of conflict is assumed to be negatively associated with the degree of economic interdependence in a dyad. States with the highest degree of interdependence should be the least likely to undertake the use of force to resolve disputes.

It is important to note that adherents to this theory do not suggest that economic integration per se reduces the likelihood of conflict, but rather that states with bilateral economic relationships have an additional suite of options to create credible impressions on other states short of the use of force. This additional suite of options should improve overall communication between economically integrated states and thus reduce the potential for miscalculation.

WHAT IS THE CONNECTION BETWEEN ECONOMIC INTEGRATION, ECONOMIC CRISES AND CONFLICT?

In February 2009, the US Director of National Intelligence Dennis Blair reported to the US House of Representatives that 'the primary near-term security concern of the United States is the global economic crisis and its geopolitical implications' (Blair, 2009, p. 2). Blair testified that weak economic conditions resulting from the crisis could lead to protectionism, domestic instability, refugee flows and a general questioning of US leadership in the world. Without coordinated action on a global level, Blair warned that 'economic and financial crises [may] spiral into broader geopolitical tensions' (Blair, 2009, p. 3).

Does academic scholarship support such a direct connection between economic conditions and security consequences? Contemporary research on the economic-security nexus has tended to focus on the relationship between dyadic interdependence and conflict, with substantially less focus on the relationship between economic conditions and the security or defence behaviour of integrated states. This section reviews the literature with reference to two questions. First, what is the relationship between economic integration and economic crises? Second, what is the relationship between economic crises and armed conflict?

There is a growing body of literature that suggests systemic economic integration is associated with an increase in the occurrence and severity of economic crises, defined here as 'episodes of financial-market volatility marked by significant problems of illiquidity and insolvency among financial-market participants and/or by official intervention to contain such consequences' (Bordo, Eichengreen, Klingebiel, Martinez-Peria, & Rose, 2001, p. 55). Bordo et al. (2001) (see also Kose, Prasad, & Terrones, 2006) show that the frequency with which economic crises are occurring has risen dramatically in recent decades and is positively correlated with global economic integration. Indeed, the only comparable period associated with such high frequency of economic crisis was the inter-war period surrounding the Great Depression. Economic explanations for this association are varied. Some prominent economists have highlighted the destabilising role of pro-cyclicality in the global economic system, the tendency for investors to inflate bubbles during economic booms and withdraw capital during economic busts just when economies need liquidity the most. Joseph Stiglitz (2000, p. 1079) argues that 'capital market liberalization is systemically associated with greater instability, and for good reason: capital market flows are markedly pro-cyclical, exacerbating economic fluctuations'.[2]

This pro-cyclical phenomenon may appear counterintuitive. Liberalised capital markets are expected to attract foreign investment, resulting in greater wealth and a greater capacity for states to secure their own economic stability. Why then should pro-cyclicality be such a concern? Ranciere, Tornell, and Westermann (2006, p. 3332) explain the paradox:

> On the one hand, financial liberalization tends to relax borrowing constraints, leading to higher investment and higher average growth; on the other hand, it encourages risk-taking, generates financial fragility and increases the probability of financial crises, which often have severe recessionary consequences.

As bank regulations are liberalised, banks have incentives to accept greater risk in their financial portfolio, resulting in structural fragility that gives way when economic conditions deteriorate. Traditional economic theory would suggest that investors, or even states, could reduce their vulnerability to volatility through investment diversification. Interestingly, Goldstein and Pauzner (2004) find that diversification between countries becomes less useful as a measure of protection against global downturns because of an increase in the likelihood that markets will co-move or co-vary. They write,

> The fact that different countries share the same group of investors leads to the transmission of negative shocks from one part of the world to another. Thus, the realization of a financial crisis in one country can induce a crisis in other countries as well. This generates a positive correlation between the returns on investments in different countries and thus reduces the effectiveness of diversifying investments across countries. (Goldstein & Pauzner, 2004, p. 152; see also Quinn & Voth, 2008)

Pro-cyclical financial flows have also been linked to a lack of clarity in international financial markets that can lead to substantial market imperfections. Calvo and Mendoza (2000), for example, argue that globalisation as it exists today leads to the possibility of crisis by weakening incentives to gain costly information and by widening the range of portfolios in which investors mimic patterns. Because investors have less information and are more willing to follow the herd, the global system will have large capital flows and pro-cyclical patterns, leading to broad volatility among all participants in the global system.

Furthermore, the history of state responses to economic crises would appear to exacerbate the problem of opacity in the global financial system. Bailouts, stimulus packages and international crisis lending create a moral hazard problem that has the long-term impact of encouraging the inflation of bubbles, increasing the incentives for unsustainable short-term capital flows (Corsetti, Pesenti, & Roubini, 1999).

This leads to a second contention common among contemporary economic research: that interdependence leads to economic crises becoming contagious. The 'contagion' hypothesis suggests that the linkages created through global economic integration for the purpose of economic efficiency are the very same linkages through which economic and financial crises are transmitted from one state to another. In times of relative economic independence, an economic shock remains localised, affecting only or at least primarily the state where the shock originates. Yet in times of economic interdependence, shocks become contagious and are spread within the system, often in unpredictable ways. As such, states that are dependent on the global economic system are vulnerable to its ups and downs.

Glick and Rose (1999, p. 604) find support for the contagion effect theory, noting that 'trade is an important channel for contagion, above and beyond macroeconomic influences. Countries that trade and compete with targets of speculative attacks are themselves likely to be attacked'.

The counterargument to contagion is the 'risk-sharing' argument. It suggests that while trade and financial linkages may spread a crisis, this creates a cushioning effect that, overall, minimises the effects on any individual state. In other words, interdependence creates shock-absorbing linkages that soften a state's vulnerability to dramatic economic downturns (see, e.g., Kalemli-Ozcan, Sorensen, & Yosha, 2003).

Gallegati, Greenwald, Richiardi, and Stiglitz (2008) have made a convincing observation that would appear to clarify this debate. They have provided statistical modelling indicating that risk-sharing and contagion are in fact two sides of the same coin. When economic times are good, inter-linkages provide mechanisms for the diffusion of individual agents that face a liquidity crisis. A lender can request a creditor defer payment, whereas a creditor can then transfer this cost on to other agents. As such, the system would absorb the crisis. When liquidity is relatively more scarce during down times, a sufficiently large negative shock will use those very same inter-linkages to transmit that shock to other agents in the system. As a result, 'risk-sharing is beneficial only when the overall economic environment is favourable, while in harsh times it might be better to stay alone ... [Linkage during market downturns] becomes socially detrimental: not only is it that the expected number of defaults is higher when the economic agents are connected, but defaults become a systemic failure' (Gallegati et al., 2008, pp. 5, 16).

Kose, Prasad, and Terrones (2009) considered the same question and found only mild support for risk-sharing and only among developed, industrial economies. They found no evidence that developing, non-industrial countries are able to share risk. The authors break relatively new ground in suggesting why this is the case for non-industrial states:

> One possibility is that these countries rely more on less stable capital such as bank loans and other forms of debt that may not allow for efficient risk sharing. Indeed, when we break up stocks of external assets and liabilities into different categories — FDI, portfolio equity, portfolio debt, etc. — we find that the underlying composition of capital flows influences the ability of developing countries to share risk. In particular, external debt appears to hinder the ability of emerging market economies to share their consumption risk. (Kose, Prasad, & Terrones, 2009, p. 259)

One reason why interdependent states may not be well-suited to share risk is due to the fact that interdependence leads to economic specialisation and reliance on external financing. Gande, John, and Senbet (2008) and Corsetti et al. (1999) provide conceptual and analytical links between specialisation, moral hazard and contagion.

Thus, the answer to the first question set out at the beginning of this section, whether economic integration and economic crises are linked, seems reasonably well-established. Substantial recent scholarship indicates a positive association between interdependence and economic crises. What then about the second question? Is there a correlation between economic crises and armed conflict? The impacts at an individual level and on a state level are intuitive and well-documented (see, e.g., Richards & Gelleny, 2006). Rodrik (1997a, 1997b), among others, argues that instability in the global economic system contributes to social disintegration and political conflict. Social unrest, regime change and even civil war have directly resulted from the vagaries of economic integration.[3]

Less intuitive is how periods of economic decline may increase the likelihood of external conflict. Political science literature has contributed a moderate degree of attention to the impact of economic decline and the security and defence behaviour of interdependent states. Research in this vein has been considered at systemic, dyadic and national levels. Several notable contributions follow.

First, on the systemic level, Pollins (2008) advances Modelski and Thompson's (1996) work on leadership cycle theory, finding that rhythms in the global economy are associated with the rise and fall of a pre-eminent power and the often bloody transition from one pre-eminent leader to the next. As such, exogenous shocks such as economic crises could usher in a redistribution of relative power (see also Gilpin, 1981) that leads to uncertainty about power balances, increasing the risk of miscalculation (Fearon, 1995). Alternatively, even a relatively certain redistribution of power could lead to a permissive environment for conflict as a rising power may seek to challenge a declining power (Werner, 1999). Separately, Pollins (1996) also shows that global economic cycles combined with parallel leadership cycles impact the likelihood of conflict among major, medium and small powers, although he suggests that the causes and connections between global economic conditions and security conditions remain unknown.

Second, on a dyadic level, Copeland's (1996, 2000) theory of trade expectations suggests that 'future expectation of trade' is a significant variable in understanding economic conditions and security behaviour of states. He argues that interdependent states are likely to gain pacific benefits from trade so long as they have an optimistic view of future trade relations. However, if the expectations of future trade decline, particularly for difficult to replace items such as energy resources, the likelihood for conflict increases, as states will be inclined to use force to gain access to those resources. Crises could potentially be the trigger for decreased trade expectations either on its own or because it triggers protectionist moves by interdependent states.[4]

Third, others have considered the link between economic decline and external armed conflict at a national level. Blomberg and Hess (2002) find a strong correlation between internal conflict and external conflict, particularly during periods of economic downturn. They write,

> The linkages between internal and external conflict and prosperity are strong and mutually reinforcing. Economic conflict tends to spawn internal conflict, which in turn returns the favour. Moreover, the presence of a recession tends to amplify the extent to which international and external conflicts self-reinforce each other. (Blomberg & Hess, 2002, p. 89)

Economic decline has also been linked with an increase in the likelihood of terrorism (Blomberg, Hess, & Weerapana, 2004), which has the capacity to spill across borders and lead to external tensions.

Furthermore, crises generally reduce the popularity of a sitting government. 'Diversionary theory' suggests that, when facing unpopularity arising from economic decline, sitting governments have increased incentives to fabricate external military conflicts to create a 'rally around the flag' effect. Wang (1996), DeRouen (1995), and Blomberg, Hess, and Thacker (2006) find supporting evidence showing that economic decline and use of force are at least indirectly correlated. Gelpi (1997), Miller (1999), and Kisangani and Pickering (2009) suggest that the tendency towards diversionary tactics are greater for democratic states than autocratic states, due to the fact that democratic leaders are generally more susceptible to being removed from office due to lack of domestic support. DeRouen (2000) has provided evidence showing that periods of weak economic performance in the United States, and thus weak Presidential popularity, are statistically linked to an increase in the use of force.

In summary, recent economic scholarship positively correlates economic integration with an increase in the frequency of economic crises, whereas political science scholarship links economic decline with external conflict at systemic, dyadic and national levels.[5] This implied connection between integration, crises and armed conflict has not featured prominently in the economic-security debate and deserves more attention.

This observation is not contradictory to other perspectives that link economic interdependence with a decrease in the likelihood of external conflict, such as those mentioned in the first paragraph of this chapter.

Those studies tend to focus on dyadic interdependence instead of global interdependence and do not specifically consider the occurrence of and conditions created by economic crises. As such, the view presented here should be considered ancillary to those views.

CAN STATES SIGNAL EFFECTIVELY DURING ECONOMIC CRISES?

The rationalist theory of war suggests that 'war is costly and risky, so rational states should have incentives to locate negotiated settlements that all would prefer to the gamble of war' (Fearon, 1995). However, states are not always able to find negotiated settlements, and inter-state war does occur, often because states are uncertain about the private information of other states, such as resolve and capabilities, which can lead to miscalculation, escalation and conflict. Costly signalling, including through the use of economic costly signals as described above, is a means of overcoming uncertainty. However, economic costly signalling theorists have not described under what conditions economic costly signals are useful for settling disputes short of the use of force. For example, how useful is signalling among divergent types of political systems (autocratic and democratic), economic systems (capitalist and socialist) and dependency levels (asymmetric and co-dependent)? Each of these conditions are worthy of further study.

This section considers the impact of economic crises on the practicality of ECST. I propose that economic crises have a dichotomous effect on the utility of economic costly signals. On the one hand, crises decrease the willingness of states to undertake economic costly signals because they are relatively more costly during crises. On the other hand, the very fact that they are more costly should increase the efficacy of such signals should they be used. However, the potential for states to 'underbalance' against foreign threats, including by declining to send economic costly signals, also increases as a result of economic crises. This tendency undermines the practical utility of ECST during and following economic crises.

As economic growth becomes scarce, its value increases to states and their societies. Negative economic shocks, therefore, increase the costs of economic costly signals, because those signals further undercut the prospects for economic growth at a time when it is scarce. A corollary of this argument would be that a state that enjoys strong economic stability can accept economic (trade and financial) costs vis-à-vis a potential adversary with less relative repercussion than an economically weakened state. At times of general economic growth, accepting some economic costs for the sake of national security is a more palatable policy adjustment than during times of economic weakness.

Along with increasing economic (monetary) costs, the political costs of economic costly signals also increase as a result of economic crises. Economic stability is a key public good for which leaders of states, particularly in open societies, are held responsible. Given that leaders desire to retain power, and given that leaders consider their political survivability when crafting foreign policies (Bueno de Mesquita, Smith, Siverson, & Morrow, 2003), leaders are thus unlikely voluntarily to undermine economic recovery during and following economic crises. In other words, domestic political interests in economic growth are relatively stronger during an economic crisis, leading to a greater probability that a political leader would be punished by an electorate or selectorate for undermining foreign trade and financial linkages that promote economic growth.[6]

This problem of increased costs ought to be particularly acute for states that increase their role in the economy as a mechanism of supporting economic recovery from a crisis. That is, governments have a strong interest in immediate stabilisation of the domestic economy during a crisis. They may undertake interventionist policies such as economic stimulus packages, bailouts for vulnerable industries or even nationalisation of companies that are particularly important for the country's overall economic health. As a result, the involvement of the state in commerce, trade and financial flows tends to increase during economic crises as it takes a more activist role in directing the economy's recovery. In the most recent economic crisis of 2007–2009, French President Nicholas Sarkozy went so far to announce that 'laissez-faire is dead', an emotive claim that can be attributed to political posturing rather than historical clairvoyance. Nevertheless, it does poignantly convey how an economic crisis can draw governments into new levels of engagement and commitment in the private sector.

The increasing government role in the economy can lead to a blending of national and private sector interests: governments want to protect their investments. The problem for economic signalling is that states begin to act on this new set of interests in their foreign policies. The government is incentivised to ensure public funds are not lost, reducing its willingness to allow the very industries it has propped up to suffer for the sake of foreign policy posturing. The result is a further internal constraining of a state's capacity to undertake economic costly signals. The link between changes in the amount of a government's intervention in its domestic economy and changes in its foreign policy is an area worthy for further study in the economic-security literature.

Yet another perspective of how economic crises increase the costs of signalling can be observed among the broader international audience. Where many states depend on a single system for their economic well-being, the costs of any one state signalling within that system impact the many. In periods of economic health, a costly move by one state would likely have little impact on the integrity of the system. However, during an economic crisis when the entire system is under duress, adverse economic moves by those relatively important to the functioning of the entire system could be interpreted by third-party states as undermining their own economic well-being.

This external constraint is thus manifested as diplomatic audience costs. Indeed, one could posit that the aggregate level of importance of an interdependent dyad to crisis recovery would be inversely related to their willingness to take punitive economic measures. Pressure by third-party states on the dyad to support the integrity of the system through continued integration would be at a maximum during a period of economic crisis.

Although states may be less inclined to undertake economic costly signals, the simple fact that they are so costly during an economic crisis should indicate that, if undertaken, the signal itself will be more credible and thus more effective. A receiving (targeted) state that recognises the severity of the cost assumed by the sending state ought to be more convinced of the genuine nature of the signal. The efficacy of the signal is made stronger by the elevated cost. One can therefore come to the conclusion that economic crises strengthen the conditions for economic costly signals to be successful.

There is, however, another trend at play. Economic crises tend to fragment regimes and divide polities. A decrease in cohesion at the political leadership level and at the electorate level reduces the ability of the state to coalesce a sufficiently strong political base required to undertake costly balancing measures such as economic costly signals. Schweller (2006) builds on earlier studies (see, e.g., Christensen, 1996; Snyder, 2000) that link political fragmentation with decisions not to balance against rising threats or to balance only in minimal and ineffective ways to demonstrate a tendency for states to 'underbalance'. Where political and social cohesion is strong, states are more likely to balance against rising threats in effective and costly ways. However, 'unstable and fragmented regimes that rule over divided polities will be significantly constrained in their ability to adapt to systemic incentives; they will be least likely to enact bold and costly policies even when their nation's survival is at stake and they are needed most' (Schweller, 2006, p. 130).

Papayoanou (1997) observes this tendency in British, French and American behaviour towards Germany in the 1930s. The Great Depression led states to become inward-looking, prioritising domestic economic interests above external national security threats. The inherent weakness in the disparate political outlooks that coincided with the economic crisis hindered their ability to balance effectively against Germany. Indeed, in the case of Great Britain, Papayoanou indicates that even though the political elite wanted to break Britain's strong economic ties with Germany for fear of 'sleeping with the enemy', a weak political base and relatively stronger interests in domestic economic growth bound the hands of the British government. Great Britain thus elected not to undertake economic costly signals despite the presence of a clear and growing threat. Papayoanou (1997, pp. 114–115) concludes that when 'status quo powers have strong economic links with threatening powers, weaker balancing postures and conciliatory policies by status quo powers, and aggression by aspiring revisionist powers, are more likely'.

Underbalancing (in this case, by not sending economic costly signals) during economic crises is consistent with a growing body of literature on the influence of domestic 'veto players' on the decision to use force. Veto players are those vested interests within an electorate or selectorate that have the authority to resist change in status quo policies. The tendency to underbalance is disproportionately strong in states with large numbers of veto players, a situation more prevalent in democracies than autocracies. Where relatively higher numbers of veto players exist within a polity, the opportunity to change status quo economic and trade policies, for example, through costly signalling, decreases (Tsebelis, 2002; Mansfield, Milner, & Pevehouse, 2008; St. Marie, Hansen, & Tuman, 2006; MacIntyre, 2001; Walsh, 2007).

In summary, I hypothesise that the occurrence of an economic crisis increases the cost associated with ECST and thus decreases the willingness of states to send economic costly signals. Although the fact that increased costs should make the signal more effective, scholarship on underbalancing theory and veto player theory provide rationale for why economic crises may inhibit the use of economic costly signals, even in the face of a direct threat.[7]

CONCLUSION

The logic of ECST supports arguments for greater economic interdependence to reduce the likelihood of conflict. This chapter does not argue against the utility of signalling theory. It does, however, suggest that when considering the occurrence of and conditions created by economic crises, ECST logic is dubious as an organising principle for security policymakers. The discussion pulls together some distinct areas of research that have not yet featured prominently in the ECST literature. Studies associating economic interdependence, economic crises and the potential for external conflict indicate that global interdependence is not necessarily a conflict-suppressing process and may be conflict-enhancing at certain points. Furthermore, the conditions created by economic crises decrease the willingness of states to send economic costly signals, even though such signals may be most effective during an economic crisis.

These two points warrant further consideration in the debate over ECST and, more broadly, theories linking interdependence and peace. The debate takes on particular importance for policymakers when considering the increasingly important US–China relationship and the long-term prospects for peace in the Asia-Pacific. Recent US policy towards China, such as the 'responsible stakeholder' approach, assumes that greater interdependence with China should decrease the likelihood for conflict. Some have even suggested that the economic relationship is necessary to ensure strategic competition does not lead to major war (see, e.g., Kastner, 2006).

If US or Chinese policymakers do indeed intend to rely on economic interdependence to reduce the likelihood of conflict, much more study is required to understand how and when interdependence impacts the security and the defence behaviour of states. This chapter contributes some thoughts to that larger debate.

NOTES

1. Notable counterarguments include Barbieri (1996), Gowa (1994), and Levy and Ali (1998).
2. Official statements have focused on this explanation as well. See, for example, Bernanke (2009).
3. For a dissenting study, see Elbadawi and Hegre (2008).
4. Note that Skaperdas and Syropoulos (2001) argue that states will have a greater incentive to arm against those with which it is interdependent to hedge against coercion. This argument could be extended to include protectionism in extreme cases. Crescenzi (2005) both challenges and agrees with Copeland's theory by suggesting that a more important indicator is the exit costs involved in terminating an economic relationship, which could be a function of the availability of alternatives.
5. There is also substantial research to indicate that periods of strong economic growth are also positively correlated with a rise in the likelihood of conflict. Pollins (2008) and Pollins and Schweller (1999) provide excellent insights into this body of literature.

6. States may have other reasons for undermining foreign trade and financial linkages, such as through domestic pressure to 'protect' industries. But the act of protectionism is motivated by economic and/or political interest. It should not be confused with the act of sending economic costly signals, which is motivated by a desire to avoid conflict.

7. A separate question is whether states can indeed signal clearly in a globalised context characterised by high levels of investment diversification and complex multilateral dependencies. Yang, Askari, Forrer, and Teegen (2004) and Angeletos, Hellwig, and Pavan (2006) provide some worthwhile thoughts on the matter.

ACKNOWLEDGMENTS

The author would like to thank Brian Pollins, Ben Goldsmith, Jurgen Brauer and Stewart Woodman for their helpful comments on earlier versions of this chapter.

REFERENCES

Angeletos, G. M., Hellwig, C., & Pavan, A. (2006). Signaling in a global game: Coordination and policy traps. *Journal of Political Economy*, *114*(3), 452–484.

Barbieri, K. (1996). Economic interdependence: A path to peace or a source of conflict? *Journal of Peace Research*, *33*(1), 29–49.

Bernanke, B. (2009). Financial reform to reduce systemic risk. Speech presented at the Council on Foreign Relations, 10 March, Washington, D.C. Available at http://www.federalreserve.gov/newsevents/speech/bernanke20090310a.htm. Retrieved on 18 February 2009.

Blair, D. (2009). Annual threat assessment of the intelligence community. Testimony before the Senate Select Committee on Intelligence, 12 February. Available at http://www.dni.gov/testimonies/20090212_testimony.pdf

Blomberg, S. B., & Hess, G. D. (2002). The temporal links between conflict and economic activity. *Journal of Conflict Resolution*, *46*(1), 74–90.

Blomberg, S. G., Hess, G. D., & Thacker, S. (2006). On the conflict-poverty nexus. *Economics and Politics*, *18*(3), 237–267.

Blomberg, S. G., Hess, G. D., & Weerapana, A. (2004). Economic conditions and terrorism. *European Journal of Political Economy*, *20*(2), 463–478.

Bordo, M., Eichengreen, B., Klingebiel, D., Martinez-Peria, M. S., & Rose, A. K. (2001). Is the crisis problem growing more severe? *Economic Policy*, *16*(32), 53–82.

Bueno de Mesquita, B., Morrow, J. D., & Zorick, E. R. (1997). Capabilities, perception, and escalation. *American Political Science Review*, *91*(1), 15–27.

Bueno de Mesquita, B., Smith, A., Siverson, R. M., & Morrow, J. D. (2003). *The logic of political survivability*. Cambridge, MA: MIT Press.

Calvo, G. A., & Mendoza, E. G. (2000). Rational contagion and the globalization of securities markets. *Journal of International Economics*, *51*(1), 79–113.

Christensen, T. J. (1996). *Useful adversaries: Grand strategy, domestic mobilization, and Sino-American conflict, 1947–1958*. Princeton, NJ: Princeton University Press.
Copeland, D. C. (1996). Economic interdependence and war: A theory of trade expectations. *International Security*, *20*(4), 5–40.
Copeland, D. C. (2000). Trade expectations and the outbreak of peace: Détente 1970–74 and the end of the Cold War 1985–91. In: J. M. Blanchard, E. D. Mansfield & N. M. Ripsman (Eds), *Power and the purse: Economic statecraft, interdependence and national security* (pp. 15–58). London, England: Frank Cass and Company.
Corsetti, G., Pesenti, P., & Roubini, N. (1999). What caused the Asian currency and financial crisis? *Japan and the World Economy*, *11*(3), 305–373.
Crescenzi, M. J. C. (2005). *Economic interdependence and conflict in world studies*. Lanham, MD: Lexington Books.
DeRouen, K. R., Jr. (1995). The indirect link: Politics, the economy, and the use of force. *Journal of Conflict Resolution*, *39*(4), 671–695.
DeRouen, K. R., Jr. (2000). Presidents and the diversionary use of force: A research note. *International Studies Quarterly*, *44*(2), 317–328.
Elbadawi, I., & Hegre, H. (2008). Globalization, economic shocks, and internal armed conflict. *Defence and Peace Economics*, *19*(1), 37–60.
Fearon, J. D. (1994). Domestic political audiences and the escalation of international disputes. *American Political Science Review*, *88*(3), 577–592.
Fearon, J. D. (1995). Rationalist explanations for war. *International Organization*, *49*(3), 379–414.
Fearon, J. D. (1997). Signaling foreign policy interests. *Journal of Conflict Resolution*, *41*(1), 68–90.
Gallegati, M., Greenwald, B., Richiardi, M. G., & Stiglitz, J. E. (2008). The asymmetric effect of diffusion processes: Risk sharing and contagion. *Global Economy Journal*, *8*(3), 1–20. Available at http://www.bepress.com/cgi/viewcontent.cgi?article = 1365&context = gej. Retrieved on 15 November 2009.
Gande, A., John, K., & Senbet, L. (2008). Bank incentives, economic specialization, and financial crises in emerging economies. *Journal of International Money and Finance*, *27*(5), 707–732.
Gartzke, E. (2003). The classical liberals were just lucky: A few thoughts about interdependence and peace. In: E. D. Mansfield & B. M. Pollins (Eds), *Economic interdependence and international conflict: New perspectives on an enduring debate* (pp. 96–110). Ann Arbor, MI: University of Michigan Press.
Gartzke, E. (2005). Economic freedom and peace. In: *Economic freedom of the world: 2005 Annual report*. Washington, DC: CATO Institute.
Gartzke, E., & Li, Q. (2003). War, peace, and the invisible hand: Positive political externalities of economic globalization. *International Studies Quarterly*, *47*(4), 561–586.
Gartzke, E., Li, Q., & Boehmer, C. (2001). Investing in the peace: Economic interdependence and international conflict. *International Organization*, *55*(2), 391–438.
Gelpi, C. (1997). Democratic diversions: Governmental structure and the externalization of domestic conflict. *Journal of Conflict Resolution*, *41*(2), 255–282.
Gilpin, R. (1981). *War and change in world politics*. Cambridge, England: Cambridge University Press.
Glick, R., & Rose, A. K. (1999). Contagion and trade: Why are currency crises regional? *Journal of International Money and Finance*, *18*(4), 603–617.

Goldstein, I., & Pauzner, A. (2004). Contagion of self-fulfilling financial crises due to diversification of investment portfolios. *Journal of Economic Theory*, *119*(1), 151–183.

Gowa, J. (1994). *Allies, adversaries, and international trade*. Princeton, NJ: Princeton University Press.

Hegre, H. (2000). Development and the liberal peace: What does it take to be a trading state? *Journal of Peace Research*, *37*(1), 5–30.

Kalemli-Ozcan, S., Sorensen, B. E., & Yosha, O. (2003). Risk sharing and industrial specialization: Regional and international evidence. *The American Economic Review*, *93*(3), 903–918.

Kastner, S. L. (2006). Ambiguity, economic interdependence, and the US strategic dilemma in the Taiwan Strait. *Journal of Contemporary China*, *15*(49), 651–669.

Kisangani, E. F., & Pickering, J. (2009). The dividends of diversion: Mature democracies' proclivity to use diversionary force and the rewards they reap from it. *British Journal of Political Science*, *39*(3), 483–515.

Kose, M. A., Prasad, E. S., & Terrones, M. E. (2006). How do trade and financial integration affect the relationship between growth and volatility? *Journal of International Economics*, *69*, 176–202.

Kose, M. A., Prasad, E. S., & Terrones, M. E. (2009). Does financial globalization promote risk sharing? *Journal of Development Economics*, *89*(2), 258–270.

Kydd, A. (2005). *Trust and mistrust in international relations*. Princeton, NJ: Princeton University Press.

Levy, J. S., & Ali, S. (1998). From commercial competition to strategic rivalry to war: The evolution of the Anglo-Dutch rivalry, 1609–52. In: P. F. Diehl (Ed.), *The dynamics of enduring rivalries*. Urbana, IL: University of Illinois Press.

MacIntyre, A. (2001). Institutions and investors: The politics of the economic crisis in Southeast Asia. *International Organization*, *55*(1), 81–122.

Mansfield, E. D., Milner, H. V., & Pevehouse, J. C. (2008). Democracy, veto players and the depth of regional integration. *World Economy*, *31*(1), 67–96.

Mansfield, E. D., & Pollins, B. M. (2003). In: *Economic interdependence and international conflict: New perspectives on an enduring debate* (pp. 1–28). Ann Arbor, MI: University of Michigan Press.

Miller, R. A. (1999). Regime type, strategic interaction, and the diversionary use of force. *Journal of Conflict Resolution*, *43*(3), 388–402.

Modelski, G., & Thompson, W. R. (1996). *Leading sectors and world powers: The coevolution of global politics and world economics*. Columbia, SC: University of South Carolina Press.

Morrow, J. D. (1999). How could trade affect conflict? *Journal of Peace Research*, *36*(4), 481–489.

Morrow, J. D. (2003). Assessing the role of trade as a source of costly signals. In: E. D. Mansfield & B. M. Pollins (Eds), *Economic interdependence and international conflict: New perspectives on an enduring debate* (pp. 89–95). Ann Arbor, MI: University of Michigan Press.

Oneal, J. R., & Russett, B. M. (1997). The classical liberals were right: Democracy, interdependence, and conflict, 1950–85. *International Studies Quarterly*, *41*(2), 267–294.

Papayoanou, P. A. (1997). Economic interdependence and the balance of power. *International Studies Quarterly*, *41*, 113–140.

Pollins, B. M. (1996). Global political order, economic change, and armed conflict: Coevolving systems and the use of force. *American Political Science Review*, *90*(1), 103–117.

Pollins, B. M. (2008). Globalization and armed conflict among nations. *Conflict Management and Peace Science, 25*(3), 191–205.

Pollins, B. M., & Schweller, R. L. (1999). Linking the levels: The long wave and shifts in U.S. foreign policy. *American Journal of Political Science, 43*(2), 431–464.

Quinn, D. P., & Voth, H. J. (2008). A century of global equity market correlations. *American Economic Review, 98*(2), 535–540.

Ranciere, R., Tornell, A., & Westermann, F. (2006). Decomposing the effects of financial liberalization: Crises vs. growth. *Journal of Banking and Finance, 30*(12), 3331–3348.

Richards, D. L., & Gelleny, R. D. (2006). Banking crises, collective protest, and rebellion. *Canadian Journal of Political Science, 39*(4), 1–25.

Rodrik, D. (1997a). *Globalisation, social conflict and economic growth*. Prebisch Lecture delivered to UNCTAD, October 24, Geneva, Switzerland.

Rodrik, D. (1997b). *Has globalization gone too far?* Washington, DC: Institute for International Economics.

Russett, B. M., & Oneal, J. R. (2001). *Triangulating peace: Democracy, interdependence, and international organizations*. New York, NY: W.W. Norton.

Schweller, R. L. (2006). *Unanswered threats*. Princeton, NJ: Princeton University Press.

Skaperdas, S., & Syropoulos, C. (2001). Guns, butter, and openness: On the relationship between security and trade. *American Economic Review, 91*(2), 353–357.

Snyder, J. (2000). *From voting to violence: Democratization and nationalist conflict*. New York, NY: W.W. Norton.

St. Marie, J. J., Hansen, K. N., & Tuman, J. P. (2006). The Asian economic crisis and bureaucratic development: A veto player analysis. *International Relations of the Asia-Pacific, 7*(1), 1–22.

Stein, A. A. (2003). Trade and conflict: Uncertainty, strategic signaling, and interstate disputes. In: E. D. Mansfield & B. M. Pollins (Eds), *Economic interdependence and international conflict: New perspectives on an enduring debate* (pp. 111–126). Ann Arbor, MI: University of Michigan Press.

Stiglitz, J. (2000). Capital market liberalization, economic growth, and instability. *World Development, 28*(6), 1075–1086.

Tsebelis, G. (2002). *Veto players: How political institutions work*. New York, NY: Russell Sage Foundation.

Walsh, J. I. (2007). Do states play signaling games? *Cooperation and Conflict, 42*(4), 441–459.

Wang, K. H. (1996). Presidential responses to foreign policy crises: Rational choice and domestic politics. *Journal of Conflict Resolution, 40*(1), 68–97.

Werner, S. (1999). Choosing demands strategically: The distribution of power, the distribution of benefits, and the risk of conflict. *Journal of Conflict Resolution, 43*(6), 705–726.

Yang, J., Askari, H., Forrer, J., & Teegen, H. (2004). U.S. economic sanctions: An empirical study. *International Trade Journal, 18*(1), 23–62.

CHAPTER 13

TERRORISM, TARGETED ECONOMIC SANCTIONS AND INADEQUATE DUE PROCESS: THE CASE OF THE SECURITY COUNCIL'S 1267 SANCTIONS REGIME

Christopher Michaelsen

ABSTRACT

Purpose – *The chapter seeks to contribute to the discourse concerning the United Nations Security Council's role in strengthening a rules-based international system and maintaining international peace and security under the rule of law. Its particular purpose is to examine the Security Council's Al-Qaida and Taliban sanctions regime (1267 regime) from a rule of law and due process perspective.*

Methodology – *To this end, the chapter reviews the 1267 regime's controversial listing and de-listing procedure and identifies shortcomings in relation to traditional due process guarantees. It then discusses reform options available to the Security Council as far as forms and modalities of an effective review mechanism are concerned.*

Economics of War and Peace: Economic, Legal, and Political Perspectives
Contributions to Conflict Management, Peace Economics and Development, Volume 14, 225–241

ISSN: 1572-8323/doi:10.1108/S1572-8323(2010)0000014017

Findings – *The chapter has two main findings. First, it concludes that the 'individualisation' of Security Council sanctions in terms of targeting individuals directly has not been accompanied by the creation of a means for the new targets to appeal the measures imposed on them. Second, it finds that a lack of political will has so far prevented comprehensive reform of the 1267 regime but that such reform is becoming increasingly urgent. The chapter suggests that reform initiatives need to address the value, effectiveness and sustainability of the 1267 regime more broadly. The Security Council, in particular, needs to consider what it is prepared to give up to maintain the 1267 regime as an effective UN sanctions regime, or whether it is prepared to give up the 1267 regime to maintain the authority it interprets to have from the UN Charter.*

INTRODUCTION

This chapter discusses the increasing use of sanctions since 1990 to enforce the United Nations (UN) Security Council decisions and the evolution of 'smart sanctions'. These sanctions are targeted towards specifically identified individuals and other entities in an attempt to avoid devastating effects on the whole population of targeted states. The chapter also outlines the development of sanctions under resolution 1267 (1999) which target terrorism-related activity. These stop supply, sale and transfer of military equipment and freeze the assets of entities associated with Al-Qaida, Osama bin Laden and/or the Taliban. The chapter discusses this sanctions regime from a rule of law and due process perspective, arguing for reform to provide sanctions targets with appropriate appeals and review mechanisms. This is becoming urgent to ensure the effectiveness and sustainability of the new sanctions regime.

The UN Security Council enjoys greater powers under the UN Charter than any other international organ in history to maintain international peace and security (Frowein & Kirsch, 2002). Yet, the tools that the Council has at its disposal are relatively few. The Charter essentially provides for two kinds of coercive measures (Chapter VII). Article 41 of the Charter authorises the Council to decide which measures *not* involving the use of armed force are to be employed to effect its decisions. Such measures include 'complete or partial interruption of economic relations and of rail, sea, air, postal, telegraphic, radio, and other means of communication, and the severance of diplomatic relations'. On the contrary, the Council can authorise the use of force if it considers that measures provided for in Article 41 are inadequate (Article 42).

From 1946 until 1990, Cold War politics prevented the Security Council from exercising the powers envisaged by those who drafted the UN Charter. For instance, the Council only imposed Article 41 sanctions twice in that period, against Southern Rhodesia in 1966 and against South Africa in 1977. The end of the Cold War, however, saw the Council using its Chapter VII powers to greater extent. Sanctions, in particular, were imposed on States that threatened international peace and security to comply with Security Council decisions. Since 1990, the Council has initiated no less than 23 sanction regimes. As Jeremy Farrall has noted, UN sanctions now form a prominent feature of the international relations landscape (Farrall, 2007). The reason for the Council's increasing use of its Article 41 powers is obvious: the use of non-military measures provides clear benefits in terms of avoiding military risks and costs.

These benefits notwithstanding, it became apparent in the 1990s that there were severe disadvantages to comprehensive sanctions regimes that were imposed on States as a whole. For instance, comprehensive sanctions had devastating effects on the innocent population without effecting any change of policy by the regime in power. Some of the most notorious cases in this regard include Iraq, Haiti and Yugoslavia. In response to severe criticism against these sanctions regimes, a process was started to develop a more targeted system of sanctions, also called smart sanctions (Cortright & Lopez, 2000). In contrast to comprehensive economic sanctions, targeted sanctions are not imposed on States or entire populations, but on specifically identified individuals and other entities. Generally, these individuals are political and military leaders and individuals close to a regime, or individuals associated with rebel groups.

In 1999 the Security Council initiated a sanctions regime to combat individuals and entities engaged in terrorism-related activity. Adopting resolution 1267 (1999), the Council required all UN Member States to freeze the assets of, prevent the entry into or transit through their territories by, and prevent the direct or indirect supply, sale and transfer of arms and military equipment to any individual or entity associated with Al-Qaida, Osama bin Laden and/or the Taliban. A decade later, the Council continues to consider the 1267 sanctions regime as 'an important tool under the Charter of the United Nations in the maintenance and restoration of international peace and security'. Adopting resolution 1822 (2008), it stressed the need for 'robust implementation' of the 1267 regime as a 'significant tool in combating terrorist activity'.

This chapter examines the 1267 sanctions regime from a rule of law and due process perspective. It argues although the individualised Security Council sanctions enable members to target individuals directly, these targets do not have access to a mechanism to appeal the measures imposed on them. To this end, the chapter first introduces briefly the 1267 regime's controversial listing and de-listing procedure and identifies shortcomings in relation to traditional due process guarantees. The chapter then discusses reform options available to the Security Council for forms and modalities of an effective review mechanism. It concludes that a lack of political will has so far prevented comprehensive reform. Nonetheless, the chapter argues that such reform is becoming increasingly urgent and that it is essential in this context to address the value, effectiveness and sustainability of the 1267 regime more broadly.

THE 1267 SANCTIONS REGIME TARGETING TERRORISM

The 1267 targeted sanctions regime was first established by the Security Council in resolution 1267 (1999). This resolution was partly adopted in response to the 1998 bombings on the US embassies in Kenya and Tanzania. One of the key features of the 1267 regime is a 'Consolidated List' maintained by the 1267 Committee, a sub-committee of the Security Council. As of 25 January 2010, 501 individuals or entities were included in the list which consists of the following four sections:

a) individuals associated with the Taliban (137 individuals)
b) entities and other groups and undertakings associated with the Taliban (none)
c) individuals associated with Al-Qaida (256 individuals)
d) entities and other groups and undertakings associated with Al-Qaida (108 entities).

All States are required to freeze assets of individuals and entities included in the list as well as to enforce travel bans. They may request the 1267 Committee to add names to this list and the Committee also considers submissions by States to delete names from it. This listing and de-listing mechanism, however, has been subject to considerable controversy. The controversies mainly stem from the fact that the sanctions regime, although preventive by design, is punitive by impact. Indeed, measures such as the freezing of assets constitute serious criminal sanctions that traditionally warrant proper safeguards. The 1267 listing and de-listing procedure, however, does not provide for any judicial or quasi-judicial protection. As a consequence, the regime continues to be criticised for its lack of respect for internationally recognised standards of due process including the right to a fair hearing, the right to judicial review and the right to an effective remedy (Johnstone, 2008).

Targeted individuals or entities are not informed before being listed and thus do not have any opportunity to stop being listed by demonstrating that this would be unjustified. Even *after* an individual or entity is listed, Member States are not obliged to provide detailed information to the person or entity concerned about reasons for their inclusion. States are merely encouraged 'to inform, to *the extent possible*, and *in writing where possible*, individuals and entities included on the Consolidated List of the measures imposed on them, the Committee's Guidelines, and, in particular, the listing and de-listing procedures contained herein and the provisions of resolution 1452 (2002)'.

On 30 June 2008, the Security Council, in resolution 1822 (2008), introduced several improvements in this regard directing the Committee, inter alia, to make accessible on its website a narrative summary of reasons for listing. Nonetheless, targeted individuals and entities remain unable to access detailed information about their listing.

Further concerns stem from the fact that targeted individuals and entities are not granted any hearing and cannot have the listing decision reviewed by an independent body. Initially they were not even allowed to petition the Committee for de-listing. Such petitions could only be submitted to governments, which in turn could bring the issue to the attention of the Committee. However, following on from proposals made by France and the United States (and other countries) and by the Analytical Support and Sanctions Monitoring Team, Security Council resolution 1730 (2006) created a 'focal point' within the UN Secretariat responsible for processing submissions by listed persons requesting sanctions be lifted. Although this now enables affected persons to submit petitions directly and independently of diplomatic protection through their governments, it does not give them the right to participate or to be heard in the review process, nor does it constitute an independent review mechanism. No legal or quasi-legal rules exist that would oblige the Committee to grant a request if specific conditions are met. On the contrary, the Committee removes people from the list at its discretion with the consent of all its members. Therefore, the focal point has had limited effect in so far as providing due process guarantees, and actual number of petitions are concerned (Verbeke, 2007).

Moreover, listed individuals and entities have very limited possibilities to challenge a listing before national courts and tribunals. This is mainly due to the obligations of UN Member States as stipulated by Articles 25, 103 and 105 of the UN Charter. Article 25 obliges Member States to comply with Chapter VII resolutions by the Security Council (like resolution 1267 and subsequent resolutions). Article 103 clarifies that obligations under the UN Charter – including binding obligations under Article 25 – prevail over 'any other international agreement' unless obligations contained therein constitute general principles of international law. This also includes national law implementing international obligations under international human rights treaties such as the International Covenant on Civil and Political Rights (ICCPR) or the European Convention on Human Rights. In addition, even in the event that people can have recourse to national courts, the UN enjoys absolute immunity from every form of domestic legal proceedings as stipulated by Article 105, paragraph 1, of the UN Charter, the General Convention on the Privileges and Immunities of the United Nations and other agreements (Fassbender, 2006; Marty, 2007).

Despite the improvements made to the listing and de-listing mechanism over the years, the procedure continues to raise serious concerns in relation to fundamental human rights. It has also been criticised by human rights groups as well as by leading legal scholars and practitioners (Almqvist, 2008; Cameron, 2006; Scheinin, 2006). In particular, it has been argued that the procedure raises serious fundamental human rights concerns including the right to judicial review, the right to procedural fairness, the right to a hearing and the right to an effective remedy (Van den Herik & Schrijver, 2006). A number of studies and reports by eminent international scholars have thus called for clear, fair and transparent procedures (Cameron & Nordback, 2003; OSCE-ODIHR, 2007). This includes, in particular, that individuals and/or entities included on the Consolidated List are informed promptly about their inclusion and that these matters are heard by a relevant decision-making body.

The issue of sanction-related listing and de-listing and due process has not only been the subject of intensive debate in policy and academic circles but has also featured prominently in several legal cases, at national and international level. Legal challenges have been presented to the national courts of Belgium, Italy, Switzerland, The Netherlands, Pakistan, Turkey, the United Kingdom, Germany and the United States of America (1267 Monitoring Team, 2009). Several cases have also been brought before the Courts of the European Communities in Luxemburg. In the cases of *Kadi* (2005), *Yusuf* and *Al Barakaat* (2005), *Ayadi* (2006) and *Hassan* (2006), the European Court of First Instance (CFI) upheld the legality of the EU regulations implementing the 1267 counter-terrorism sanctions regime and found that it generally lacked the power to judicially review resolutions by the UN Security Council. However, these findings were rejected in an opinion issued in January 2008 by one of the eight Advocates General assisting the Court. Similarly, the European Court of Justice (ECJ), in the appeal cases of *Kadi* and *Al Barakaat*, found that the Courts of the European Communities have jurisdiction to review the implementation of UN Security resolutions, and furthermore, that the contested EC regulation violated fundamental rights as recognised by Community law (Michaelsen, 2009).

Handing down its decision in *Kadi and Al Barakaat* on 3 September 2008, the ECJ confirmed that the Council of the EU was competent to adopt the regulation on the basis of the articles of the EC Treaty that it chose. Even if the CFI made certain errors in its reasoning, its final conclusion that the Council was competent to adopt that regulation was not incorrect (paras. 234–236). However, the ECJ found that the CFI erred in law in ruling that the Community courts had, in principle, no jurisdiction to review the internal lawfulness of the contested regulation (paras. 327–328). It held that the Court's review of whether any Community measure was valid in the light of fundamental rights needed to be considered to be the expression of a constitutional guarantee stemming from the EC Treaty as an autonomous legal system, which may not be prejudiced by an international agreement (para. 316). The ECJ clarified that the review of lawfulness ensured by the Community courts applied to the Community act intended to give effect to the international agreement at issue and not to the international agreement itself.

The ECJ then undertook this analysis and examined whether the regulation(s) of the Council of the EU implementing the UN Security Council's 1267 sanctions regime violated Mr Kadi's and Al Barakaat's fundamental rights as protected by Community law. It found that the rights of the defence, in particular the right to be heard, and the right to effective judicial review of those rights, were 'patently not respected' (para. 334). The Court pointed out that the effectiveness of judicial review meant that the Community authority in question must communicate to the person or entity concerned the grounds on which the measure at issue was based, so far as possible, either when that measure was decided on or, at the very least, as soon as possible after that decision. This would enable those persons or entities to exercise their right to bring an action within the periods prescribed. However, the regulation at issue provided no procedure for communicating the evidence justifying the listing either at the same time as or after that inclusion. At no time did the Council of the EU inform

Mr Kadi and Al Barakaat of the evidence adduced against them to justify the initial inclusion of their names in the list (paras. 345–348).

In addition, the ECJ held that the infringement of Mr Kadi and Al Barakaat's rights of defence also gave rise to a breach of the right to a legal remedy, in as much as the appellants were also unable to defend their rights in satisfactory conditions before the Community courts (paras. 349–352). Furthermore, the Court found that freezing funds constituted an unjustified restriction of Mr Kadi's right to property (paras. 354–371). According to the Court, the restrictive measures imposed by the regulation(s) of the Council of the EU amounted to restrictions of that right, which could, in principle, be justified (paras. 354, 356). However, the regulation in question was adopted without furnishing any guarantee enabling Mr Kadi to put his case to the competent authorities (para. 369). Such a guarantee would have been necessary to ensure respect for his right to property, having regard to the general application and continuation of the freezing measures affecting him.

OPTIONS AND INITIATIVES TO ENSURE DUE PROCESS FOR SANCTION TARGETS

The ECJ's decision in *Kadi and Al Barakaat* and recently published studies and reports on sanctions-related listing and de-listing procedure demonstrate that the current mechanism is subject to serious shortcomings, in particular, in relation to guarantees of due process. Among the due process rights, it is specifically the right to a hearing and the right to judicial review (including the right to an effective remedy) that are engaged by the listing and de-listing procedure. Over the years, the 1267 Committee has made a series of improvements to its procedures that have addressed some of the concerns expressed about the fairness of the sanctions. These include establishing a focal point as well as several technical amendments. Nevertheless, new or additional procedures and safeguards are urgently needed to ensure that due process rights are respected.

Security Council resolution 1822 (2008) contained some welcome changes in relation to the review of listings of individuals and entities. For example, it requires the 1267 Committee to conduct a review of all names on the Consolidated List by 30 June 2010 in which the relevant names are circulated to the designating States and States of residence and/or citizenship, where known, pursuant to the procedures set forth in the Committee guidelines, to ensure the Consolidated List is as updated and accurate as possible.

However, despite these notable improvements, the current procedure remains inadequate and does not amount to a genuine and effective mechanism of judicial control by an independent tribunal as required by internationally recognised standards of due process.

A number of scholars have identified alternative forms and modalities of an effective review mechanism (Fassbender, 2006; Biersteker & Eckert, 2006; Cameron, 2003). The proposals include the establishment of:

a) an independent international arbitral panel, court or tribunal
b) an ombudsman office
c) an inspection panel following the model of the World Bank Inspection Panel
d) a commission of inquiry
e) a committee of experts serving in their personal capacity (as it exists, for instance, in accordance with Article 28 of the ICCPR).

In general, the proposals can be classified into two categories: The first category includes those mechanisms that would be fully independent of the Security Council. The second category includes review mechanisms that would be set up under the auspices of the Security Council. The advantages of proposals in the first category are obvious. Instruments such as an independent arbitral panel, court or tribunal would arguably fulfil the requirements of effective judicial review as required by international human rights law and by general principles of due process. However, in practice, the establishment of an independent arbitral panel, court or tribunal appears almost impossible to achieve given the political and practical sensitivities involved. In fact, it is highly unlikely that the Security Council will be prepared to accept a fully independent judicial authority that scrutinises its actions. This was also noted by the 1267 Committee's Analytical Support and Sanctions Monitoring Team that has pointed out that:

> [i]t is difficult to imagine that the Security Council could accept any review panel that appeared to erode its absolute authority to take action on matters affecting international peace and security, as enshrined in the Charter. This argues against any panel having more than an advisory role, and against publication of its opinions, to avoid undercutting Council decisions. It would argue too for the Council retaining authority to select or approve the membership of a review body. (1267 Monitoring Team, 2008, para. 41)

Proposals for review mechanism under the authority of the Security Council include:

- extending the responsibilities of the 1267 Committee's Analytical Support and Sanctions Monitoring Team

- establishing an ombudsman office
- creating a review panel under the authority of the Security Council.

In 2006, for instance, Denmark proposed that the Committee establish an independent review mechanism, in the form of an ombudsman, which could accept petitions directly from listed parties claiming they were unjustly included on the Consolidated List and unable to get de-listed. The ombudsman would have had the authority to consider those petitions, as well as other cases raised at his or her initiative, and to make recommendations to the Committee that would endorse or disregard them. Thus, the ombudsman's decision would not have been binding on the sanctions committee. Procedurally, the ombudsman would have been accessible by listed individuals, but there would not have been a formal hearing, nor would the ombudsman have had access to non-redacted statements of case. This modest proposal was not considered officially by the Security Council.

In May 2008, Denmark, Germany, Liechtenstein, The Netherlands, Sweden and Switzerland put forward a proposal inspired by the example of the World Bank inspection panels to establish a review panel of three to five independent, impartial and judicially qualified persons to review listing decisions (Discussion Paper, 2008). The panel would be governed by general principles of international law concerning fair procedure, and it would be composed of persons experienced in handling confidential information. The review panel members would be proposed by the Secretary-General and appointed by the Security Council. The panel would review de-listing requests and take a decision within a certain timeframe, that is three months. Petitioners would be able to request a de-listing decision through the focal point. The proposal also stipulates that the Committee, all Member States and all relevant international organisations would cooperate with the panel 'to the fullest extent possible, in particular by providing any relevant information or evidence' (Discussion Paper, 2008.) The review panel would report its findings and recommend to the 1267 Committee either de-listing or rejecting the petition. The panel recommendations would be published as soon as they were submitted to the Committee. The final decision, however, would rest with the Committee. In addition, the proposal stipulates that the Committee 'shall *ex officio* keep the listing decisions under constant review, re-evaluating them on a regular basis, the intervals to be decided by the Committee, in particular in the light of new information submitted by Member States' (Discussion Paper, 2008, p. 1).

While having an ombudsman office and/or a review panel under the authority of the Security Council would significantly improve the existing listing and de-listing procedure, it is unlikely that the two mechanisms would fulfil the requirements of effective due process. As Amnesty International put it in an open letter of 3 June 2008 to all members of the Security Council regarding the May 2008 proposal, the review panel option in question 'does not go far enough to meet minimum guarantees of fairness and transparency required, notably in respect of the outcome of the proposed review mechanism and the nature of the information provided to challenge a listing' (Amnesty International, 2008). Both mechanisms would not have the power to grant appropriate relief as the final decision on whether to de-list or not would rest with the 1267 Committee. This also stands in contrast to the requirements as set out in the 2008 *Kadi and Al Barakaat* decision of the ECJ.

In addition, it is questionable whether the review panel as described in the May 2008 proposal would be sufficiently independent as its members would be appointed by and serve under the authority of the Security Council. It is also unclear to what extent the panel would have access to all relevant information. The proposal does not compel Member States to submit evidence in support of listing decisions. It is difficult to see how the review panel may submit a listing decision to thorough scrutiny when it is dependent on Member States providing access to information in a quasi-voluntary manner. This, in turn, has significant implications for guarantees of the right to a hearing and the right to effective judicial review.

Although the review mechanism stipulated by the May 2008 proposal was a significant improvement, it arguably falls short of fulfilling several due process requirements of international law. These have been identified by the ECJ in *Kadi and Al Barakaat* and by various academic studies and reports, legal cases and other reports. Although it is commendable that the issue was brought to the attention of the Security Council, the proposal's timing was problematic. The proposal failed to take into account the arguments to be made in *Kadi* and *Al Barakaat*. It would have perhaps been wiser – for political and practical reasons – to wait for the outcome of the (then pending) appeal cases in Luxemburg before submitting the proposal to the Security Council. On the contrary, as Liechtenstein's Permanent Representative to the UN, Christian Wenaweser, has pointed out, at time the proposal was submitted to the Security Council, it was unclear at what date the ECJ was going to hand down its decision (Wenaweser, 2008). Consequently, a conscious decision was made to engage the Council in May 2008 to allow it to take note of the proposal before the 30 June 2008 meeting reviewing the 1267 regime.

THE LACK OF POLITICAL WILL FOR PROCEDURAL REFORM

Neither the Danish ombudsman proposal of 2006 nor the 2008 review panel proposal of the group of like-minded states found any resonance with the Security Council. In fact, there appears to be a lack of political will among Security Council members, in particular among the permanent members, to initiate comprehensive reform. The apparent lack of political will may have several reasons. One of them may be based on the perception that the due process shortcomings of the 1267 regime are negligible as they only affect a relatively small number of alleged terrorists and their associates. What is more, one could argue that there are much more serious human rights violations being committed each day, so why not focus on other, more urgent, policy questions?

This perception, however, is flawed. The shortcomings of the 1267 regime do not only affect listed individuals and entities but have much broader implications. In particular, they demonstrate that the 'individualisation' of Security Council measures in the context of targeted sanctions has not come with corresponding due process safeguards. As such the debate on the due process concerns of the 1267 regime is not only about individual justice for Mr Kadi, the Al Barakaat Foundation or other listed individuals and entities. Rather, as Larissa van den Herik has noted, it is also 'about the system that we want to build: if we want to go beyond the State and target the individual, we should also give the individual standing to defend himself' (Van den Herik, 2009). The issue is thus also related to the Security Council's credibility. As the Council is becoming more and more concerned with human rights violations, it is problematic that its own practice raises serious concerns in relation to traditional due process guarantees.

Notwithstanding the lack of political will to initiate comprehensive reform, practical obstacles and political sensitivities have also prevented significant progress. These include the problem of independent review of Security Council decisions as well as evidentiary problems. The latter allegedly arise as many listing decisions are based on intelligence information that states are reluctant or unwilling to share or to submit to scrutiny. As the 1267 Committee's Monitoring Team (2008, para. 41) noted,

> Although [a review] panel might be allowed access to the confidential statements of case presented to justify listings, Committee members also draw on intelligence and law-enforcement information available to them nationally or through other sources, including information obtained through bilateral exchanges, which could not easily be made available to reviewers.

This problem is part of a classical challenge faced in the context of judicial review and counter-terrorism, that is, whether and to what extent classified intelligence information can be used and/or disclosed in court. It is beyond question that the protection of sensitive sources and of important intelligence information is a legitimate state interest. However, there are mechanisms available to address this issue in a way that also maximises concern for fair trial rights and due process guarantees. These include in particular closed court proceedings and vetted or security-cleared counsel. The latter option was also emphasised by the UN Special Rapporteur on the promotion and protection of human rights while countering terrorism in his 2006 report to the UN General Assembly in which he recommended that 'consideration should be given to means through which a listed entity can still challenge the evidence against it' (Scheinin, 2006). As far as a review panel is concerned, closed court proceedings appear to be a particularly viable option. Such proceedings would protect intelligence and law-enforcement information as well as guarantee fundamental aspects of the right to a hearing (which includes the right to be informed) and of the right to judicial review.

In addition, the 1267 Committee's Monitoring Team has recently argued that the *Kadi and Al Barakaat* decision 'has changed the terms of the debate' on the review of listings (Monitoring Team, 2009). In its ninth report on 13 May 2009, the Monitoring Team took the view that the action by national and regional courts such as the ECJ had pre-empted the discussion on an independent review mechanism to be established by the Security Council. Apparently arguing that such mechanism was no longer necessary, the Monitoring Team (2009) noted that:

> The fact that European courts have joined American courts in asserting their jurisdiction over national implementation procedures means that in this context they will in effect offer an independent review of listing decisions by the Committee when these are challenged before them. Other national and regional courts may decide to take similar action.

The Monitoring Team's view is problematic in that it ignores some significant pitfalls of exclusive reliance of domestic systems for review. First, not all UN Member States have equally strong judiciaries. This means that exclusive reliance on domestic review mechanisms may lead to selectiveness. Moreover, there is a risk of fragmentation where different national courts come to opposing conclusions on the propriety of a specific listing. Also, this approach has significant normative flaws. For example, there is the question of what the consequence of an adverse national decision should be.

The Security Council is not bound by domestic decisions, nor are its subsidiary organs. According to the Monitoring Team, the 1267 Committee should give a national decision 'due weight'. But this may not be enough. The credibility of the 1267 Committee may be seriously hampered if it maintains persons listed when national courts, after reviewing all available evidence, have decided that a listing is unjustified. Such situations may also put governments in untenable situations.

CONCLUSION

The Security Council considers Al-Qaida and the Taliban to be serious threats to international peace and security and most Council members continue to believe that the sanctions regime represents an essential tool for the prevention of terrorist acts. As the outgoing Belgian Chair of the 1267 Committee, Jan Grauls (2008), has remarked at the Security Council meeting on 15 December 2008:

> I do not think there is any doubt in anyone's mind that terrorism remains one of the most serious threats to international peace and security. The sanctions regime against Al-Qaida, the Taliban and their associates is still one of the most important tools of the international community in the fight against terrorism. In that light, it is important that Member States use this tool to the fullest extent possible by proposing the names of key actors for listing and complying fully with the sanctions measures.

Nevertheless, the fallibility of the 1267 regime and its Consolidated List has undermined support. Despite several improvements to the Consolidated List that include the establishment of a 'focal point' within the UN Secretariat as well as measures introduced by resolution 1822 (2008) – sanctioned individuals and entities to be notified, reasons for listing posted on the Committee's website and all names on the Consolidated List reviewed on 30 June 2010 – the listing and de-listing mechanism continues to raise serious concerns in relation to internationally recognised requirements of due process. These concerns specifically stem from the insufficient protection of the right to a fair hearing, the right to judicial review and the right to an effective remedy as contained in the constitutions of UN Member States as well as in leading international human rights instruments.

It is clear establishing an independent review mechanism would ease such concerns to a significant extent. However, although some UN Member States seem to be somewhat receptive to such changes, some of the Council's permanent members remain cautious about accepting any procedure or an outside independent panel that would, as they see it, erode the authority of the 1267 Committee. The discourse on appropriate review mechanisms of the listing and de-listing procedure thus appears in a quandary. Proposals that would fulfil the due process requirements of international human rights law are politically infeasible, whereas proposals that may gain support from the Security Council contain shortcomings as far as internationally guaranteed due process rights are concerned.

Rather than limiting the discourse on the legal, political and technical challenges of the listing and de-listing mechanism per se, it is essential to address the value, effectiveness and sustainability of the 1267 regime more broadly. The international community as a whole, and the permanent members of the Security Council in particular, need to consider what they are prepared to give up to maintain the 1267 regime as an effective UN sanctions regime, or whether they are prepared to give up the regime to maintain the authority that they interpret to have from the UN Charter.

Tough questions need to be asked in this context, questions that have implications beyond the operation of the 1267 regime. These include an assessment of whether the 1267 regime is in fact an 'essential tool' in the fight against terrorism, and furthermore, whether this tool is actually effective. A thorough review of the 1267 regime must further include an analysis of its strategic impact. To what extent does it damage the credibility and acceptance of other UN targeted sanctions regimes? Also, does the 1267 regime impede the ability of the Security Council, and more broadly of the United Nations, to play a role in identifying national human rights shortcomings in counter-terrorism law and policy of UN Member States? These questions need to be addressed as a matter of urgency. Otherwise, the 1267 sanction regime will continue to lose support. This, in turn, may have serious consequences for the credibility and effectiveness of other UN targeted sanctions regimes. Such a development has the potential to weaken one of the few tools that the Security Council has at its disposal to maintain international peace and security.

POST SCRIPTUM

On 17 December 2009, the Security Council adopted resolution 1904 (2009). This resolution contains significant improvements in procedures for sanctions targeting. It creates an ombudsperson mechanism within the 1267 sanctions committee that draws heavily on the proposal made by Denmark in 2006. The resolution also establishes new listing and de-listing procedures that enhance due process. These measures are a response to recent court rulings like the ECJ's *Kadi and Al Barakaat* decision and pressures for reform from states in Europe and elsewhere. Nonetheless, it is questionable whether the ombudsperson mechanism fulfils the requirements of effective due process, and it remains to be seen whether courts like the ECJ will consider this mechanism sufficient.

REFERENCES

Almqvist, J. (2008). A human rights critique of European judicial review: Counter-terrorism sanctions. *International & Comparative Law Quarterly*, *57*(3), 303–332.

Amnesty International. (2008). Open letter to all members of the Security Council – Listing and de-listing of suspected terrorists under Security Council's sanctions regime, 3 June 2008, Ref.: UN/NYt/057/08 (letter on file with author).

Analytical Support and Sanctions Monitoring Team. (2006). *Fifth Report*, UN Security Council, S/2006/750.

Analytical Support and Sanctions Monitoring Team. (2008). *Eighth Report*, UN Security Council, S/2008/324.

Analytical Support and Sanctions Monitoring Team. (2009). *Ninth Report*, UN Security Council, S/2009/245.

Ayadi v Council of the EU (2006) (T-253/02) ECR II-2139.

Biersteker, T., & Eckert, S. (Eds). (2006). *Strengthening targeted sanctions through fair and clear procedures*. Watson Institute for International Studies. Available at http://www.watsoninstitute.org/pub/Strengthening_Targeted_Sanctions.pdf

Cameron, I. (2003). European Union anti-terrorist blacklisting. *Human Rights Law Review*, *3*(2), 225–246.

Cameron, I. (2006). *The European convention on human rights, due process and United Nations Security Council counter-terrorism sanctions*. Report for the Council of Europe. Available at http://www.coe.int/t/e/legal_affairs/legal_co-operation/public_international_law/Texts_&_Documents/2006/I.%20Cameron%20Report%2006.pdf

Cameron, I., & Nordback, K. (2003). EU blacklisting: The Renaissance of imperial power, but on a global scale. *European Business Law Review*, *14*, 111–142.

Cortright, D., & Lopez, G. (Eds). (2000). *The sanctions decade: Assessing UN strategies in the 1990s*. Boulder, CO: Lynne Rienner.

Discussion Paper. (2008). Improving the implementation of sanctions regimes through ensuring 'fair and clear procedures' (on file with author).

Farrall, J. M. (2007). *United Nations sanctions and the rule of law*. Cambridge: Cambridge University Press.

Fassbender, B. (2006). Targeted sanctions and due process. Humboldt-Universität zu Berlin, Study commissioned by the United Nations, Office of Legal Affairs, Office of the Legal Counsel. Available at http://www.un.org/law/counsel/Fassbender_study.pdf

Frowein, J. A., & Kirsch, N. (2002). Introduction to chapter VII. In: B. Simma, et al. (Eds), *The charter of the United Nations: A commentary* (Vol. I, pp. 701–716). Oxford: Oxford University Press.

Grauls, J. (2008). Briefing of chairman of the Security Council committee established pursuant to resolution 1267 (1999) concerning Al-Qaida and the Taliban and Associated Individuals and Entities, to the Security Council on 15 December 2008, UN Security Council, 6043rd meeting, Doc S/PV.6043.

Hassan v Council of the EU (2006) (T-49/04) ECR II-52.

Johnstone, I. (2008). The UN security council, counter-terrorism and human rights. In: A. Bianchi & A. Keller (Eds), *Counterterrorism: Democracy's challenge* (pp. 335–353). Oxford: Hart.

Kadi and Al Barakaat v Council of the European Union and Commission of the European Communities (2008) (C-402/05 P) and (C-415/05 P).

Kadi v Council of the EU (2005) (T-315/01) ECR II-3649.

Marty, D. (2007). UN Security Council black lists – Introductory memorandum. Committee on Legal Affairs and Human Rights, CoE, PACE, AS/Jur (2007) 14 (19 March 2007).

Michaelsen, C. (2009). Kadi and Al Barakaat v Council of the EU – The incompatibility of the UN Security Council's 1267 sanctions regime with European due process guarantees. *Melbourne Journal of International Law, 10*(1), 329–345.

OSCE-ODIHR. (2007). *Final Report of the Expert Workshop on Human Rights and International Cooperation in Counter-Terrorism organized by the OSCE-ODIHR and the OHCHR in Triesenberg, Liechtenstein*, 15–17 November 2006, ODIHR.GAL/14/07. Available at http://www.osce.org/documents/odihr/2007/02/23424_en.pdf

Scheinin, M. (2006). *Report of the special rapporteur on the promotion and protection of human rights while countering terrorism*. UN General Assembly, A/61/267.

Van den Herik, L. (2009). *From comprehensive to smart sanctions and ensuring their proper application and implementation*. Paper presented at the Seminar on Improving the Effectivity and Legitimacy of UN Targeted Sanctions. Dutch Ministry of Foreign Affairs, Kurhaus, The Hague, 25 May.

Van den Herik, L., & Schrijver, N. (2006). Human rights concerns in current targeted sanctions regimes from the perspective of International and European law. In: T. Biersteker & S. Eckert (Eds), *Strengthening targeted sanctions through fair and clear procedures* (pp. 9–23). Watson Institute for International Studies at Brown University. Available at http://www.watsoninstitute.org/pub/Strengthening_Targeted_Sanctions.pdf

Verbeke, J. (2007). Briefing of chairman of the security council committee established pursuant to resolution 1267 (1999) concerning Al-Qaida and the Taliban and Associated Individuals and Entities, to the Security Council on 14 November 2007, UN Security Council Doc S/PV.5779. Available at http://www.un.org/sc/committees/dfp.shtml

Wenaweser, C. (2008). Oral remarks at the seminar. Countering terrorism through domestic and international sanctions listing. A rule of law perspective. Session 3, held at the Washington College of Law, American University, Washington, DC, 15 September. Available at http://media.wcl.american.edu/Mediasite/Viewer/?peid = e8613fd1-e1e0-4054-bdb2-b0c33ffac555

Yusuf and Al Barakaat v Council of the EU (2005) (T-306/01) ECR II-3533.

CHAPTER 14

COMPENSATION FOR CIVILIAN CASUALTIES IN ARMED CONFLICTS AND THEORY OF LIABILITY

Minako Ichikawa Smart

ABSTRACT

Purpose – *The purpose of this chapter is to highlight the current limitations in compensating the civilian victims of armed conflicts and to examine the possibility of extending this practice.*

Methodology/approach – *The first half of the chapter employs legal and political analysis of the current framework of international law and the practice of the United States. The latter half of the chapter examines the literature on theory of liability in economics and philosophy.*

Findings – *The framework of international law, which does not require compensation for the victims of lawful attacks, is increasingly at odds with the current trend in which military force is used by a powerful state against a much weaker state on the grounds that the local population would benefit from the operation. The system developed by the United States is the most extensive and can form a model for other states and international institutions. Keating's analysis of enterprise liability can be applied to compensation of victims in military operations that are deemed to be*

Economics of War and Peace: Economic, Legal, and Political Perspectives
Contributions to Conflict Management, Peace Economics and Development, Volume 14, 243–259

ISSN: 1572-8323/doi:10.1108/S1572-8323(2010)0000014018

beneficial to the population. Economic analysis, on contrary, suggests that compensation of civilian victims has minimal effect on the level of risks.

Originality/value – *This chapter makes a unique contribution by applying theory of liability to a situation that widely diverges from the context in which the theory has developed. It critically examines the current practice and proposes a morally preferable and economically sustainable alternative model.*

INTRODUCTION

Minimising civilian casualties and providing remedies for civilian victims have become essential elements of recent military operations in Iraq and Afghanistan. Although these practices are developing among states participating in international military operations, compensation scheme coverage is limited, and there is a lack of coordination among states participating in the same operation (Human Rights Watch, 2009; Campaign for Innocent Victims in Conflict [CIVIC], 2008). One reason for insufficient compensation is that the current framework of international law does not require compensation for the damage caused by incidental and proportional attacks (i.e. 'collateral damage'). Another reason is that states are reluctant to admit legal liability for damages caused in armed conflict. Most states provide compensation only when negligence has been established and offer limited amount of payment variously called 'condolence' or 'ex-gratia' payments (Human Rights Watch, 2009; CIVIC, 2008). Even in the United States, which allows compensation on the basis of causation rather than negligence, many civilian victims are denied compensation as the claims caused by 'combat activities' are precluded, as discussed later.

This chapter challenges these assumptions limiting the practice of civilian compensation by the following methods. The chapter first outlines the framework of international law and then examines the compensation mechanism developed by the United States, which provides the most extensive remedy for civilian victims, with a specific focus on the clause of 'combat exclusion'. The latter half of the chapter investigates the literature on tort liability to propose that analysis of both economic and philosophical aspects of tort liability supports compensating all civilian victims without regard to negligence on the part of the injurer, particularly in the case of a military operation where a powerful state uses force against a much weaker state that has not initiated the conflict.

PROTECTING CIVILIANS IN INTERNATIONAL HUMANITARIAN LAW

The idea that civilians, who do not take direct part in hostilities, should be protected in armed conflicts forms an integral part of international humanitarian law (IHL). The principle of distinction, which prohibits direct attack of civilians, and the principle of proportionality, which requires that incidental damages to civilians should be proportional to the anticipated military advantage, have been derived from the *jus in bello* framework of the just war tradition, setting out just conduct in wars. These principles have been written into specific rules of positive international law, including the Hague Conventions and the Geneva Conventions, and many of the rules are considered to have developed into customary law.

Although the principle of distinction establishes the fundamental principle that civilians should be distinguished from combatants, the principle of proportionality determines whether unintended attacks are lawful. It is codified in Article 51(5)(b) of Additional Protocol I to the Geneva Conventions (1977), which prohibits 'an attack which may be expected to cause incidental loss of civilian life, injury to civilians, damage to civilian objects, or a combination thereof, which would be excessive in relation to the concrete and direct military advantage anticipated'. The principle is considered to be a customary rule binding on all states (Henckaerts & Doswald-Beck, 2005, pp. 47–48). What constitutes 'excessive' damage, however, is relative to the specific situation and the subjective understanding of the commander. Human Rights Watch, an authoritative international human rights organisation, accepts that a higher number of civilian casualties might be justifiable under the laws of war if the target has high strategic value (Human Rights Watch, 2007, Section VI).

In addition to the principles of distinction and proportionality, the obligation to take precautions during military operations is also part of civilian protection rules of IHL. This is an important indication that precaution in armed conflict is conceivable, contrary to the assumption that any notion of care is alien to the conduct in armed conflict, which underlies the states' denial of legal liability for civilian casualties. The rule was first set out in the 1907 Hague Convention (IX), and later codified in Article 57 of the Additional Protocol I, which stipulates that 'constant care shall be taken to spare the civilian population, civilians and civilian objects'. Attack is permitted if the defender deliberately uses civilians as human shields, although the principle of proportionality still applies (Henckaerts & Doswald-Beck, 2005, p. 71).

CIVILIAN COMPENSATION IN INTERNATIONAL HUMANITARIAN LAW

Although IHL does contain obligation for compensation, it is limited to damages caused by unlawful acts prohibited by IHL, based on the principle of state responsibility in international law. A state, as a subject of international law, bears responsibility for its conduct in breach of international law and is required to make reparation for the injury caused by its wrongful act. So long as compensation is based on this idea, it is impossible to oblige a state to compensate for damages caused by lawful attacks deemed to be incidental and proportionate. Article 91 of Additional Protocol I stipulates specific obligation in IHL:

> A Party to the conflict which violates the provisions of the Conventions or of this Protocol shall, if the case demands, be liable to pay compensation.

As part of the process of 'humanisation' of IHL after World War II, it has become possible for the victims to claim compensation themselves, moving away from the conventional understanding in international law that damages could only be claimed by states (Meron, 2006, pp. 248–249). Although compensations have been successfully claimed by individuals through inter-state arrangements and the unilateral act of responsible states, attempts to seek compensation in national courts often face difficulties (Henckaerts & Doswald-Beck, 2005, pp. 541–543). The most common hurdle is the principle of sovereign immunity, which exempts sovereign states from judicial proceedings in national courts (Henckaerts & Doswald-Beck, 2005, pp. 544–545). A recent example of this is the failure of the victims of abuse in Abu Ghraib prison to receive compensation from the US government (United States District Court for the District of Columbia, 2005).

A further problem arises from the link between compensation of the victim and criminal prosecution of the injurer, which is increasingly at odds with insurgency operations characteristic of warfare in the 21st century. In many of the events where civilians have been directly attacked based on the mistaken but reasonable perception that they might have been enemies, it is not necessarily appropriate to hold the attacker criminally liable, even if the victims might deserve to be compensated (Cassese, 2008).

The current framework of IHL reflects the conventional notion of inter-state conflict between two states of comparable military and economic power. As long as both sides inflict reciprocal (incidental) damage on the opponent's population, it might make sense to expect each state to provide remedy for its citizens. However, it is at odds with military operations characteristic of the post–Cold War era, in which a powerful state uses force against a much weaker state that has not initiated the conflict. As IHL would apply to all types of states and non-state parties to armed conflict, it is not appropriate to lay down generalised obligations of compensation under IHL. What is more practical is to supplement IHL with practices at national as well as at international levels.

THE US FOREIGN CLAIMS SYSTEM AND ITS LIMITS

The Foreign Claims Act (FCA, 10U.S.C. § 2734) system developed by the United States is considered to be the most extensive system of compensating civilian victims. The FCA authorises commanding officers to appoint the Foreign Claims Commission, which can approve or reject claims made by victims. Acceptance of payment is considered full and final settlement, releasing the United States and its employees from further liabilities. The system is limited by 'combat exclusion', which precludes compensation for damages caused by combat activities, although 'condolence payment' can be offered to some of the excluded cases.

The FCA was enacted shortly after the United States entered World War II and is still in effect today, after undergoing a series of amendments. It came to public attention in 2007 when the American Civil Liberties Union (ACLU) obtained documents concerning claims filed in Afghanistan and Iraq under the Freedom of Information Act and made them accessible through their homepage (American Civil Liberties Union, 2007a). Researchers and journalists investigating the data revealed confusion and contradictions in the manner individual cases had been handled (Witt, 2008; von Zielbauer, 2007). However, it is important to note that the system, with all its flaws, provides a significant supplement to the current framework of international law and is considered to be the most extensive among the existing mechanisms.

The FCA stipulates that a claim may be made against the Untied States for personal injury or death of an inhabitant of a foreign country, if the damage is 'caused by, or is otherwise incident to noncombat activities' of the military or is caused by a military personnel (10U.S.C. § 2734 (a)(3)). It is important to note that the simple fact that the damage was caused by the US forces is sufficient, without requiring negligence to be established. This policy is confirmed in the training manual for Navy lawyers, which states that in the context of FCA, 'the acts that caused the loss *need not be wrongful or negligent*' (Naval Education and Training Professional Development and Technology Center, 2003, pp. 12–21, emphasis added). The guiding policy document of the Department of the Army also distinguishes between damage which 'results from non-combat activity' and damage from a 'negligent act or omission' of military personnel (US Department of the Army, 2008, 10-3a), implying that it is not necessary to establish negligence to make a claim through the FCA system.

In tort law, rendering the injurer liable for all damages caused is called a strict liability rule, as opposed to a negligence rule, which makes the injurer liable only where there is evidence that the injurer acted negligently. As with most strict liability schemes, the FCA is accompanied by the principle of contributive or comparative negligence, which takes into account negligent or wrongful conduct on the part of the claimant (US Department of the Army, 2008, 10-4Aa). Although the FCA's choice of strict liability, judging from its historical origin, seems to be based on its flexibility (Witt, 2008), it benefits victims as it allows them to claim compensation without establishing negligence. The scope of compensation is significantly limited by the rule of combat exclusion.

CASES OF COMBAT EXCLUSION UNDER THE FOREIGN CLAIMS SYSTEM

The concept of combat exclusion is outlined in paragraph (b)(3) of the FCA, which states that a claim may be allowed only if it 'did not arise from action by an enemy or result directly or indirectly from an act of the armed forces of the United States in combat'. The guiding policy document of the Department of the Army defines 'combat activities' as '[a]ctivities resulting directly or indirectly from action by the enemy, or by the Armed Forces of the United States engaged in armed conflict, or in immediate preparation for impending armed conflict' (US Department of the Army, 2008, p. 119). The broad definition of 'combat activities' allows wide discretion for the armed forces to make payments to advance strategic gains without giving the victims the right to compensation (Witt, 2008, pp. 9–11).

The documents disclosed by the ACLU, despite some inconsistency, reveal some patterns in cases rejected on the ground of combat exclusion. Among 490 viable claims, 233 of the 404 rejected cases were based on 'combat exclusion' (CIVIC, 2007, p. 4; Witt, 2008, p. 12). Diverse cases of claims denied under 'combat exclusion' can be divided into two categories.

The first is where the victim happened to be present when the US force was engaged in a combat with insurgents or suspected terrorists. This category covers various situations such as being caught up in crossfire, being shot by a stray bullet or being bombed while at home during a raid. Claims have been denied under 'combat exclusion' simply because the Coalition Forces' record suggested that there had been fighting in the area (American Civil Liberties Union, 2007b; Army Bates 197–200; Army Bates 623–628), or on the assumption that the military must have been responding to enemy attack (American Civil Liberties Union, 2007b; Army Bates 656–659; Army Bates 1535–1538).

The second category of claims denied under 'combat exclusion' involves cases of the military forces directly attacking a civilian as a result of mistaking him/her for an enemy. This covers situations such as a driver failing to stop at a checkpoint or driving too close to the military vehicle and a pedestrian whose bag was mistaken for a bomb. Cases where victims had been killed by warning shots were sometimes rejected under combat exclusion (American Civil Liberties Union, 2007b; Army Bates 1097–1100; Army Bates 1175–1179). Unlike in the first category, there is no fighting before the military's act that results in damage to the victim, although categorising these cases as combat activities is understandable in insurgency wars in which it has become increasingly difficult to distinguish between civilians and combatants.

JUSTIFYING COMBAT EXCLUSION

From the perspective of compensating the victims, justifying the exclusion of combat-related claims in a scheme designed for compensation in armed conflict can appear puzzling. Combat exclusion, however, is not unique to the FCA. It is also embedded in other claims systems under the Military Claims Act (10U.S.C. § 2733) and the Federal Tort Claims Act (FTCA, 28U.S.C. §§ 2671–2680). Although legal justification for combat exclusion is not given in the FCA or related documents, it has been discussed in court in the context of the FTCA. Since the FTCA, unlike the FCA, partially waives sovereign immunity, it is possible to file a lawsuit against the US government under this law. An important difference between the FTCA and the FCA is that the former requires negligence on the part of the government or government employees who had caused damage, while the FCA is based on strict liability.

Justification of combat exclusion has also been outlined in the 1992 *Koohi* case in which damages were considered for families of passengers in an Iranian civilian aircraft shot down by the United States during the Iran–Iraq conflict. In this case, the judge commented extensively on how combat exclusion can be justified in the context of the FTCA. The question at issue in the *Koohi* case (US Court of Appeals 9th Cir., 1992) was whether the damages caused resulted from a combat activity, in which case sovereign immunity could not be waived. The judge affirmed that the act of shooting down a civilian aircraft as a result of mistaking it for a missile constituted a combat activity.

The judgment provided three reasons why combat exclusion was necessary for the FTCA (US Court of Appeals 9th Cir., 1992, paragraph 17). First was the claim that duty of care, which is central to tort law, cannot be expected from the military forces engaged in combat.

> The reason, we believe, is that one purpose of the combat activities exception is to recognize that during wartime encounters no duty of reasonable care is owed to those against whom force is directed as a result of authorized military action. (US Court of Appeals 9th Cir. 1992, paragraph 24)

This appears to be a legitimate argument, pointing out that duty of care as assumed in tort law could not be expected in a relationship between the military forces and the victim of attack. The attacker is only required to do what is feasible even though there is duty of precaution in IHL. It is not up to the civil court to determine the appropriate level of care in the context of armed conflict. However, this does not explain why combat exclusion is necessary for the FCA system, which is an administrative procedure through which victims claim compensation on the basis of strict liability, that is, based on causation rather than negligence.

The other two reasons justifying combat exclusion were less convincing (US Court of Appeals 9th Cir., 1992, paragraph 17). The second argument claimed it would make little sense to compensate a few enemy citizens when overwhelming violence has been intentionally inflicted on both sides. This position fails to take into account that IHL distinguishes between attacks on combatants and attacks on civilians and that intentional killing of civilians constitutes a grave violation. The third point, that military personnel should not be punished for their failure to protect the enemy civilians, is more defendable. However, it should not rule out compensating the victims without linking it to negligence on the part of the injurer.

Further consideration was given to the notion of combat exclusion in such compensation matters in a case filed by detainees of Abu Ghraib prison against the private contractors involved in torture and abuse. This case, *Ibrahim v. Titan* (US District Court for the District of Columbia, 2005) mentioned the *Koohi* case. Although the judge repeated *Koohi*'s statement that duty of care did not apply in combat situations, the argument was based on the idea that military decisions of the Federal government should not be subject to lawsuit. The judge was not opposed, in principle, to compensating the plaintiffs in a way that would not challenge sovereign immunity and did not exclude the possibility of lawsuit against the private contractors on the basis of common law tort.

CAMPAIGN FOR UNRESTRICTED COMPENSATION

In 2007, the Campaign for Compensation was launched by the Campaign for Innocent Victims in Conflict (CIVIC), an organisation devoted to protection of civilian victims in armed conflict, and five partner organisations. Their goal is to create a new claims system through which all civilian victims in conflict can receive compensation. According to the Campaign's homepage, the Civilian Claims Act is being drafted by US Senator Patrick Leahy (Campaign for Compensation, 2007). Rather than replacing the FCA, the Civilian Claims Act seeks to work alongside it, as a permanent claims system covering damages caused by combat activities of US forces. Details of the program are yet to be disclosed, and it is difficult to predict how the campaign will proceed. The proposal involves substantial payments to foreign nationals where there is no existing legal obligation. Still, it is significant that the emerging norm that all civilian victims should be compensated is developing into a political movement in the United States.

THEORY OF LIABILITY AND CIVILIAN VICTIMS IN ARMED CONFLICT

The previous section has argued that justifications for 'combat exclusion', including the assumption that duty of care does not apply in a combat situation, do not hold in the context of an administrative claims system like the US FCA system. It also referred to the emerging norm that all civilian victims should be compensated. This section will investigate the literature on tort liability in economics and philosophy to assess whether it supports the proposal of extending compensation to all civilian victims.

Regulating Dangerous Activities

One important function of tort law is to reduce accidents by deterring dangerous activities and creating incentives to take appropriate level of care (Shavell, 1984, p. 357; Landes & Posner, 1984, p. 417). In a basic model of economic analysis, due care is considered to be the level of care which minimises the social costs, which can be calculated by adding the total cost of damage suffered by the victim and the sum of the cost of care paid by the potential injurer to reduce risks. In other words, optimal level of care is reached when reduction in expected damages equals marginal cost of care (Landes & Posner, 1984, pp. 418–419; Shavell, 1984, pp. 358–359). Some propose setting optimal level of care at a point where the sum of social costs equals the total of expected social benefits arising from the dangerous activities (Coase, 1960; Gilead, 1997).

This model can be applied to the context of use of force to the extent that it is a dangerous activity that is permitted by society under certain circumstances. It is particularly suited for analysing military operations aimed at benefiting the international community or the local population by achieving peace or humanitarian protection. Quite clearly, two basic assumptions in the economic model are at odds with the situation in armed conflict. First is the assumption that the probability of an accident depends on level of care and activities (Landes & Posner, 1984, p. 419). In cases where tort law is used for regulating activities, the possibility of accidents is expected to decrease as the injurers and the victims increase the level of care by investing in safety equipment, taking more precautions, or reducing the level of risky activities. In armed conflict, while risk reduction can be expected as a consequence of using certain military technology, such as more precise targeting, and by training in civilian protection, there is a limit to how much precaution can be taken without risking the lives of the soldiers. The second assumption is that it is possible to calculate social costs and benefits on the basis of utilities equated with wealth or income. In the context of armed conflict, damages suffered by the victims and the costs of care borne by the injurers and the victims cannot be added up to calculate the social costs as the injurers and the victims do not form a common society as assumed in most economic models. It is also difficult to convert the social benefits of the activities into monetary value at a time when economic exchanges have been severely disrupted.

Although the model does not seem suited for calculating the optimum level of care in armed conflict, some findings of the economic analysis can be used in assessing the impact of civilian compensation on the society.

According to Shavell, strict liability with a defence of contributory negligence is preferred when the injurer has greater influence on the possibility of accidents. On the contrary, negligence is preferred when the injurer and the victim equally contribute to the risks. It is based on the idea that once the appropriate level of care is established, the level of activities determines the level of risks. As Shavell illustrates, by using the example of pedestrians and motorists, under negligence, potential injurers (motorists) have no incentive to reduce the level of activities, as they would not be held liable so long as they exercise due care. On the contrary, potential victims (pedestrians) would reduce their activities, as they would have to bear the losses if the injurers were not negligent. In contrast, under strict liability, potential injurers would be motivated to reduce the level of activities to minimise the chance of accidents, although potential victims would have no incentive to reduce the level of activities (Shavell, 1980, pp. 6–7; Faure & Wang, 2006, pp. 183–184).

This model might be useful in assessing whether compensation for civilian victims would have a negative impact on the society by over-deterring the military forces or under-deterring the victims. Under-deterrence becomes a problem to the extent that the activity level of the victim contributes to the probability of accidents. For example, the probability of accidents between motorists and pedestrians could be reduced to zero if there were no pedestrians on the street. However, Shavell (1980, p. 24) argues that it is neither practical nor desirable to control victims' activities that are typically entirely routine in nature.

Analysing the FCA claims rejected on the basis of 'combat exclusion' suggests little ground to believe that compensating victims for their losses would increase the chance of incidental damages. In the first category of rejected cases, namely, situations where the victims were caught in crossfire or bombed during the raid, there seems to be little they could have done to prevent the accidents, especially if they were attacked while at home. As for the second category, that is, cases where the victims were mistaken for enemies, risks could theoretically be reduced by avoiding passing checkpoints and staying at home, but again as Shavell argues, it is neither practical nor desirable to control the victims' routine activities. Accidents still happened under the current situation where the victims are not compensated, and there is little ground to believe that accidents would increase as the result of compensation.

The next question is whether over-deterrence of the armed forces would limit the level of military operations. Here, we limit our analysis to states with sufficient economic resources to compensate the victims, focusing specifically on military operations conducted by a powerful state against a much weaker state. Considering the economic power of the states with leading roles in such military operations and the gap in economic standard between the attacking state and the target state, it appears that the impact of compensation modelled on the US FCA system would be limited. According to Witt (2008, p. 14), the total cost of claims paid in Afghanistan and Iraq combined (USD 32 million) constitute 0.0032 per cent of the total costs of the Iraq war (USD 1 trillion). Even if USD 11,000, the highest award for death among the files released by the ACLU, were paid for each of the 9,270 civilian deaths caused by the US-led forces between March 2003 and March 2005 (Iraq Body Count, 2005), it would amount to approximately USD 100 million, still 0.01 per cent of the total costs of the war.

Military forces are more likely to be motivated to minimise civilian casualties by political pressures and strategic considerations than by cost. Colonel James Garrett (2008, p. 25), who has commanded operations in Afghanistan, proposes that in determining whether to attack a target, the commander should assess whether the expected military advantage would exceed the potential civilian casualties and the 'associated negative impact to the military operation as a whole'. The US Army's Field Manual on counter-insurgency emphasises the specific importance of protecting civilians in counter-insurgency operations:

> Fires that cause unnecessary harm or death to noncombatants may create more resistance and increase the insurgency's appeal—especially if the populace perceives a lack of discrimination in their use. The use of discriminating, proportionate force as a mindset goes beyond the adherence to the rules of engagement. (US Department of the Army, 2006, Chap. 7, p. 7)

In the view of the US Army, compensating civilian victims, rather than preventing otherwise legitimate and beneficial operations, is expected to partially offset the political and strategic costs of civilian casualties (US Department of the Army, 2006, pp. 5–23). The implication of this is that while the economic impact of compensation on the level of care and activities is limited, the military forces are likely to be motivated by political and strategic considerations to minimise civilian casualties and compensate the victims.

Fair Distribution of Cost and Benefit

The philosophical aspect of tort liability concerns how cost and benefit arising from risky activities should be allocated among the members of the society. As Coleman & Ripstein (1995, p. 94) argue, tort law, along with distributive institutions, is concerned with allocating misfortune and its burdens fairly across the society. Conventionally, it was believed that tort law, based on *corrective justice*, should be distinguished from *distributive justice* (Avraham & Kohler-Hausmann, 2006, pp. 182–183; Coleman & Ripstein, 1995, p. 93). However, it is clear that consideration about fair distribution of costs and benefits among the parties involved is unavoidable in designing a tort mechanism (Coleman & Ripstein, 1995, p. 96; Avraham & Kohler-Hausmann, 2006, pp. 211–212).

Although the literature normally assumes that all parties, that is, the injurer, the victim and the population as a whole, belong to the same society, it is possible that the injurer comes from another society. By extension of this logic, it is possible to regard the military forces operating in another country as one of the parties among which costs and benefits of the dangerous activity should be shared. Gregory Keating's (2005) analysis of enterprise liability appears to have a potential to be applied to the case of civilian casualties in armed conflict.

Keating's analysis involves three parties: the enterprise, the victim and the population. The enterprise puts the population at risk by its gainful activities, from which the population would benefit in the long run. An accident will happen despite the care taken by the enterprise, and the victim is singled out to suffer the harm caused by the accident. In a case like this, he considers that strict liability borne by the enterprise ensures fair distribution of costs and benefits among all parties. It is fair for the victim, who had to shoulder the cost of the risky activity alone. It is a fair price for the enterprise to pay for its freedom to impose risks upon the population, and it results in fair distribution of the costs and benefits among the population, as the costs unfairly imposed on the victim have been repaired by the compensation. According to Keating (2005, p. 9), payment of compensation to the victim is a condition for legitimate conduct of a risky activity.

This is an interesting interpretation of the strict liability norm, which sees compensation as reparation for the suffering of the victim caused by the risk justified by utilitarian calculations. This line of argument can be applied to civilian casualties in humanitarian military operations. The military forces can be equated with the enterprise engaging in gainful activities to the extent that the decision to undertake the military operation was taken voluntarily, on the basis of calculation of costs and benefits. Although the military operation is expected to benefit the population in the long run, civilian casualties are inevitable, and the victims pay the cost by loss of life, injury and property damage. If we apply the reasoning in Keating's enterprise liability, it is fair to expect the military forces to cover the costs so long as they have voluntarily chosen to impose risks on the population. Cost of compensation is not likely to change the initial cost/benefit calculation as we have seen earlier. Even if the population benefits in the long run, it should not be expected to bear the costs of the risks imposed without consent.

This formula would apply to a case where the military operation has not benefited the population, so long as the decision to take military action was made voluntarily. However, it would not apply if the population was partly responsible for starting the conflict by initiating an attack or directly provoking the attacker. Responsibility can be shared by the militaries of multiple states in a case where an operation is conducted by a coalition or an alliance. In a case where the operation is authorised by the Untied Nations and member states are called upon to contribute their forces, it will be required to establish a special fund for compensation at the institutional level. In this case, the United Nations as an institution, rather than the states contributing to the mission, is equated with the enterprise.

CONCLUDING REMARKS

This chapter has demonstrated that compensating civilian casualties in armed conflict without regard to criminal liability or negligence is supported by the literature of tort liability, even though it is not required under the current framework of international law. Economic analysis suggests that strict liability is preferred when the injurer has greater influence on the possibility of accidents, which applies in conflict situations. In a case where a powerful state uses force against a much weaker state that has not initiated the conflict, the cost of compensation makes limited impact on the level of care and activities, although political and strategic considerations are likely to motivate the military forces to minimise civilian casualties and to compensate the victims. The implication of this is that compensating all civilian casualties, despite incurring substantial cost, has the potential of facilitating a legitimate operation, partially offsetting the political and strategic costs of civilian casualties.

Philosophical analysis of tort liability suggests that providing compensation for all civilian casualties on the basis of strict liability is a precondition for legitimate conduct of a risky activity such as a military operation. Military forces would be required to compensate the victims *even if* the population as a whole benefited from the military operation. If the population did not benefit from the operation, the military forces would still be required to compensate the victims, but in this case, compensation would not be sufficient for justifying imposing unnecessary risks on the population. In other words, compensation is a necessary but not sufficient condition for a fair military operation.

To combine the findings of economic and philosophical analyses, compensating all civilian casualties is required from the perspective of fairness, while the cost of compensation would not have the negative impacts of over-deterring military forces or under-deterring victims. Where the overall operation is perceived to be fair by the local population, there is a higher chance that the operation will be facilitated by local support.

The FCA system developed by the United States can provide a good model to be followed by other states, although 'combat exclusion' will have to be lifted for its benefits to be fully realised. A coordinated system should be developed for multilateral operations so that victims who suffered similar damages would receive the same treatment (Human Rights Watch, 2009). It would also become necessary to develop a special mechanism and funds for operations authorised by the United Nations.

This chapter has focused on use of force by a powerful state against a much weaker state that has not initiated the conflict. Economic analysis of deterrence assumes that the potential injurer has sufficient resources to compensate the victims. If the potential damage exceeds the assets of the potential injurer, there is a possibility that the injurer is under-deterred (Landes & Posner, 1984, p. 420; Faure & Wang, 2006, p. 184). The model of enterprise liability assumes that the risk is unilaterally imposed upon the population, which precludes its application to conventional inter-state conflicts or intra-state conflicts between rival groups. In many of the recent inter-state and intra-state conflicts, direct and intentional attacks of civilians are prevalent. Compensating victims of direct and indirect attacks by the enemy forces, insurgents and militias would require a different approach, such as assistance provided by the post-conflict government. Examples of this are the President's Fund and the Martyrs Fund provided by the government of Afghanistan (CIVIC, 2008).

REFERENCES

American Civil Liberties Union. (2007a). ACLU releases US Army documents that depict American troops' involvement in civilian casualties in Iraq and Afghanistan. Available at http://www.aclu.org/natsec/31540prs20070904.html. Retrieved on 23 June 2009.

American Civil Liberties Union. (2007b). Documents received from the Department of the Army in response to ACLU freedom of information act request. Available at http://www.aclu.org/natsec/foia/log.html. Retrieved on 23 June 2009.

Avraham, R., & Kohler-Hausmann, I. (2006). Accident law for egalitarians. *Legal Theory*, *12*, 181–224.

Campaign for Compensation. (2007). Frequently asked questions. Available at http://www.campaign4compensation.org/About%20Us.html. Retrieved on 23 June 2009.

Campaign for Innocent Victims in Conflict. (2007). Adding insult to injury: US military claims system for civilians. Available at http://www.civicworldwide.org/storage/civic/documents/civic%20-%20casualties%20white%20paper.pdf. Retrieved on 23 June 2009.

Campaign for Innocent Victims in Conflict. (2008). Afghanistan's war victims. Available at http://www.civicworldwide.org/storage/civic/120508%20afghanistan%20war%20victims.pdf. Retrieved on 24 November 2009.

Cassese, A. (2008). Under what conditions may belligerents be acquitted of the crime of attacking an ambulance? *Journal of International Criminal Justice*, *6*, 385–397.

Coase, R. H. (1960). The problem of social cost. *Journal of Law and Economics*, *3*, 1–44.

Coleman, J., & Ripstein, A. (1995). Mischief and misfortune. *McGill Law Journal*, *41*, 91–130.

Faure, M., & Wang, H. (2006). Economic analysis of compensation for oil pollution damage. *Journal of Maritime Law and Commerce*, *37*, 179–217.

Garrett, J. F. (2008). Necessity and proportionality in the operation enduring freedom VII campaign. Strategic Research Project, US Army War College. Available at http://www.dtic.mil/cgi-bin/GetTRDoc?AD = ADA479007&Location = U2&doc = GetTRDoc.pdf. Retrieved on 23 June 2009.

Gilead, I. (1997). Tort law and internalization: The gap between private loss and social cost. *International Review of Law and Economics*, *17*, 589–608.

Henckaerts, J.-M., & Doswald-Beck, L. (2005). *Customary international humanitarian law*. Cambridge: Cambridge University Press.

Human Rights Watch. (2007). The human cost: The consequences of insurgent attacks in Afghanistan. Available at http://www.hrw.org/en/reports/2007/04/15/human-cost. Retrieved on 23 June 2009.

Human Rights Watch. (2009). Letter to NATO to investigate compensation for civilian casualties in Afghanistan. Available at http://www.hrw.org/en/news/2009/04/02/letter-nato-investigate-compensation-civilian-casualties-afghanistan. Retrieved on 24 November 2009.

Iraq Body Count. (2005). A dossier of civilian casualties 2003–2005. Available at http://reports.iraqbodycount.org/a_dossier_of_civilian_casualties_2003-2005.pdf. Retrieved on 23 June 2009.

Keating, G. C. (2005). *Fairness and two fundamental questions in the tort law of accidents*. University of Southern California, Olin Working Paper no. 99-21. Available at http://papers.ssrn.com/paper.taf?abstract_id = 200778. Retrieved on 23 June 2009.

Landes, W. M., & Posner, R. A. (1984). Tort law as a regulatory regime for catastrophic personal injuries. *Journal of Legal Studies*, *13*, 417–434.

Meron, T. (2006). *The humanization of international law*. Leiden: Martinus Nijhoff Publishers.

Naval Education and Training Professional Development and Technology Center. (2003). Legalman NAVEDTRA 14351, Pensacola FL.

Shavell, S. (1980). Strict liability versus negligence. *Journal of Legal Studies*, *9*, 1–25.

Shavell, S. (1984). Liability for harm versus regulation of safety. *Journal of Legal Studies, 13*, 357–374.
US Court of Appeal 9th Cir. (1992). *Koohi v. United States, 976F.2d 1328.*
US Department of the Army. (2006). FM 3-24 Counterinsurgency, Department of the Army, Washington D.C.
US Department of the Army. (2008). AR 27-20 legal services: Claims. Available at http://www.army.mil/usapa/epubs/pdf/r27_20.pdf. Retrieved on 23 June 2009.
US District Court for the District of Columbia. (2005). *Ibrahim v. Titan, 391F.* Supp. 2d 10.
von Zielbauer, P. (2007). Confusion and discord in US compensation to civilian victims of war. *The International Herald Tribune*,12 April 2007. Available at http://www.nytimes.com/2007/04/12/world/americas/12iht-abuse.1.5246758.html. Retrieved on 23 June 2009.
Witt, J. F. (2008). *Form and substance in the law of counterinsurgency damages.* Columbia Law School, Public Law & Legal Theory Working Paper Group no. 08-181. Available at http://ssrn.com/abstract = 1096587. Retrieved on 23 June 2009.

PART IV
CONCLUSIONS

CHAPTER 15

ECONOMIC FACTORS IN PEACE AND WAR: A DISCUSSION

Benjamin E. Goldsmith

ABSTRACT

Purpose – *The main purpose is to provide ideas about an intellectual framework for considering the role of "economic factors" in conflict and to suggest some potentially useful future areas of research. I selectively reference some relevant findings from the other chapters in this volume.*

Methodology/approach – *This chapter is speculative, but raises important issues. It might seem that economic factors should be considered "hard" constraints on the dynamics of large-scale conflict and peace, whereas political factors are "soft." I propose the opposite. I argue that we should consider political factors as causally primary and economic factors as contingent on them. I present statistical analyses that call into question some recent research on the apparent primacy of economic factors in international conflict.*

Findings – *These models challenge a strong belief in the primacy of a "capitalist peace" or "economic peace" over political factors such as democracy. But my purpose here is no more than to suggest that this is a promising area for further inquiry. Economic factors are of course hugely important, but they are filtered through norms and institutions, which are political creations. If the basic logic of my thinking holds, similar results would be obtained for studies of civil conflict initiation and escalation.*

Economics of War and Peace: Economic, Legal, and Political Perspectives
Contributions to Conflict Management, Peace Economics and Development, Volume 14, 263–282

ISSN: 1572-8323/doi:10.1108/S1572-8323(2010)0000014019

Originality/value of paper – *This chapter raises the issue of the appropriate place of economic and political factors in understanding organized conflict at various levels of analysis. It suggests how the chapters in this volume help advance thinking about the relationship between economic factors and conflict in this context and provides some novel empirical results to suggest the plausibility of the argument that economic factors may be less theoretically fundamental than political ones.*

The main purpose in this chapter is to provide ideas about an intellectual framework within which to consider the role of "economic factors" in conflict and to suggest some potentially useful future areas of research based on these ideas. I see this chapter as speculative, but raising important issues. Although it might seem that economic factors should be considered "hard" constraints on the dynamics of large-scale conflict and peace, whereas political factors are "soft," in the sense that they are malleable and vary with the context, I propose the opposite. I argue that we should consider political factors as causally primary and economic factors as contingent on them, in the processes that lead to organized violence within and between societies such as states. However, although I favor this argument, I am more concerned to point out the theoretical importance of the issue for conflict analysis and to begin to sketch the logic on both sides.

I selectively reference the findings from the other chapters in this volume, when they relate to the themes I address, and place them in perspective by suggesting how they contribute to existing knowledge about the roles of economic factors in domestic and international war. Because organized violent conflict within and between states has complex causes, it is especially important to clarify as much as possible the theoretical hierarchy of different types of factors. Empirical analysis, statistical or qualitative, must be theory driven to provide valid tests of causation. But with so many factors to consider, and so many potential ways in which causal processes might unfold, there is a danger that analysts will focus on their favorite models among competing, and equally statistically significant, findings (Beck, King, & Zeng, 2000). Thus careful theorizing about the causes of various types of conflict is essential, even as our data, analytical tools, and bank of cumulative findings become more sophisticated. The chapters in this volume are helpful in this regard, because they suggest a range of new ideas or new applications of existing concepts. In this chapter, I attempt a further modest contribution by focusing on the issue of the relative position of economic and political factors in conflict processes.

Toward the end of the chapter, I present some statistical analyses that call into question some recent research on the apparent primacy of economic factors in international conflict. Fundamentally, I float an argument that the things we tend to term "economic" are of necessity embedded in norms and institutions in all human interactions, and these norms and institutions can be termed "political." For this reason, the effects of economic factors on serious civil or international conflict should be thought of as conditioned by, and secondary to, at least some fundamental political factors. However, I also point out some of the potential logic of a primacy of economics argument. Although I recognize that it is reasonable to argue that economic factors are actually primary, for example because they most directly relate to the very survival, sustenance, and welfare of humans, I try to make the case that behavior driven by even the most basic human needs is nevertheless conditioned by politics, even at the individual level of analysis, but still more plausibly at the level of larger aggregations such as ethnicities and states. It is also possible that the political and economic factors are of equal weight, but I do not dwell on this possibility here.

Whether or not they are contingent on political factors, there are numerous ways in which economic factors might be causally related to conflict within and among countries. One way to think about this is to consider various levels of analysis, as has been common in the field of international relations for decades.[1] For example, economic causes might be located at the sub-state, state, bilateral, regional, or systemic level, and the conflict or peace outcomes could also be considered at each of these levels. Most extant studies of economics and conflict probably focus on the sub-state or state levels regarding civil war, and the bilateral or dyadic level for international war. Several chapters in this book suggest how the regional or even systemic levels might be considered. Robbani's chapter in this volume explicitly focuses on formalized regional economic integration as a factor in international conflict. Royal's chapter considers the integrated global economic system as a layer of economic dynamics and political considerations, which could alter perceptions and strategic calculations of states in bilateral bargaining situations, including disagreements that threaten to escalate to war. Needless to say, there is no guarantee that conflict at different levels, such as civil war and inter-state war, will have similar or even related causal processes involving economic factors. And of course, there are different types and intensities of conflict, which often need to be considered separately (e.g., Cederman, Buhaug, & Rod, 2009; Goldsmith, 2006; Regan & Norton, 2005).

Another way in which one might consider economic factors as possible causes of conflict is to specify which particular aspects of economic activity and outcomes have positive or negative effects on the likelihood of specific types of conflict. Most of the debates in the current literature center around these sorts of distinctions. Thus, for civil war, is it greed, grievance (often due to economic injustice), or both, which matter (Berdal & Malone, 2000)? For international war, is it economic interdependence (Xiang, Xu, & Keteku, 2007), or domestic market institutions (Gartzke, 2007; Mousseau, 2009), foreign investment and open finance (Gartzke, 2007), or some other factor(s) which matter? Although most consideration of the relationship between economics and conflict has focused on relatively constant, or slow-changing, factors such as trade or investment flows, Royal's chapter in this volume points to short-term, volatile factors such as economic crises, as potentially important. This suggests another question: should analysts not only pay attention to underlying economic variables that help create the dry forest, but also consider proximate economic factors that could provide the spark? Although there are unlikely to be simple answers to these and similar questions, properly understanding the role played by specific economic activities and outcomes is a central challenge, and a necessity, for analysts.

Of course, to develop theoretical expectations about economics and conflict, both the levels of analysis and the type(s) of economic activities or outcomes must be specified.

This volume suggests some relatively novel approaches such as considering the regional and systemic levels of analysis, rather than just the dyadic, or bilateral, level, regarding inter-state conflict. In this volume, we also encounter a wide range of economic factors, from private military contractors to international trade, to arms export controls, to economic sanctions. But before expanding on any of these specifically, it seems useful to step back and ask a more fundamental question. Collier and Hoeffler's (2004, p. 563) seminal work led to their conclusion that "economic variables, which could proxy some grievances but are perhaps more obviously related to the viability of rebellion, provide considerably more explanatory power" for civil wars than more political variables. The political factors they considered, especially a lack of political rights, did not prove to be strong correlates of civil war in their data. Regarding causes of international conflict, Gartzke (2007, p. 166) has recently asserted that "[e]conomic development, capital market integration, and the compatibility of foreign policy preferences supplant the effect of democracy in standard statistical tests of the democratic peace." But, what are "economic" and "political" factors, and how should we consider them in relation to conflict?

ECONOMICS, POLITICS, AND CONFLICT

Webster's dictionary (1996) gives us the following definitions. Economic: "pertaining to the production, distribution, and use of income, wealth, and commodities." Political: "exercising or seeking power in the governmental or public affairs of a state, municipality, etc." I minimally elaborate these concepts to clarify how I think of them and to support further discussion.

I define the "economic" as involving material goods and services, and money used to facilitate their exchange. A relevant aspect for conflict is that this often has to do with physical sustenance and welfare of humans. The currencies are money or barter.

I define the "political" as involving moral, ethical, and normative "goods," and in the present context especially their implications for distribution or redistribution of economic factors in ways that the nominal owners of those factors might not choose. A relevant aspect for conflict is that politics often has to do with, or is supposed to be related to, establishing a just social order among people or groups in a society. The currencies are power and authority.

Although prolific bank robber Willie Sutton supposedly was motivated to rob banks "because that's where the money is," Robin Hood's criminal activities can be said to have social justice as their central goal. By my definition, Sutton's crimes had economic causes, whereas Hood's had political ones.

With these definitions, I do not intend to imply that economists, political scientists, or other analysts should or do limit their inquiries to one type of factor or another.[2] I only intend to draw distinctions between these two types of causal elements. The specifics of the definitions, of course, determine the conclusions. My contention is that making the distinction between these types of factors is analytically useful – it is at least prominent in the current conflict literature. Economic and political factors are of course closely related in conflict situations, and it is important to recognize that the dividing line between them is necessarily blurry. It goes without saying that political outcomes such as violence have economic consequences, as Brauer and Marlin demonstrate in this volume, and it would follow that economic considerations loom large in the decision calculus leading to intrastate and inter-state conflict.

But, how can we think about the relative causal position of economics and politics in conflict? I suggest that political power dynamics are logically more fundamental. For example, although Hall and Wylie in their chapter make a logically consistent argument, and point to important dynamics around export control of military technology, it seems important to consider the actual imbalances and disparities that usually accompany the relationship between arms exporters and their customers. It is often the case that they are allies and that one state is a great power with a large economy, whereas the other is smaller on both counts (these conditions hold for the U.S.–Australia case examined in their chapter). In such circumstances, the security concerns that the indigenously developed technology will be turned against the country with export controls (an ally and great power), and the realistic chance of the smaller importer becoming a serious competitor on the international arms trade market (given the political linkages and economies of scale of large arms purchases from countries with fully developed military industries), might not be very large. But these are logical and empirical questions that show the value of Hall and Wylie's provocative and interesting analysis and deserve further exploration by researchers.

I focus on what drives people's decisions, assuming that all conflict factors operate in some way through the decisions of citizens and/or elites. I suppose that the economic realm sits within the political realm in human affairs. Even in the case of basic survival, this can be logically supported. Humans may put other values ahead of their very physical existence, which I assume is the most fundamental sort of economic motivation: food, shelter and other physical necessities of life. If one believes strongly enough, one may choose to starve to death for the sake of justice or morality, or not commit violence that one feels is wrong, such as killing a child, even if one's life itself is at stake. This is a political choice (as I have defined it), which becomes more obviously political as the level of social aggregation increases beyond individuals and small groups, to ethnicities and states. No doubt, some or even most might violate what they believe are their scruples in such situations, but the fact that at least some people would actually die rather than commit serious injustice or do something immoral, is enough to support the idea that economic behavior may be understood to operate within political bounds. The fact that most people probably recognize some sorts of political limits to their economic choices, such as accepting some degree of progressive tax for the sake of others' welfare, makes the case stronger.

This could be so, at least, if there were not similar economic bounds for political life. I argue that the economic bounds are not as strong, and not logically similar, such that political conditioning of economic choices is more fundamental to human decisions at the individual and group levels than economic conditioning is for political choices. I do not yet want to claim that the argument is beyond reproach. But if it is correct, then it provides a logical foundation to expect that political factors associated with serious intrastate and inter-state conflict should be more fundamental, and more powerful, causes of these outcomes, than economic factors.

Is the logic that would have economic considerations temper political choices parallel or reciprocal to that which suggests that economic choices are politically framed? Economic choices may require some political context for humans. Even the purchase of some daily goods in a grocery store can be seen as happening within a political context. If there is no great injustice involved that one knows of, one can make the economic transaction. If the store is owned by a morally repugnant individual, or a politically dangerous one, one might decide to boycott the store. If the product is made by a company one takes exception to for their investments in Zimbabwe, one might boycott the product.

Do political choices require an economic context? In fact, one would like to choose between right and wrong, just and unjust, without considering the economic constraints. But there are almost always economic constraints. Are these constraints of economic reality, such as not being able to feed all the hungry or employ all the unemployed, equally or more fundamental to human decisions than the political constraints I have discussed?

Of course, it seems common for individuals and leaders to alter their political beliefs, or to alter social institutions, for the sake of economic outcomes. A candidate for office may support building a new sports arena that he previously opposed, if he can receive campaign donations from construction companies for taking this position. A socialist leader might agree to privatize heavy industry if the state needs immediate revenue. My purpose here is to raise these issues, rather than resolve the question. But, I am more persuaded by the argument that economic choices are fundamentally conditioned by the political context, whereas political choices are more immune, though of course not totally so, from straightforward economic imperatives. Politics goes farther in defining what is economically valuable, than economics does in defining what is politically valuable.

One way to think about this is to ask about the implications of hypothetically lifting these different types of constraints on choice. Is there an equality of logic or consequences for lifting economic restraints on political choices (we can feed the hungry, because it will cost us nothing) and lifting political constraints on economic ones (we can take the oil by force, because the people who own it now are not our concern)? I suggest that we usually want to free ourselves from economic constraints, since they have no fundamental value in and of themselves, while we hold as more fundamental the political constraints we have, even if we adhere to them with astounding imperfection.

My argument is potentially undermined, but I would say ultimately reinforced, by the fact that political values can change, whereas basic economic logic, tied to physical human needs, is not so malleable over time and place. We might rationalize abandoning the goal of national statehood for the sake of a steady supply of energy resources from a neighboring region. But this will require redefining the national identity in some way, which would then begin to constitute a new set of norms and institutions. The key question is the extent to which such norms and institutions, although malleable, can condition economic choices, and shape our understanding of the value represented. If they are fully malleable based on maximizing economic utility, then economic factors will clearly be the more important. But, if norms and institutions are guided by some underlying human sense of justice, morality, fairness or the like, then there is considerable scope for hard constraints being defined by some basic political values. This can be so, in the extreme, to the point that any pretense of a basic logic we would call "economic" must be abandoned, as in the case of the hunger striker who dies for her cause. The extent to which it is so, on a broader social scale, in the context of situations of potential violent conflict, is the pertinent question, but I will not claim to be able to answer now.

Although I cannot decisively claim that economic imperatives do not have an equal or greater fundamental conditioning effect on political choices, the core of my preferred argument is that political considerations are closer to the ultimate decision-making determinants of humans than are economic considerations.

James Lee Ray (1989) has argued that some basic dynamic of "moral progress" might be moving human society to abandon war, in much the same way as it has largely abandoned slavery. Ken Binmore (2005) – in the spirit of Rawls and even Kropotkin – has recently argued that the evolution of the concept of justice is fundamental to patterns of human behavior, and changes in these patterns, providing the norms that guide human behavior in politics, economics, and other spheres. By my definition, norms of justice are rightly termed political factors, and especially at the societal and state level, I think this is uncontroversial. The people we call politicians, working within the political system, make the laws and appoint the courts to adjudicate for citizens over all manner of issues, including economic ones, based on ideas of what is just, weighing the interests of all members of society.

Kenneth Waltz's (1979) basic insight about the primacy of force being the result of anarchy in international politics is also potentially important here. When organized large-scale violence is a plausible outcome, the ordered realm of hierarchy, in which rule of law and economic institutions will function and allow relatively open or regularized economic activity, cannot be considered to exist. In an anarchic environment, political-military resources will dominate. The way economic interactions take place, if they do at all, will be fundamentally altered. Thus, the economic relationship between the US and the USSR during the Cold War was fundamentally conditioned by the normative and institutional environment, which developed in a world of international anarchy. The relationship between post-Soviet Russia and the United States is much different, because the politics and military calculations have changed. Similarly, as intrastate tensions tend toward the use of large-scale organized violence, the government's hierarchical authority cannot be said to dominate, and anarchy better defines the situation. The role of economic factors in the dynamics of escalation to civil war, or achievement of peace, will be conditioned by the basic anarchy that allows the possibility of violence to begin with.

INTERNAL CONFLICT

The chapters in this volume point to a number of ways in which economic factors contribute to, or ameliorate, organized violent conflict within states. Piggott's discussion of Indonesian separatist movements implies that grievance alone does not lead to terrorist tactics. Key conditioning factors appear to be ideology, and organizational capacity of the groups seeking to alter the status quo. These political factors, in other words, condition the role of economic (and other political) factors. Hunt's chapter regarding Iran reminds us that international economic factors, such as fluctuation in the oil price, can have complex and hard-to-predict effects on domestic political conflict. She suggests that the important filter is perceptions of gain or loss among competing domestic groups, and I would add that the reference point is not one of absolute or even relative profit or wealth, but of relative position in the power structure of the state. Carmignani and Gauci's chapter shows that fiscal policy can have an important effect on the success of post-conflict stabilization of African Civil Wars. The importance of increased government spending, financed by either grants or debt, suggests that meeting basic economic needs of the population has a strong effect on this outcome. But this might also indicate that the appearance of good governance and significant state capacity could be an important political asset facilitating successful post-conflict transitions. Somewhat similarly, Ladley and Williams point to the importance of efficient and appropriate management of aid funds, and the potential of credible and well-functioning institutions, outside of the full sovereign control of the recipient state, to achieve such good governance and avoid the recurrence of conflict.

In the ongoing and evolving debate, and potentially disparate empirical findings, the economically based arguments have recently been deemphasized. For example, recent results from the Political Instability Task Force (Goldstone et al., 2010) make the case for the importance of national political institutions, whereas Collier, Hoeffler, and Rohner (2009, p. 23) find that "the new evidence goes considerably beyond supporting key results of our previous work about the primacy of economic variables in the risk of civil war. While not decisive, it clearly points towards the proposition that feasibility rather than motivation is decisive." More important than treating conflict analysis as a sort of horse race among competing variables, however, is to expand our thinking about the entire process of internal organized violence and civil war, to develop empirical expectations more solidly grounded in theories of such conflict. For example, if it is the case that violent rebellion may happen wherever it is feasible, as Collier, Hoeffler, and Rohner contend, is this so for all societies, or for some identifiable subgroup, and what is it that distinguished those social, political, and/or economic systems from others? Is insecurity built in to some societies in a structural or cultural way?

INTERNATIONAL CONFLICT

In an important review of a range of research, Mansfield and Pollins (2003) highlight the traditional debate over the effects of international economic interdependence on inter-state conflict. But, although the theoretical and empirical debate about the role of trade in international conflict, if any, continues, in a sense it might be superseded by recent research into the relationship between other economic factors and conflict between states.

Some of the current international conflict literature is turning away from political causes and toward economic ones, but also moving away from the focus on international trade. Krishner (2007) provides evidence that the banking sector is consistently anti-war, across time and in different states, for the basic reason that banks desire macroeconomic stability to make profits. McDonald's (2009) *The Invisible Hand of Peace* focuses on domestic institutions of capitalism and argues that there is a capitalist peace with stronger fundamental effects than the democratic peace, based on private property and market competition, which reduce imperial impulses, decentralize politics, and make governments inclined to compromise to avoid the costs of war.

Clearly this recent literature contradicts my assertions about the primacy of politics. In this volume, Robbani's chapter might also be seen as supporting the primacy of economics, since it may be economic logic that drives the success of Regional Integration Agreements (RIA). However, first, these are institutions created out of political processes. Second, Robbani does not control for shared membership in general International Governmental Organizations (IGO), even more politically driven groupings. Thus, a further question for the analysis is whether RIAs have a pacific effect above and beyond the general effect (if it exists) of joint IGO memberships for a dyad.

For the purposes of this volume, his theoretical emphasis on the expectation of future economic benefits is also important – this supposedly gives states added incentives to avoid militarized conflict. What is perhaps most interesting is the use of a security community argument in this vein of liberal analysis. But it is normative and institutional structure that is essential. Security communities do not exist everywhere; they have multiple and complex causes, but the single essential element seems essentially political: the "we feeling" or common identity Deutsch, Burrell, and Kann (1957) described.

Royal's skeptical comments regarding the consistently pacifying effects of trade due to the signaling it facilitates during crises are worth considering, not only for the specific points made, but also for the broader conceptual source of the arguments: the international economic system, and how it changes, should be considered even in dyadic-level thinking about international conflict. But that system exists in any given form, and changes, based in part on the decisions of states about how to regulate and manage it. Mansfield's (1994) earlier work on the concentration of power in the system might be an important relevant guide here. Crises are open to manipulation for security or other political purposes, just as free trade is, if dominant actors have sufficient leverage.

An emphasis of this volume has been legal perspectives on the economics of conflict. Michaelsen provides a prescient account of the United Nations Security Council (UNSC) sanctions regime and some of its shortcomings. But, the risk here is to succumb to an apolitical approach to the UN system and international law. The UNSC is a supremely political entity, more than a legal one. To infuse greater due process, respect for rights, and ultimately greater legitimacy into UNSC sanctions regimes, Michaelsen is correct from my perspective to argue that great-power political and intelligence concerns need to be addressed. He is also correct to point to the overall effectiveness of the regime as the key outcome. Any spill-over effects of its loss of credibility into other enforcement or human-rights agendas of the UN should be the ultimate guide. Economic sanctions are an important tool, but of uncertain effect. From my perspective, sanctions' effectiveness should be mainly contingent on political factors.

Smart raises important and difficult normative issues, in addition to describing the extant and evolving international and US legal regimes surrounding compensation for civilian casualties. However, one issue that remains to be addressed is that of moral hazard tied to compensation. Smart strongly argues that political and tactical factors are more important determinants of the effort the military will take to avoid civilian casualties, while the economic costs of compensation of the victims or their surviving relatives are negligible. Could the positive effect on "legitimacy" of the overall campaign that compensation delivers, according to Smart, actually encourage the military decision makers to accept more risk of civilian harm or death, given that it has an economic tool to minimize any negative tactical or political effects? This is an issue that is morally troubling from a number of perspectives, but deserves further empirical, theoretical, and ethical scrutiny. The economic logic is not in question, from my perspective, but the political dynamics are.

I also point to the ease with which the concept of collective responsibility might be misleadingly applied in such contexts. Certainly the members of military organizations, rebel groups, invading, invaded, and occupied governments might be treated as bearing responsibility for the actions and choices of the organization as a whole. But Smart is perhaps not careful enough in discussing the concept of the responsibility of members of an invaded or occupied country's civilian population for actions or choices that some civilians might have taken. It seems clear under principles of international humanitarian law and general logic that the obligation to pay compensation to particular individuals in a population is not negated if "the population was partly responsible for starting the conflict," assuming that there is no way to know about the responsibility of specific individuals in question.

THE ECONOMIC TURN IN INTERNATIONAL CONFLICT RESEARCH: SKEPTICAL COMMENTS AND SOME EVIDENCE

In sum, I expect economic factors to be strong, but not fundamental, in their causal relationship to conflict. I argue that norms of justice and institutions for governance constrain and impose limits on human behavior in the most basic ways. When the most important, highest-stake decisions are made, the motivations tend to be more political than economic. Or, more precisely, economic motives must be filtered through political understandings, usually contained in norms and institutions.

If this is the case, correlations between more purely economic factors such as trade or investment flows and the incidence of intrastate or inter-state conflict may be apparent, but conceptually (if not in the available data and measures) there should be some political conditioning factor that is more closely tied to the conflict or peace outcome. Furthermore, as the decision process becomes more risky, or the chance of serious conflict becomes higher, political factors should loom larger. In this section, I present some evidence regarding international conflict consistent with this argument and troubling for the primacy-of-economics perspective.

I will not argue that these few models are more than suggestive; they are certainly not decisive. However, they are at least strong indications that my perspective is plausible, because they show the potential fragility of statistical results supporting the recent economic turn in "liberal peace" type arguments. Specifically, I use variables the same as, or quite similar to, those used by Gartzke (2007) in his capitalist peace analysis and by Mousseau (2009) in his contract-intensive-economies peace argument. One key point is that proper specification of political and economic factors in statistical models is essential, but of course also quite challenging, as most analysts, including Collier and Hoeffler (2004), recognize.

In my first set of statistical models, I examine only the variables suggested by Gartzke's capitalist peace arguments. I show that, as the conflict process becomes more serious, and the chance of large-scale hostility increases, political factors become more determinant of outcomes, economic factors less so. Table 1 provides evidence of this.

What have I done differently from Gartzke? Most importantly, I have measured the political factor(s) more precisely. Rather than the standard "weak-link" measure of the lower democracy score of a dyad, three variables are used, which I have elsewhere argued, with extensive evidence, better capture the important aspects of a difficult concept, "dyadic" regime type (Goldsmith, Chalup, & Quinlan, 2008). Thus, "Degree of joint democracy" is a scale of the degree to which both states in the dyad are democratic, but importantly, it does not confound this with the more general concept of political similarity (or distance), which the weak-link measure demonstrably does. I also include a measure of "Political distance" that simply tracks the absolute value of the difference in Polity IV scores for the two states in the dyad. And I also include a "Joint autocracy dummy" that controls for

Table 1. Logit Models of Conflict Initiation, 1975–2001.

	MID Initiation t+1		Fatal MID Initiation t+1		251 MID Initiation t+1	
	Coefficient		Coefficient		Coefficient	
Trade dependence (lower)	−18.066	*18.829*	−0.694	*24.506*	−458.767	*253.461*
Interests	−1.215	*0.416***	−0.746	*0.707*	−0.477	*0.893*
GDPpcLow	0.000	*0.000*	−0.000	*0.000*	−0.000	*0.000*
GDPpcLowContig	−0.000	*0.000****	−0.000	*0.000*	−0.000	*0.000*
EconGlobLow	−0.041	*0.009****	−0.024	*0.016*	0.033	*0.017*
Minor powers	−0.837	*0.230****	0.242	*0.500*	−0.598	*0.533*
Alliance *S* score	−1.094	*0.345***	−1.474	*0.606**	−0.711	*0.630*
Distanceln	−0.460	*0.113****	−0.598	*0.189***	−1.019	*0.245****
Joint IGO memberships	0.040	*0.010****	0.029	*0.013**	−0.001	*0.021*
Degree of joint democracy	−0.047	*0.039*	−0.132	*0.060**	−0.278	*0.073****
Political distance	0.000	*0.016*	−0.004	*0.025*	−0.036	*0.028*
Joint autocracy dummy	−0.941	*0.391**	−1.519	*0.854*	––	
Contiguity	2.959	*0.344****	2.861	*0.609****	0.985	*0.865*
Power parity	−0.051	*0.333*	−0.399	*0.481*	−0.016	*0.569*
cwpceyrs	−0.107	*0.018****	−0.278	*0.064****	−0.271	*0.111**
cwpceyrs2	0.001	*0.000****	0.011	*0.003****	0.013	*0.005***
cwpceyrs3	−0.000	*0.000**	−0.000	*0.000****	−0.000	*0.000***
Constant	1.398	*1.288*	0.856	*1.901*	3.503	2.298
N	106311		106311		97278	
Wald chi2(18, 18, 17)	1194.65		564.64		308.87	
Probability >chi^2	0.0000		0.0000		0.0000	
Pseudo R^2	0.3045		0.2348		0.1166	

Note: Logit models with clustering on dyads and robust standard errors in italics.
–– inidicates variable dropped due to "perfect prediction" of failure.
*$p \leq .05$, **$p \leq .01$, ***$p \leq .001$.

the robust, if less-reported, finding in the literature that there is a probabilistic authoritarian peace. This is also important to include because its omission dilutes the more linear nature of the democratic peace effect.

The variables for trade dependence, interests, GDP per capita, and GDP per captia interacted with Contiguity follow Gartzke's specifications.[3] The variable EconGlobLow is not exactly the same as Gartzke's Financial Openness indicator, but is based on a measure of Economic Globalization for each country. It should be substantially similar to Gartzke's indicator based on IMF assessments. It is a combination of indicators of financial and trade flows, and restrictions on commerce, for each country, measured by the KOF index of globalization (http://globalization.kof.ethz.ch/).

The results are consistent with my expectations. Although economic factors are significant and generally in the expected direction as predictors of the onset of all militarized inter-state disputes (MIDs, any threat or use of force), their significance declines as the dependent variable is restricted to the initiation of more serious MIDs. For fatal MIDs (in which at least one battle-related death occurred) and for MIDs that incurred over 250 battle deaths, no economic factors are significant. The story for the political factors is almost the mirror image of this. The degree of joint democracy is not significant in its effect on all MIDs, but is significant at the .05 level for fatal MIDs and at an even higher level for those incurring over 250 deaths. Political distance is never significant, but joint autocracy is significant for all MIDs and actually drops from the model for the most serious MIDs due to "perfect prediction" (discussed later).

The pattern is robust to the inclusion of Mousseau's "contract intensive economies" (CIE) variables, based on his own data.[4] The results in Table 2 show that when the CIE variables are added to the models in Table 1, economic factors are again more important for lower-intensity conflicts and much less so for conflicts with few or many fatalities. The CIEone variable, which indicates that at least one state in a dyad is a contract-intensive economy, is never significant when other economic factors are controlled. The indicator for two CIE states in a dyad, CIEboth, is significant for all MIDs, in the predicted pacific direction, and, as Mousseau (2009) also finds, drops out of other models due to "perfect prediction." However, this does not necessarily indicate the CIEboth is a very powerful cause of peace.

Joint CIE's (CIEboth) perfect prediction, much touted by Mousseau, is perhaps not as statistically impressive as it sounds. And it is not unique – both joint Autocracy (in my models, as noted) and jointly wealthy dyads above $15,000 GDPpc (ppp) exhibit the same effect (not shown). The key substantive point for CIEboth is that it is measured in a way that actually loses information. The variable could be continuous, since it is based simply on the density of life insurance and other contracts. But, Mousseau chooses to set an arbitrary level at which a society seems to have a lot of such contracts, and thus the dichotomous variable as specified has zero observations of "1" that coincide with the initiation of a MID. However, it has many observations of "0" that also coincide with peace – so perfect prediction is in this sense a misnomer. It is correspondence with the lack of a MID, given the presence of two states above the arbitrary CIE threshold. The same is true for GDP per capita of $15,000. The large amount of

Table 2. Logit Models of Conflict Initiation with CIE Variables, 1975–2001.

	MID Initiation t+1		Fatal MID Initiation t+1		251 MID Initiation t+1	
	Coefficient		Coefficient		Coefficient	
Trade dependence (lower)	2.796	*15.390*	17.877	*29.637*	−400.664	*251.636*
Interests	−1.086	*0.415***	−1.265	*0.655*	−0.785	*0.882*
GDPpcLow	0.000	*0.000****	0.000	*0.000*	−0.000	*0.000*
GDPpcLowContig	−0.000	*0.000****	−0.000	*0.000**	−0.000	*0.000*
EconGlobLow	−0.048	*0.009****	−0.025	*0.016*	0.032	*0.018*
CIEboth	−2.670	*0.739****	−−		−−	
CIEone	0.137	*0.309*	−0.682	*0.412*	−0.426	*0.490*
Minor powers	−0.813	*0.225****	0.194	*0.526*	−0.629	*0.553*
Alliance S score	−0.904	*0.348***	−1.462	*0.614**	−0.701	*0.630*
Distanceln	−0.421	*0.108****	−0.604	*0.191***	−1.006	*0.248****
Joint IGO memberships	0.047	*0.011****	0.032	*0.013***	0.000	*0.021*
Degree of joint democracy	−0.054	*0.036*	−0.105	*0.059*	−0.249	*0.082***
Political distance	−0.007	*0.016*	−0.001	*0.024*	−0.034	*0.028*
Joint autocracy dummy	−0.925	*0.389**	−1.416	*0.854*	−−	
Contiguity	2.988	*0.386****	2.889	*0.624****	1.005	*0.854*
Power parity	−0.224	*0.324*	−0.530	*0.471*	−0.069	*0.572*
cwpceyrs	−0.104	*0.017****	−0.271	*0.064****	−0.268	*0.111**
cwpceyrs2	0.001	*0.000****	0.011	*0.003****	0.013	*0.005***
cwpceyrs3	−0.000	*0.000**	−0.000	*0.000****	−0.000	*0.000***
Constant	0.618	*1.283*	1.067	*2.035*	3.509	*2.352*
N	106311		100350		91317	
Wald chi^2 (20, 19, 18)	1297.49		548.91		286.91	
Probability>chi^2	0.0000		0.0000		0.0000	
Pseudo R^2	0.3116		0.2353		0.1131	

Note: Logit models with clustering on dyads and robust standard errors in italics.
−− inidicates variable dropped due to "perfect prediction" of failure.
$^*p \leq .05$, $^{**}p \leq .01$, $^{***}p \leq .001$.

missing data for life insurance contracts, one of the two components of Mousseau's variable, makes this at least a questionable finding.

But perhaps the more appropriate test of my expectations is to consider the bargaining process more directly. This can be done with a selection model (Heckman, 1979). Extensive analysis with Heckman models on very similar data has indicated that selection bias is an issue for analysis of fatal MIDs

Table 3. Selection Models of MID Initiation and Escalation, 1975–2001.

Selection into MID	Coefficient	
Total dyadic trade	0.004	*0.003*
Interests	−0.447	*0.102****
GDPpcLow	0.000	*0.000***
GDPpcLowContig	−0.000	*0.000****
EconGlobLow	−0.015	*0.002****
Minor powers	−0.291	*0.066****
Alliance S score	−0.378	*0.099****
Distanceln	−0.178	*0.031****
Joint IGO memberships	0.014	*0.002****
Degree of joint democracy	−0.022	*0.010**
Joint autocracy dummy	−0.442	*0.116****
Contiguity	1.242	*0.086****
cwpceyrs	−0.039	*0.004****
cwpceyrs2	0.001	*0.000****
cwpceyrs3	−0.000	*0.000****
Constant	−0.015	*0.303*
Outcome: Fatal MID	**Coefficient**	
Total dyadic trade	−0.001	*0.005*
Interests	−0.249	*0.254*
GDPpcLow	−0.000	*0.000*
GDPpcLowContig	−0.000	*0.000***
EconGlobLow	−0.006	*0.003*
Minor powers	0.043	*0.156*
Alliance S score	−0.616	*0.204***
Distanceln	−0.184	*0.062***
Joint IGO memberships	0.010	*0.004*
Degree of joint democracy	−0.044	*0.023**
Joint autocracy dummy	−0.650	*0.241***
Contiguity	1.268	*0.182****
cwpceyrs	−0.046	*0.018***
cwpceyrs2	0.002	*0.001**
cwpceyrs3	−0.000	*0.000*
Constant	−0.718	*0.609*
N	106311	
Log likelihood	−1639.60	
Probability $>\text{chi}^2$	0.0000	
Wald chi^2 (15)	1185.58	

Note: Sartori selection model, standard errors in italics.
$^{*}p \leq .05$, $^{**}p \leq .01$, $^{***}p \leq .001$.

and MIDs at higher levels of violence, since states select themselves into lower-level conflict (any MID) in a non-random way (i.e., the rho statistic is significant; Goldsmith, 2009). I use Sartori's (2003) technique that does not require the exclusion of any variable from the outcome process. This accounts for the process of conflict initiation and escalation more directly and allows me to focus on the important stage of escalation to MIDs that incur at least one battle death, without selection bias in the results.[5]

The results again demonstrate the pattern of an important role for political factors, both joint democracy and joint autocracy, as international conflict escalates, and a decreasing role for economic factors, with the most important of these again being per capita GDP among contiguous dyads. However, in this configuration, political factors are also important in the stage of initiation of all MIDs, whether or not they eventually escalate to more serious levels of violence (Table 3).

I am willing to claim that these models call into question a strong belief in the primacy of a "capitalist peace" or "economic peace" over political factors such as democracy. But my purpose here is no more than to suggest that this is a promising area for further inquiry. The still speculative conclusion that is suggested is that causes and cures of violent international conflict are fundamentally political. Economic factors are of course hugely important, but they are filtered through norms and institutions, which are political creations. If the basic logic of my thinking holds, similar results would be obtained for studies of civil conflict initiation and escalation.

The final point I want to make, with regard to this volume of diverse, creative, and thought-provoking studies of the relationship between economics and militarized conflict, is certainly not that economic factors are unimportant for understanding conflict. Rather, as many of the chapters imply, further careful theorizing based on creative new thinking about existing findings and concepts seems warranted for understanding how economic factors fit into the complex processes leading to large-scale violence within and among states.

NOTES

1. Mansfield and Pollins (2003) have considered the levels-of-analysis issue for theories of international trade and war between states.

2. To elaborate, it is important to acknowledge that these brief definitions are not intended to describe the scientific fields of economics or political science. I readily acknowledge that economists are interested in human and social choice, exchange, and behavioural dynamics across a wide range of topics that I would not attempt to

limit or define (e.g., http://www.vanderbilt.edu/AEA/students/WhatIsEconomics.htm). My purpose in providing this limited definition of economic *factors* is to explicitly highlight the roles of such factors, often characterized by connection to money or material goods, for the purpose of their consideration as a class, which might be distinguished from another class of factors commonly characterized as 'political' in content. I thank Jurgen Brauer for suggesting that this distinction be acknowledged and clarified, and for useful comments on other parts of this chapter as well, although this should not imply his full agreement with the arguments it contains.

3. The data sources are Gleditsch trade data for Total dyadic trade and Trade dependence (imp+exp/GDP) (http://privatewww.essex.ac.uk/~ksg/exptradegdp.html); Gartzke's own data for Interests (http://dss.ucsd.edu/~egartzke/); World Bank data and KOF data for GDP per capita and Economic Globalization (Pippa Norris, Democracy Timeseries Data Release 3.0, January 2009, http://www.hks.harvard.edu/fs/pnorris/Data/Data.htm). Other variables as described in Goldsmith (2009); cwpceyrs variables are a cubic polynomial of the years each dyad is at peace, to account for linear and non-linear temporal dependence (Carter & Signorino, 2007).

4. http://home.ku.edu.tr/~mmousseau/ (retrieved on January 2010).

5. It is important to note that these models proved fragile with this dataset, and Heckman and Sartori models frequently failed to converge on any results. Thus, not all variables are included in the model; total dyadic trade is substituted for trade interdependence; and escalation to the much rarer 251 deaths or greater MID level is not presented.

REFERENCES

Beck, N., King, G., & Zeng, L. (2000). Improving quantitative studies of international conflict. *American Political Science Review*, *94*(1), 21–35.

Berdal, M. R., & Malone, D. M. (2000). *Greed and grievance: Economic agendas in civil wars*. Boulder, CO: Lynne Rienner Publishers.

Binmore, K. (2005). *Natural justice*. Oxford, UK: Oxford University Press.

Carter, D., & Signorino, C. S. (2007). *Back to the future: Modeling time dependence in binary data*. Working Paper, University of Rochester.

Cederman, L. E., Buhaug, H., & Rod, J. K. (2009). Ethno-nationalist dyads and civil war a GIS-based analysis. *Journal of Conflict Resolution*, *53*(4), 496–525.

Collier, P., & Hoeffler, A. (2004). Greed and grievance in civil war. *Oxford Economic Papers: New Series*, *56*(4), 563–595.

Collier, P., Hoeffler, A., & Rohner, D. (2009). Beyond greed and grievance: Feasibility and civil war. *Oxford Economic Papers: New Series*, *61*(1), 1–27.

Deutsch, K. W., Burrell, S. A., & Kann, R. A. ([1957]1969). *Political community and the North Atlantic area: International organization in the light of historical experience*. New York: Greenwood Press.

Gartzke, E. (2007). The capitalist peace. *American Journal of Political Science*, *51*(1), 166–191.

Goldsmith, B. E. (2006). A universal proposition? Region, conflict, war, and the robustness of the liberal peace. *European Journal of International Relations*, *12*(4), 533–563.

Goldsmith, B. E. (2009). *More to fight about, or more reasons not to fight?:International trade, bargaining, peace, and war*. Unpublished manuscript, University of Sydney.

Goldsmith, B. E., Chalup, S. K., & Quinlan, M. J. (2008). Regime type and international conflict: Towards a general model. *Journal of Peace Research, 45*(6), 743–763.

Goldstone, J. A., Bates, R. H., Epstein, D. L., Gurr, T. R., Lustik, M. B., Marshall, M. G., Ulfelder, J., & Woodward, M. (2010). A global model for forecasting political instability. *American Journal of Political Science, 54*(1), 190–208.

Heckman, J. (1979). Sample selection bias as a specification error. *Econometrica, 47*, 153–161.

Krishner, J. (2007). *Appeasing bankers: Financial caution on the road to war*. Princeton, NJ: Princeton University Press.

Mansfield, E. D. (1994). *Power, trade, and war*. Princeton, NJ: Princeton University Press.

Mansfield, E. D., & Pollins, B. M. (2003). Interdependence and conflict: An introduction. In: E. D. Mansfield & B. M. Pollins (Eds), *Economic interdependence and international conflict: New perspectives on an enduring debate* (pp. 1–28). Ann Arbor, MI: University of Michigan Press.

McDonald, P. J. (2009). *The invisible hand of peace: Capitalism, the war machine, and international relations theory*. Cambridge, UK: Cambridge University Press.

Mousseau, M. (2009). The social market roots of democratic peace. *International Security, 33*(4), 52–86.

Ray, J. L. (1989). The abolition of slavery and the end of international war. *International Organization, 43*(3), 405–439.

Regan, P. M., & Norton, D. (2005). Greed, grievance, and mobilization in civil wars. *Journal of Conflict Resolution, 49*(3), 319–336.

Sartori, A. E. (2003). An Estimator for some binary-outcome selection models without exclusion restrictions. *Political Analysis, 11*, 111–138.

Waltz, K. N. (1979). *Theory of international politics*. New York: McGraw-Hill.

Webster's. (1996). *Webster's new universal unabridged dictionary*. New York: Barnes and Noble Books.

Xiang, J., Xu, X., & Keteku, G. (2007). Power: The missing link in the trade conflict relationship. *Journal of Conflict Resolution, 51*(4), 646–663.

ABOUT THE AUTHORS

Aditya Agrawal is a scholarship graduate from Bond University (2006, first class honors in Management Science) and the 2007–2008 summer scholar at the Strategic and Defence Studies Centre, Australian National University. He commenced work at the University College, Australian Defence Force Academy in June 2008 and is currently reading for his doctorate in military outsourcing. Previously he has worked with both the corporate sector and the government departments. He has published in scholarly journals and peer-reviewed conferences and was awarded the Best Paper Prize at the national Australian Conference on Information Systems (ACIS 2007).

Jurgen Brauer, Ph.D., is professor of Economics, James M. Hull College of Business, Augusta State University, Augusta, GA, USA, and visiting professor of Economics at the economics departments of the Universidad del Rosario, Bogotá, Colombia, and Chulalongkorn University, Bangkok, Thailand. He is co-editor of *The Economics of Peace and Security Journal* and the *Studies in Defense and Peace Economics* book series with Routledge, London, UK.

Fabrizio Carmignani holds a Ph.D. from Glasgow University and he is currently senior lecturer at the School of Economics of the University of Queensland (UQ). Before joining UQ, he worked for the Regional Economic Commissions of the United Nations in Africa and Europe. His research interests focus on political economy, economic development, macroeconomics and applied economics. He has published his work in journals such as the *Journal of Macroeconomics*, the *European Journal of Political Economy*, the *Journal of African Economies*, the *Scottish Journal of Political Economy* and the *Journal of International Money and Finance*.

Adrian Gauci joined the United Nations Secretariat through a National Competitive Examination for economists in 2001. Since then, Adrian Gauci has been stationed in the Economic Commission for Africa within the Social Policy and Poverty unit. In this context, he has analysed and monitored Africa's progress towards the Internally Agreed Development Goals, backed by background papers on the determinants of persistent and chronic poverty on the continent. In this regard, Adrian Gauci has, among other aspects, investigated the poverty conflict nexus resulting in various publications on the economic and social profile of low-income African countries.

Benjamin E. Goldsmith is a senior lecturer in the Department of Government and International Relations at the University of Sydney. His research and teaching are in the areas of international relations, comparative foreign policy and political psychology. He is the author of the book *Imitation in International Relations: Observational Learning, Analogies, and Foreign Policy in Russia and Ukraine* as well as articles in leading academic journals including *European Journal of International Relations*, *Journal of Conflict Resolution*, *Journal of Peace Research*, *Journal of Politics*, and *Security Studies*.

Peter Hall is emeritus professor in the School of Business at the Australian Defence Force Academy campus of The University of New South Wales, Canberra, Australia. His most recent book is *Defence Procurement and Industry Policy: A Small Country Perspective*, London, Routledge, 2010, co-authored with Stefan Markowski and Robert Wylie.

Brendan Howe is associate director of the Institute for Development and Human Security and Associate Professor of International Relations at Ewha Womans University, South Korea. He previously held positions at Sydney University, the East-West Center, Beijing Foreign Studies University, and Universiti Malaysia Sarawak. He is associate editor of the *International Studies Review* and has researched and published extensively on security and development, security decision-making and Asian security operating environments.

Jennifer S. Hunt is a Ph.D. candidate at the Centre for International Security (CISS), University of Sydney, Australia. She holds a Master's Degree from CISS and completed her undergraduate studies at the University of North Carolina at Chapel Hill, USA.

Minako Ichikawa Smart holds a Ph.D. in Politics and International Relations from Keele University in the UK and currently holds academic positions at the Centre for International Security Studies and the Department of Government and International Relations at the University of Sydney. She specialises in legal and normative aspects of international relations, with a particular interest in the context of armed conflict. Before moving to Sydney, she was an assistant professor at Tokyo University of Social Welfare in Japan.

Andrew Ladley is adjunct professor in the School of Government at Victoria University of Wellington, New Zealand. He has recently completed a term as a Senior Expert Mediator (Constitutional Arrangements) for the United Nations Mediation Support Unit.

John Tepper Marlin, Ph.D., is adjunct professor at the Stern School of Business, New York University, New York. Previously, he served the City of New York as Chief Economist, Office of the Comptroller, and in private consulting practice.

Christopher Michaelsen is a research fellow at the Law Faculty of the University of New South Wales (UNSW), Sydney. He teaches and specialises in public international law, human rights and international security. Before joining UNSW, he served as a Human Rights Officer (Anti-Terrorism) at the Organization for Security and Cooperation in Europe (OSCE). He is the co-author of *International Law and the Use of Force: A Documentary and Reference Guide* (Praeger Security International, 2009).

Dele Ogunmola is a doctoral student in Peace Studies at The University of New England, Armidale, Australia. He had been a lecturer in Lead City University, Ibadan, Nigeria, and his articles have appeared in learned journals.

Leanne Piggott is the Deputy Director of the Centre for International Security Studies where she heads up the Centre's Energy Security program. She is a specialist on the Middle East, with a particular interest in governance reform and security in the region, and is the author of the book *The Arab-Israeli Conflict: A Timeless Struggle*. Her other recent publications include *The Evolving Terrorist Threat to Southeast Asia: A Net Assessment*, a jointly authored book published by the RAND Corporation. Leanne is a member of the Australian Government's Foreign Affairs Council and the Editorial Advisory Board of the Department of Foreign Affairs and Trade.

Golam Robbani Lecturer, Department of Accounting and Information Management, University of Maastricht, the Netherlands.

Jedidiah Royal is the director of Cooperative Threat Reduction at the US Department of Defense. He is an MPhil candidate at the University of New South Wales, Australian Defence Force Academy.

Keiran Sharpe is senior lecturer at the School of Business, University of New South Wales at the Australian Defence Force Academy. His research interests are in the theory of decision-making, the theory of action and in the history of economic thought.

Helen Ware is professor of Peace Studies at the University of New England where she teaches aspects of peace building to distance education students from Afghanistan to the Solomon Islands. She was previously Australian High Commissioner to Zambia, Malawi and Namibia and Ambassador to Angola. She has also worked as a senior AusAUD official, human rights researcher and coordinated a research consortium that united field researchers in 12 African countries.

Jessie Williams Ph.D. candidate in the area of post-conflict transformation, in the School of Government at Victoria University of Wellington, New Zealand. She is also a researcher at VUW's Institute of Policy Studies.

Robert Wylie lectures at the Australian Defence Force Academy campus of The University of New South Wales, Canberra, Australia, specialising in public policy analysis, development and advice with particular reference to defence. His research interests centre on innovation in defence capability development.

AUTHOR INDEX

SUBJECT INDEX

Printed and bound by CPI Group (UK) Ltd, Croydon, CR0 4YY

16/09/2026

14963402-0006